❧ MILTON AND THE

MILTON AND THE VICTORIANS

ERIK GRAY

CORNELL UNIVERSITY PRESS
Ithaca and London

First published 2009 by Cornell University Press

Printed in the United States of America

Library of Congress Cataloging-in-Publication Data

Gray, Erik Irving, 1972–
    Milton and the Victorians / Erik Gray.
        p. cm.
    Includes index.
    ISBN 978-0-8014-4680-1 (cloth : alk. paper)
    1. Milton, John, 1608–1674—Influence.   2. Milton, John, 1608–1674—Criticism and interpretation—History. 3. English literature—19th century—History and criticism. 4. Criticism—Great Britain—History—19th century. I. Title.
    PR3588.G675   2009
    821'.4—dc22
2008044215

Parts of chapter 2 have previously appeared as "Nostalgia, the Classics, and the Intimations Ode: Wordsworth's Forgotten Education," *Philological Quarterly* 80, no. 2 (Spring 2001), reprinted with permission from the editor of *Philological Quarterly;* and "Faithful Likenesses: Lists of Similes in Milton, Shelley, and Rossetti," *Texas Studies in Literature and Language* 48, no. 4 (2006): 291–311, reprinted with permission from the University of Texas Press.

Cornell University Press strives to use environmentally responsible suppliers and materials to the fullest extent possible in the publishing of its books. Such materials include vegetable-based, low-VOC inks and acid-free papers that are recycled, totally chlorine-free, or partly composed of nonwood fibers. For further information, visit our website at www.cornellpress.cornell.edu.

Cloth printing   10 9 8 7 6 5 4 3 2 1

❧ CONTENTS

❦ ACKNOWLEDGMENTS

I am deeply indebted to Joseph Wittreich, who very generously read through my entire manuscript on three separate occasions, and who by his comments and suggestions, as much as by his example, has made this a better book. A number of friends and colleagues have provided much-needed help and advice for which I am very grateful, including Abe Stoll, Chris Rovee, Marah Gubar, Gerhard Joseph, Sharon Marcus, David Kastan, David Yerkes, my research assistant Katie Deutsch, and several anonymous readers. I am particularly grateful to Amanda Claybaugh and Denise Gigante, both of whom offered constant encouragement, and both of whom kindly agreed on short notice to read through late versions of several chapters. Peter Potter at Cornell University Press has been wonderfully supportive and helpful throughout. This book was begun during a sabbatical leave from Harvard University, and completed during a leave from Columbia University that I spent at Clare Hall, Cambridge, and I wish to thank all three institutions for their generous support; Columbia also provided welcome assistance through its Summer Grant Program in the Humanities. Parts of chapter 2 have previously appeared in *Philological Quarterly* and *Texas Studies in Literature and Language;* I am thankful to the editors of those journals for permission to reprint.

Finally, this book is dedicated to my parents, whose influence is obvious and has always been good.

❧ EDITIONS AND ABBREVIATIONS

Unless otherwise noted, all quotations from Milton's poetry refer to the following:

Milton: Complete Shorter Poems. Ed. John Carey. 2nd ed. London: Longman, 1997.
Milton: Paradise Lost. Ed. Alastair Fowler. 2nd ed. London: Longman, 1998.

The following abbreviations have been used for frequently cited works:

CPA: *The Complete Prose Works of Matthew Arnold*. Ed. R. H. Super. 11 vols. Ann Arbor: University of Michigan Press, 1960–77.

HSL: Gerard Manley Hopkins. *Selected Letters*. Ed. Catherine Phillips. Oxford and New York: Oxford University Press, 1991.

Life: David Masson. *The Life of John Milton: Narrated in Connection with the Political, Ecclesiastical, and Literary History of His Time*. 7 vols. London: Macmillan, 1859–94.

LT: *The Letters of Alfred Lord Tennyson*. Ed. Cecil Y. Lang and Edgar F. Shannon, Jr. Oxford: Clarendon Press, 1982–90.

M: George Eliot. *Middlemarch*. Ed. David Carroll. Oxford. Clarendon Press, 1986.

M.Enc.: *A Milton Encyclopedia*. Ed. William B. Hunter, Jr., et al. Lewisburg: Bucknell University Press, 1978–80.

Memoir: Hallam, Lord Tennyson. *Alfred Lord Tennyson: A Memoir*. London and New York: Macmillan, 1897.

Prose: *The Complete Prose Works of John Milton*. Ed. Don M. Wolfe et al. New Haven: Yale University Press, 1953–82.

❧ MILTON AND THE VICTORIANS

❧ CHAPTER 1

Dark with Excessive Bright:
The Victorian Milton

Thomas De Quincey saw more than a touch of Milton in William Wordsworth. Not long after he first met Wordsworth in 1807, De Quincey bought a commentary on *Paradise Lost* that had as its frontispiece an engraving of Milton, said to be very accurate. "Judge of my astonishment," he writes, "when, in this portrait of Milton, I saw a likeness nearly perfect of Wordsworth, better by much than any which I have since seen, of those expressly painted for himself." De Quincey showed the picture to Wordsworth's family, who agreed with him about the likeness, and even the poet himself "admitted that the resemblance was, *for that period of his life,* (but let not that restriction be forgotten,) perfect, or as nearly so as art could accomplish" (De Quincey 11:59–61). The similarities De Quincey detected between the two men were not merely physical, of course. Even Wordsworth's scrupulous reminder—that his resemblance to the engraving of Milton was subject to time—points to a concern shared by the two poets: both Milton and Wordsworth while still young wrote lyrics lamenting the swift passage of time and the loss of their youth. As Wordsworth rose to become the leading British poet of his day, often taking Milton as an acknowledged model for his verse, the comparison became irresistible. "He is the Milton of our day," John Hamilton Reynolds wrote in 1816, echoing an opinion that Samuel Taylor Coleridge, Robert Southey, Leigh Hunt, and many others had expressed.[1]

Yet by the middle of the century, when Wordsworth was Queen Victoria's poet laureate, the Miltonic precedent had apparently become less remarkable. Ralph Waldo Emerson recounts that during his journey to England in 1847–48,

> A gentleman in London showed me a watch that once belonged to Milton, whose initials are engraved on its face. He said, he once showed this to Wordsworth, who took it in one hand, then drew out his own watch, and held it up with the other, before the company, but no one making the expected remark, he put back his own in silence.[2]

Emerson's anecdote is humorous but also suggestive: clearly, times have changed. But was the Victorian Wordsworth really less Miltonic than the Romantic Wordsworth had been? Or was it rather that the comparison had now become too obvious to be worth repeating? And if Milton now seemed less immediately relevant in relation even to Wordsworth, how did he stand in relation to the new generation of Victorian poets that had succeeded?

According to a widely held critical view, Milton exerted a dominant influence on Romantic poetry; the Romantic poets in their turn begat the Victorian poets; yet Victorian poetry shows no particular, direct indebtedness to Milton. This view is primarily associated with Harold Bloom, but not exclusively. Joseph Wittreich's 1970 anthology *The Romantics on Milton,* which antedates most of Bloom's writings on influence, explicitly claims not only that the Romantics had a particular interest in Milton and valuable insights to offer, but that the Victorians did not. Whereas Romantic poets and critics responded to every aspect of Milton—his life, his thought, and his art—the Victorians were "repelled by the man and enraged variously by his terrifying theology, Puritan austerity, and subversive politics," and hence were "far narrower in outlook" (Wittreich, *Romantics,* 9). Wittreich's anthology follows a pattern set by Raymond Dexter Havens, whose *The Influence of Milton on English Poetry* (1922) similarly concludes with John Keats. The pattern has continued: not only Bloom but numerous critics, including many who

---

1. John Hamilton Reynolds, letter to Benjamin Haydon, 28 September 1816 (Woof 936). For similar comparisons, see Woof 51, 118, 334, 471, and 490.

2. The story is related in *English Traits* (Emerson 5:167). According to Emerson's notebooks, the gentleman in question was Sir Charles Fellowes, but the exact date of the episode is not known.

in other respects strongly disagree with Bloom, assume that Milton's direct influence on poetry skips a generation or perhaps ends altogether after the later Romantics. Between 1975 and 1980 there existed a journal titled *Milton and the Romantics;* a journal entirely dedicated to Milton and the Victorians would be difficult to imagine. The dozens of articles and monographs dedicated to Milton's relationship to Romanticism find their parallel in the large body of criticism describing Romantic influence on Victorian poetry.[3] But work on Milton and the Victorians is limited to one general overview, James Nelson's *The Sublime Puritan* (1963); one more specialized monograph (focusing on a novelist), Anna K. Nardo's *George Eliot's Dialogue with John Milton* (2003); and a handful of articles.[4] By general consensus, at least implicit, Milton's sometimes overwhelming influence on forty years of English poetry came to an abrupt halt with the deaths of Keats, Percy Shelley, and Lord Byron in the 1820s.

There are two things to be said about this view: first, that it is clearly false, and second, that it is just as clearly true. It is false in that Victorian poetry is filled with echoes and allusions to Milton. The Victorian period, far from being indifferent, is well-known for its study of Milton: his lost treatise on *Christian Doctrine* was rediscovered and published only at the very end of the Romantic period (1825),[5] and the decades that followed its publication witnessed a renewed interest in Milton's writings, including prose that had long been largely neglected (Nelson 77–85). David Masson's *The Life of John Milton,* published in six enormous volumes between 1859 and 1880, remains a monument of Milton scholarship; Victorian scholarly editions, notably those of Thomas Keightley (1859) and of Masson (1874), outstripped anything

---

3. See, for instance, Andrew Elfenbein, *Byron and the Victorians;* Stephen Gill, *Wordsworth and the Victorians;* Antony Harrison, *Victorian Poems and Romantic Poets;* and James Najarian, *Victorian Keats.*

4. I discuss Nardo's book at length in chapter 5, but it is worth noting that, in addition to her discussion of George Eliot's treatment of Milton, she also dedicates an early chapter to other Victorian representations and invocations of Milton's life story, thus building on work begun by Nelson. Articles concerning Milton and Victorian poets have typically focused on single poems displaying evidence of direct influence. These articles are discussed below: those on Rossetti (Shurbutt, Vejvoda, Winters) and Hopkins (Glavin, Sobolev) in chapter 2; and those on Tennyson (Adler, Bonney, Kincaid, Sendry) in chapter 4. Also of interest is Catherine Maxwell's *The Female Sublime from Milton to Swinburne* (2001). As its title suggests, Maxwell's book is a study not so much of influence as of poetic elements shared by Milton and the Victorians—specifically, such feminized figures of poetic inspiration as Philomela, Orpheus, and Sappho. Like many critics (as I discuss below), Maxwell sees the Victorians as relating to Milton primarily through the mediation of a Romantic poet—in this case, Percy Shelley.

5. The authorship of the treatise was called into question by one critic (Thomas Burgess) soon after its publication but was not then seriously questioned again until the early 1990s. For a history of the recent controversy concerning its authorship, see Rumrich 214–21.

produced by the previous generation.[6] Milton continued to be a presence not only in scholarly but in popular imagination throughout Victoria's reign (Nelson 3–4), and it would be perverse if only the poets ignored his work. And one does not need to look very hard before finding major Victorian poems for which Milton is an obvious precursor: Christina Rossetti's "Goblin Market," Gerard Manley Hopkins's "caudated" sonnets, Alfred Tennyson's *In Memoriam.*

On the other hand, the common critical perception remains oddly true: although Milton may not have ceased to exert an influence after the deaths of Keats and Byron, he does suddenly cease to stand out from all other major precursors as he had in the past. The oddity is that the distinction between "Romantic" and "Victorian" is an artificial one, and criticism has for some years been trying to jettison these periodizations.[7] Keats is closer in date of birth to the Brownings and Tennyson than he is to Wordsworth and William Blake, yet the case of Miltonic influence seems to justify grouping him with the earlier poets and to reify the traditional Romantic-Victorian divide. Even Nelson, four chapters into his monograph, admits a dramatic falling-off of influence: "Actually there was little direct imitation of Milton during the Victorian period; in terms of quality there was nothing comparable to Keats's *Hyperion.* Scattered indications of Milton's direct influence can be observed, for instance, in some of Tennyson's early experiments, . . . but the only extensive evidence of close imitation is found in the sonnet" (Nelson 39). The examples I cite above could go either way: Hopkins's poems and *In Memoriam* are influenced less by *Paradise Lost* than by Milton's minor works, the sonnets and "Lycidas." Even "Goblin Market" displays a closer resemblance to *Comus* than to *Paradise Lost,* as Kathleen Vejvoda has described.[8] (I return to the special case of Rossetti in chapter 2.) It is difficult to deny a pattern: a list of major Romantic poems—*The Prelude, Prometheus Unbound, Hyperion*—immediately, insistently calls to mind Milton's epic, as a similar list of Victorian masterpieces—*Aurora Leigh, Idylls of the King, The Ring and the Book*—does not. If Milton was as widely read and appreciated as ever, he nevertheless seems to stand in a different relation to the Victorian poets than to the Romantics.

---

6. The major work of scholarship from the Romantic period is Henry John Todd's variorum edition, first published in 1801. But the great eras of Milton scholarship are generally acknowledged to lie on either side of the Romantic period.

7. See, for instance, the cluster of essays "Who's Carving Up the Nineteenth Century?" by Jerome McGann, Charles Rzepka, and Susan Wolfson in *PMLA* 116 (2001), 1415–41.

8. See Vejvoda, "The Fruit of Charity." Throughout this book I refer to Milton's masque as *Comus,* the name by which the Victorians themselves referred to it.

This shift is most clearly registered in the criticism of Harold Bloom. It emerges already in the central chapters of *The Ringers in the Tower,* which was published in 1971, although most of the essays that comprise it appeared earlier. The chapter "Keats and the Embarrassments of Poetic Tradition" might as well be called "Keats and Milton": Wordsworth figures briefly as a secondary "burden," and Shakespeare as an influence, though "not an embarrassment"; but Milton is throughout the essay nearly synonymous with "tradition" (Bloom, *Ringers,* 132, 136). Yet the subsequent chapter, "Tennyson, Hallam, and Romantic Tradition," does not mention Milton, even though Tennyson is described as belonging entirely with the Romantic and not the Victorian poets and as being "legitimately the heir of Keats" (146). The next chapter, "Browning's *Childe Roland:* All Things Deformed and Broken," names a number of possible influences on Browning—Shelley, above all—but once again Milton is not mentioned. As Bloom goes on to rewrite and refine his notion English poetic history, this pattern is repeated over and over again: the Romantic poets up through Keats struggle with Milton as well as with each other, but the Victorians with the Romantics alone.

This distinction is particularly striking given that according to Bloom's central thesis, formulated in *The Anxiety of Influence,* poetry depends on influence, and influence *is* Milton. "Let us attempt the experiment... of reading *Paradise Lost* as an allegory of the dilemma of the modern poet, at his strongest. Satan is that modern poet, while God is his dead but still embarrassingly potent and present ancestor, or rather, ancestral poet" (Bloom, *Influence,* 20). Milton provides not only the model for the workings of poetic influence but its historical source: the anxiety of influence has been "the covert subject of most poetry for the last three centuries"—that is, since the publication of *Paradise Lost* (148). And the originator of this poetic tradition remains its most powerful force: "If one examines the dozen or so major poetic influencers before this century, one discovers quickly who among them ranks as the great Inhibitor, the Sphinx who strangles even strong imaginations in their cradles: Milton" (32). It would seem to be essential to Bloom's argument to assert the conscious or unconscious influence of Milton beyond the first quarter of the nineteenth century, yet the list of his "descendants" always ends in the same place: "Blake, Wordsworth, Shelley,... Keats" (108). There is nothing in Bloom's theory that prevents a strong poet from struggling with several generations of ancestors at once: Keats is repeatedly depicted as wrestling with both Milton and Wordsworth, and Yeats is the anxious heir to both Shelley and Browning. Perhaps we are to understand Milton as somehow underlying the Victorians' anxious relationship with their immediate predecessors; but such influence is almost never explicitly asserted.

The omission is most egregious in *A Map of Misreading*, in which Bloom applies the theory outlined in *The Anxiety of Influence*. Once again we are reminded that Milton's Satan is the "paradigm" of the "strong poet" reacting against his precursors, and that the chief precursor is Milton himself (Bloom, *Misreading*, 37). We are reminded as well that the Romantic "psychology of belatedness" is a long-standing condition: far from distinguishing "Romanticism" from periods or movements immediately adjacent to it, Bloom applies the term to Western culture "from the mid-1740's" to the present (35–36). It is therefore natural that Bloom should take as his paradigmatic Romantic "poet-as-hero" a Victorian creation, Browning's Childe Roland (122). Yet in the chapter devoted to a reading of Browning's poem, probably the most convincing of all of Bloom's attempts to apply his theory of precursor poets, Milton is not named. According to Bloom's allegorization, Browning/ Roland is obsessed with Shelley and, to a lesser extent, with Wordsworth and Byron. On a few occasions Roland is paralleled with Satan (106, 113), but he is satanic only by courtesy of his being a quester; Bloom scrupulously avoids the implication that Browning was specifically recalling, or even resisting, Milton's figure.

Near the end of *A Map of Misreading* we get the first suggestion in Bloom's criticism of a Victorian poet directly reading or misreading Milton. Of Tennyson's Ulysses, Bloom claims, "His truest and largest ancestor is Milton's Satan in Book II of *Paradise Lost,* where the Grand Solipsist becomes the first and the greatest explorer, moving through a Chaos that accurately mirrors his soul" (157). Unlike Roland, then, Ulysses seems to be descended from Milton's devil, not just analogous to him. But this is the only exception in Bloom's writings, and it is a curious one, since Tennyson's hero is so clearly Dantean in the first place, and Homeric in the second, that Satan can figure as at best no more than a wicked uncle. When Bloom returns to Ulysses in his next book, *Poetry and Repression,* he makes no mention of Milton. The central chapters of *Poetry and Repression* are Bloom's own rewriting of those in *The Ringers in the Tower,* now informed by his own fully articulated theory of influence. Yet in one sense at least nothing has changed. In the chapter on Keats, Milton still figures preeminently, though not exclusively, as the poetic father. In the succeeding chapter, writing of Tennyson's "The Holy Grail," Bloom mentions Spenser and Milton in passing as part of a tradition of quest poetry, "but much closer are the Solitary of Wordsworth, and the Solitary's younger brothers in Childe Harold, Endymion, and, above all others, the doomed, driven poet of *Alastor*" (Bloom, *Poetry and Repression,* 169). The chapter on Browning follows suit, mentioning Milton only incidentally. That Bloom, despite his near obsession with Milton, explicitly admits the limits of his influence suggests that a significant shift really did occur in the brief period that separates the late Romantics from the first Victorian poets.

One major critical work that refuses to accept this demarcation is Sandra Gilbert and Susan Gubar's *The Madwoman in the Attic* (1979). Like Bloom, Gilbert and Gubar are centrally concerned with literary tradition, and they too cast literary history in terms of struggle and anxiety, but they notably revise Bloom's paradigm. By concentrating on nineteenth-century women writers, they not only complicate the oedipal family romance that Bloom describes but also, incidentally, seem to challenge the Romantic-Victorian divide. Part 3 of *The Madwoman in the Attic,* "How Are We Fal'n?: Milton's Daughters," includes chapters on both Mary Shelley's *Frankenstein* and Emily Brontë's *Wuthering Heights* and claims that all nineteenth-century women writers in English—Romantic and Victorian, poets and novelists—are equally "daughters of Milton." And yet Gilbert and Gubar reiterate and even reinforce the idea that Victorian writers were influenced primarily by Romantic versions of Milton, not by Milton himself. They adapt Bloom by choosing as their model for the rebellious writer, not Satan, but Eve and her double, Sin. But whereas Satan had only one progenitor against whom to struggle, Eve/Sin (in this reading) has two, God and Satan. Again, therefore, we have a model including three generations: as God is to Satan is to Eve, so Milton is to the Romantics is to Victorian women writers, who are more likely to respond to Byron and his satanic heroes than directly to Milton (Gilbert and Gubar 201–07).

Although Gilbert and Gubar claim at the outset of their section on "Milton's Daughters" that writers such as the Brontës *do* engage directly with Milton's writings (189), in most of their readings "Milton" serves rather as a metonym for the patriarchal tradition than as an individual influence. The exception is their chapter on *Frankenstein,* a Romantic work that explicitly invokes *Paradise Lost* as a precursor. But when they turn to *Wuthering Heights,* written a generation later, they change their terms. Admitting "the fact that Brontë never mentions either Milton or *Paradise Lost* in *Wuthering Heights,*" they "speculate . . . that Milton's absence is itself a presence" (252–53). Milton becomes in this chapter what Gilbert and Gubar, borrowing the term from Virginia Woolf, call a "bogey": a name to be conjured with, a stand-in for an entire cultural history. They refer, for instance, to "Milton's and Western culture's central tale of the fall of woman" (255)—"Milton" becoming a representative symptom rather than an all-too-individual presence. They do cite several plausible verbal parallels between *Wuthering Heights* and *Paradise Lost,* but the difference between the two successive chapters is nevertheless striking: where Mary Shelley engaged with Milton, her Victorian successor

struggles only with "Milton."[9] Although Gilbert and Gubar do not analyze
this distinction, it represents an important shift in attitudes. For many Victorian writers, Milton's influence is constant but diffuse. It cannot be traced
or pinpointed, as it can in *Frankenstein,* for instance, but is no less powerful
for being unlocalized.

The Bloomian model of literary struggle has often been questioned, not
just in its arcane particulars but in its broadest assumptions.[10] Miltonic influence in Bloom's books appears not only to stop abruptly after 1824 but
to skip the entire century before Blake. Dustin Griffin, among others, has
examined this lost century and discovered a very different relationship to
Milton among "writers in the ages of Dryden, Pope, and Johnson," a "sense
of detachment, friendly rivalry, and literary possibility" (Griffin ix).[11] Taking advantage of the work of Griffin and other scholars who have discussed
the continuity of the tradition between Milton and the Romantics, Lucy
Newlyn, in one of the best and most complete treatments of the subject yet,
revisits the question of the Romantic poets' use of their great predecessor.
Seeking not to counter Bloom's model but to "supplement" it (Newlyn 15),
Newlyn argues that the Romantics had two Miltons: the authoritarian one
whom they invoked by name and rebelled against, and a more open, "negatively capable" Milton whose nuances and ambiguities they appreciated and
echoed in their poetry. Newlyn's preferred term for this second relationship is "continuity" (4): Romantic poetry does not merely imitate Milton
or rebelliously revise him, but continues the tradition of multivalent allusion

---

9. The same distinction is registered in Peter McInerney's article on *Frankenstein* and *Wuthering
Heights* (the only article to appear in *Milton and the Romantics* that strays beyond 1830). Although
others treat Brontë's novel "as an example of Romantic literature," McInerney claims that *"Wuthering Heights* is not Romantic, but is instead an historical novel about Romanticism" (McInerney 10),
and hence differs from *Frankenstein* in that its satanic figure, Heathcliff, is more truly Byronic than
Miltonic.

10. See, for instance, the early response from James Rieger, who argues that Wordsworth read
Milton "typologically," hence unanxiously: "Wordsworth was typical of his time, rather than the
reverse, in his freedom from anxiety over his relationship to the mighty dead" (Rieger 202–3). In
the same volume, Joseph Wittreich describes a "tradition of prophecy," including both Milton
and the Romantics, in which the poet emphasizes "continuity between himself and his precursors,
whose visions he releases and then expands" (Wittreich, "'A Poet Amongst Poets,'" 104).

11. John T. Shawcross makes a similar argument, suggesting that eighteenth-century Miltonic
poetry has been largely misunderstood, not least because Augustan poets generally responded to
Milton as a poet of "wit" rather than of "vision" (Shawcross, *John Milton and Influence,* 66–86).
Even Walter Jackson Bate, whose *The Burden of the Past and the English Poet* (1970) in many ways
overlaps with and complements Bloom's work, sees other models at work in the eighteenth century
(and continuing into the Romantic period). Bate notes "the rediscovery, by these writers, of the use
of identification with the great in the past for confidence and security, as well as to gain strength in
one's antagonism to what is least valued in the present" (Bate 130).

that characterizes his poetry. The notion of "continuity," however, jars not with periodization. Although Newlyn does not accept Bloom's eliding of the eighteenth century and his mystification of the Milton-Romantic relationship, the parameters and the very title of her book, *Paradise Lost and the Romantic Reader,* imply that one period's response to a major predecessor may differ distinctly from that of any other period.

I agree. Terms like *Augustan, Romantic, Victorian,* though vague, have proven too useful to be abandoned, and here is a case in which these divisions appear particularly appropriate. Milton, as I have said, continued to be a major influence on Victorian poetry. One could easily compile a hefty tome of Miltonic echoes, allusions, and appreciations by the Victorian poets; their language and rhythms continue to be influenced by his, as much as by Shakespeare's or the Bible's. Yet something has altered since the early years of the century. In a letter of 1819, Keats writes, "I have but lately stood on my guard against Milton. Life to him would be death to me" (Keats, *Letters,* 2:212)—a statement that Bloom adopts as the "motto" to a whole era of poetry (Bloom, *Influence,* 32). In a letter of 1879, by contrast, Gerard Manley Hopkins casually remarks, "I hope in time to have a more...Miltonic style" (HSL 117). It would seem inadvisable to insist upon two such isolated comments were it not that they represent a larger pattern. Keats's words resemble numerous gestures by other Romantic poets, registering Milton's looming presence in their imaginations, that have no Victorian counterpart. If Milton continues to exert influence on the Victorians, but one different from his influence on the Romantics, then what is its nature? This book studies that relationship to find out what it can teach us about Victorian literature above all, but also about Romanticism, about Milton, and about forms of poetic influence.

To that end, the next two chapters both propose models, drawn principally from Milton's own writings, to help illuminate the characteristically oblique nature of Milton's influence on Victorian authors. In chapter 2 I discuss the concept of the "classic"—a work of literature so familiar that it goes without saying. Milton, I suggest, was a Victorian classic: if his influence becomes less obvious in the later nineteenth century, that is due not to his disappearance but to his pervasiveness; my primary example is Elizabeth Barrett Browning. I then consider one particular classic, the Bible, and use it as a model to describe Milton's influence on Christina Rossetti. In both cases, the classic, Victorian Milton contrasts sharply with the Romantic Milton, since he is backgrounded rather than foregrounded. Chapter 3 describes a peculiarly Miltonic method of exerting power through seeming weakness or retreat— a method employed by all of Milton's heroes, beginning with the Son in the Nativity Ode and culminating in the Son of *Paradise Regained.* This manner of exercising influence, I suggest, may be taken as a model of Milton's own relation to certain major Victorian writers, notably Matthew Arnold. Allusions to Milton in Arnold's prose and poetry are often glancing and fugitive, but they come out most strongly when Arnold is himself propounding the very Miltonic ideal of tactical retreat. In all these instances, influence is the stronger for being hidden or indirect.

Chapters 4 and 5 center on the work of two of the preeminent writers of the Victorian period. The former considers the poetry of Alfred Tennyson, who turns to Milton less for his sublime abstractions than for his more modest effects. Particularly in the first half of his career Tennyson was fascinated by Milton's concrete details, even more than by his heaven or hell; in *In Memoriam* especially, Tennyson draws upon Milton when he wishes to emphasize a sense of physical presence. Because of this focus upon the less remarkable or immediately recognizable elements of Milton's verse, his fundamental influence on the young Tennyson appears muted and diffused. *Idylls of the King,* meanwhile, imitates the Miltonic maneuver of quietly passing over a crucial originary event of the story (Satan's first turn to sin, Lancelot and Guinevere's adultery); this serves as yet another model of Milton's own influence, in this case his essential though often inconspicuous effect upon Tennyson's epic and on his poetry more generally. Chapter 5 focuses on a single work, George Eliot's *Middlemarch,* which unlike most of the other works discussed directly and repeatedly invokes both Milton's life and his writings. In the opening chapters of the novel, Dorothea Brooke pictures herself as an obedient daughter of Milton, and critics of *Middlemarch,* beginning with Gilbert and Gubar, have agreed in taking Milton as Eliot's figure for authoritative, patriarchal discourse. But Eliot connects Milton rather with discursive difficulty, invoking specifically those episodes from his life and poetry in which communication proves ineffective, haphazard, or contingent upon outward circumstances. By consistently associating Milton with failed or thwarted communication, Eliot establishes him as a precedent for her own characters, with their frequently frustrated intentions. Milton's relation to *Middlemarch* is thus more complex—and more pervasive—than has previously been described: he influenced Eliot's novel as much through his failures to write with authority as through his successes.

The concluding chapter examines the nature and history of Milton's influence more generally and suggests why the study of the Victorian Milton can be of particular value. The models of Miltonic influence that I offer in this book are largely drawn from Milton's own writings—a method that finds precedent in the works of Bloom, Gilbert and Gubar, and a number of other major critics, all of whom derive their models of poetic relations from the power relations portrayed in Milton's poetry. The popularity of this critical methodology, I argue, can be attributed to the way in which it depicts literary history as both necessarily contingent—since it is open-ended, multiple, and dependent upon forces and circumstances outside the text—and at the same time self-determined, since the precursor text contains within itself the key to its own interpretations. This is the same duality that has underlain critical debate about literary history in recent decades —a debate, in broadest terms, between a model of "intertextuality," which discounts the power of particular authors or texts in favor of more impersonal forces, and a model of "influence," which conceives of literary history in terms of individual agency. The Victorian response to Milton, however, demonstrates that these two models not only coexist but are mutually dependent. To Victorian poets, novelists, and critics, the more Milton seemed to blend into a broader historical and literary context, the more singularly powerful his presence and influence became. Studying the Victorian Milton can thus help provide a crucial insight into the workings of literary influence.

This study is necessarily selective. In the first place, it concentrates on Milton's literary reception, rather than attempting to provide a more general history of his effect upon Victorian social and material culture. This is not intended to privilege literary influence over other types of cultural influence: clearly, every aspect of Milton's reception is relevant to a full understanding of the others. But since an exhaustive account covering the whole range of Victorian culture was not possible, I have focused on Victorian authors whose work, in addition to being familiar, is particularly typical or significant in its response to Milton,[12] Secondly, this study is selective in that most of the authors I discuss are poets. I have chosen to focus in this way because Milton's influence on subsequent poetry is far greater than his influence on prose writing, and likewise because the apparent falling off of that influence in the Victorian period is more striking in the case of its chief poets than in the case of its novelists. But poetry is not a wholly independent literary tradition, and I do consider a number of prose works: in addition to the chapter on Eliot, I discuss Anthony Trollope, the criticism of Arnold, and the many less well-known critics who wrote about Milton throughout the Victorian period.

---

12. There exists a prejudice to the effect that a literary study cannot be written until a full account of the prevailing cultural climate has first been provided. But this prejudice unfairly privileges literature at the expense of other forms of culture: it suggests that popular manifestations of (say) Milton's influence can be understood without a previous analysis of his literary influence, but not vice versa. Rather, since there is a constant interchange between literary and other cultural discourses, the study of each must contribute to the other; for this purpose, the accounts by Nelson and Nardo of Victorian representations of Milton are indispensable (see above, note 4).

Rather than attempting to offer a complete survey of Milton's influence on Victorian literature, the chapters that follow, and my analyses of individual authors, aim to be representative, to provide models that may illuminate future studies, whether general or specific. In tracing Milton's influence on Victorian texts I have often relied on verbal echoes and similarities. I cite these echoes, not so much for themselves, but because they provide one of the clearest indications of an author's conscious or unconscious reminiscence of Milton and can therefore help to draw our attention to the presence of larger structural or thematic influences. For this reason I have not attempted to distinguish among different types or level of echo—allusion, borrowing, reference[13]—but have simply indicated striking verbal, rhetorical, or rhythmic similarities when they occur. The examination of these local echoes can help us understand the broader relationship between Milton and the later poet, just as the study of individual poets can provide a model or microcosm of larger trends. My ultimate goal has been to offer more complex and nuanced understandings of Milton, of his Victorian heirs, and of the nature of literary influence.

This is a work of literary history, but it is more than that. Milton holds such a prominent place in political and intellectual as well as literary history that to investigate an age's reaction to Milton is to learn a great deal about the values of that age. But the topic is compelling for other reasons besides the purely intellectual. Milton is usually thought of as an object of reverence rather than of love; the Victorians, however, recognized no such restriction, and neither do I. Thomas Babington Macaulay expresses something more than historical admiration when he concludes his essay on Milton by fantasizing about a personal encounter with the poet:

> We image to ourselves the breathless silence in which we should listen to his slightest word; the passionate veneration with which we should kneel to kiss his hand and weep upon it; the earnestness with which we should endeavour to console him, if indeed such a spirit could need consolation, for the neglect of an age unworthy of his talents and his virtues; the eagerness with which we should contest with his daughters, or with his Quaker friend Elwood, the privilege of reading Homer to him, or of taking down the immortal accents which flowed from his lips. (Macaulay 345–46)

---

13. For a thoughtful reexamination of the terminology in current use, see Gregory Machacek, "Allusion."

"These are perhaps foolish feelings," Macaulay admits abashedly, but many of his successors also evinced their love for Milton. Anna Nardo has traced a tradition in Victorian fiction in which Milton figures as a lover and "object of the erotic gaze" (Nardo 33–46). It is always fascinating to know how one's beloved is perceived by others, especially by former lovers; how much more so when the lovers are the great Victorian poets and novelists, and their object is Milton.

Is it possible to define a "Victorian Milton"? The analogous concept of the "Romantic Milton" is quite familiar, though it can be misleading; Joseph Wittreich laments the "general misunderstanding of what the Romantics said about Milton and the widespread notion that they said little about anything besides Milton's Satan" (Wittreich, *Romantics*, xi). Wittreich therefore sets out to correct this misconception, yet the anthology he compiles is by his own admission not just partial but also, in its own way, distorted. None of the Romantic poets and critics he includes "is to be mistaken for the common reader"; to the contrary, the most important of them are distinguished specifically by being *unrepresentative* of their age, since they "forge interests and formulate insights that future generations embrace and elaborate" (18). A summary of the "average" estimation of Milton in the Romantic period, Wittreich implies, might not be desirable, even if it were possible. To summarize Victorian attitudes is even more of a challenge. The term *Romantic* indicates, however indistinctly, a group of writers and thinkers sharing certain artistic methods or beliefs. *Victorian,* by contrast, is all-inclusive, since it is defined temporally rather than ideologically. The time it encompasses, moreover, is substantial; how can one summarize the collective attitude of a period that includes as representative figures characters as different as Thomas Arnold and Oscar Wilde? These objections are evident and real; yet keeping them in mind, it is nevertheless possible to describe some of the prevailing critical estimations of Milton in the later nineteenth century—a background of opinion against which the attitudes of Victorian writers, described in the following chapters, must be understood.

For this purpose James Nelson's 1963 study *The Sublime Puritan: Milton and the Victorians* remains indispensable. Nelson recognizes the impossibility of trying to provide an exhaustive survey of "so diverse and extensive" a topic and opts instead to give a representative "series of essays." Yet he does not shy away from making broad assertions about "the thought and disposition of the era from about 1820 to 1900," with a willingness to generalize that, for better or for worse, has all but disappeared from criticism in the decades since he wrote (Nelson ix). One important area of debate, as Nelson's

title indicates, was Milton's "Puritanism." Although many Victorian critics followed the major eighteenth-century biographies in objecting to the
Puritan aspects of Milton's character and his politics, others contested the
interpretation and even the pertinence of the term (Nelson 74–77). This
more nuanced assessment was partly attributable to a much wider reading of
Milton's work, including not only his *Christian Doctrine* but also a number of
other prose works that were now widely reprinted and appreciated (81–85).
One important result of the expanded canon is that, as the century wore on,
there was less of a tendency to equate Milton almost exclusively with his
epic. If most earlier criticism had been epicentric—though with such ec-
centric exceptions as Samuel Johnson's "Life of Milton," which gives ample
attention to minor works—Victorian criticism tended to be more catholic
in its scope. *Paradise Lost,* and especially Satan, continued to hold pride of
place (61–70), but the writings of Milton's middle years, the sonnets and the
pamphlets, began to seize on readers' imaginations.

The increasing willingness to engage with all aspects of Milton is reflected in the reception given to the nineteenth century's most important
work of Milton scholarship. If it is difficult to define the Victorian Milton,
it is by contrast easy enough to define the Victorian *Milton.* The year 1859,
which witnessed the publication of such characteristic Victorian works as
Edward FitzGerald's *Rubáiyát of Omar Khayyám,* Samuel Smiles's *Self-Help,*
and Charles Darwin's *The Origin of Species,* also saw the publication of the
first volume of David Masson's biography of Milton. The work immediately
attracted notice, being reviewed at length in the *North British Review,* the
National Review, the *British Quarterly Review,* the *Edinburgh Review,* and the
Dublin University Magazine; later volumes drew the attention of *Macmillan's
Magazine,* the *Quarterly,* the *Modern Review,* and others. Masson (1822–1907)
was a professor of English literature at University College, London, and
later at the University of Edinburgh; he was also a founder and editor of
Macmillan's Magazine. His work on Milton began in 1844 with an article
comparing Milton's concept of the devil to those of Luther and Goethe, and
this was followed by other essays and reviews. But his great contribution was
his six-volume *The Life of John Milton: Narrated in Connection with the Political, Ecclesiastical, and Literary History of His Time* (1859–80; a seventh volume,
containing an index, appeared in 1894). The first installment, weighing in
at nearly eight hundred pages, covers the years 1608–39. In an introductory
"Notice" and again in the "Preface" to the first volume, Masson reiterates
the promise of his subtitle: the work "is intended to exhibit Milton's Life in
its connexions with all the more notable phenomena of the period of British
history in which it was cast—its state-politics, its ecclesiastical variations, its

literature and speculative thought" (Life 1:v). It is meant to be "not merely a Biography of Milton, but also, in some sort, a continuous History of his Time" (1:xiii).

Masson clearly feels the need to apologize for the scale and method of his undertaking. He notes that "almost every Life" previously published is "written as an introductory memoir to some edition or other of the Poet's works, and on a scale corresponding to that purpose" (1:xi). On a corresponding scale, and also on a corresponding plan: earlier biographies had tended to concentrate on Milton's poetry and hence only on such historical information as pertained obviously and directly to its interpretation. Masson's decision to depict the young Milton as inextricably linked to all the "political, ecclesiastical, and literary" currents of his time implicitly challenged the image—promoted by Milton himself—that his youth was spent in isolated retirement, communing only with God and the classics. Masson includes in his initial volume a "Survey of English Literature" as it stood in 1632, running to well over a hundred pages, as well as a minutely detailed account of every religious and political controversy of which Milton might have been conscious during his years at St. Paul's, at Cambridge, and in Italy. Heretofore, Milton's life had always been written as if it were itself a poem, orderly and discrete; Masson, in true Victorian fashion, rewrites it as a loose, baggy monster, drawing in all the varied material circumstances that surrounded the poet. (Their comparable narratological methods may explain why Masson and Eliot exerted a mutual influence upon each other, as described in chapter 5.)[14] Masson promises two more volumes, covering the other two periods of Milton's life—his efforts as a political and religious polemicist (1640–60) and his major poetry (1661–74). But the work quickly ballooned, as the projected two more volumes expanded to five, each as large and as exhaustively researched as the first, and providing between them, as was soon recognized, as complete a history of the English Civil War as had yet been written.

Reviewers of the first volume were not on the whole convinced by Masson's method and its implications. The *British Quarterly* reviewer objected that however diverse Milton's life and writings may have been, his reputation rests on a few works of poetry disengaged from the rest.

> Of the millions who are familiar with his fame, and with the works upon which it reposes, and to whom his name is a "household word," an incredible proportion have never read a line of his prose writings;

---

14. For a useful comparison of the autobiographical passages in Milton's divorce tracts to prose fiction, see Annabel Patterson, "No Meer Amatorious Novel?"

and whatever reception the *Areopagitica*, the *Defensio Populi*, or the *Reason of Church Government*, may have met in his own day, the *Paradise Lost*, the *Comus*, and the *Samson*, are the productions for which posterity has crowned him with immortality. As a poet, then, mainly, although not exclusively, should Milton be presented by his biographer. (Anon., "Masson's *Life of Milton*," 187).

The same reviewer also predicts that as Masson reaches the period of the Civil War, the disproportion of history to poetry will grow, and he accurately foresees that the proposed three volumes will turn out to be insufficient (189–90). Walter Bagehot, while not wishing "to speak with censure of a book on which so much genuine labour has been expended," agrees that "it has been composed upon a principle that is utterly erroneous" (Bagehot 109). Nor was such disapproval restricted to the first volume: reviewing the second installment in 1872, Francis Turner Palgrave worried that if Masson were to continue along the same lines, "The poet would be wholly crushed beneath the vast robes and wrappings of his biography" (Palgrave 396). And yet Palgrave at the same time encourages Masson to pursue his work, recognizing the biography as already beginning to constitute "a work of national importance" (393).

This pattern consistently characterizes the reviews of Masson's work: beginning with suspicion, critics eventually came to recognize the value of an exhaustively historicized biography. John Tulloch, writing in the *North British Review*, opens his assessment of Masson's first volume in a stance of opposition. Milton, he claims, is a pure poet, whose sound is infinitely superior to his sense: "Milton's strength therefore, lay, not in the ability to rise, like Dante, to the height of 'great arguments,' but in that of so uttering matters of no very great moral, intellectual, or passionate depth, that they should have all the poetical effect of such arguments" (Tulloch 282). Given this, Masson's insistence on yoking Milton's poetry to political and intellectual history seems wrongheaded, and Tulloch memorably sums up Masson's obsessive attention to detail as "the pre-Raphaelitism of biography" (286). And yet he cannot help but admire: "The 'Life of Milton' is here written once for all. The materials—whatever defect we may find in the form in which they are placed before us—are probably exhausted, and everything that could in any way illustrate the subject, is brought into contribution, with an industry which, if it errs, does so on the safe side of excess" (285). The reviewer for the *Dublin University Magazine* agreed: "Some of Mr. Masson's critics have found fault with him for thus reversing the rights of history and biography, putting the satellite for the sun, and the sun for the satellite"; yet Masson's method, though it may be "Ptolemean," nevertheless helps us "to form our conclusion of the man and the age—how far the man helped to guide the age, and how far the age shaped and governed the man" (Anon., "Masson's *Milton*," 610–11). As the work progressed, critics began to praise it unapologetically; reviewing volume 3 in 1873, George Barnett Smith writes that "the relation of events in the national history to Milton may not always be apparent, but as he was very largely moulded by the times in which he lived, we cannot accurately gauge his character without having a clear understanding of the social and political history of the period" (Smith 537). In 1874 the *British Quarterly Review* largely reversed its skepticism of fifteen years earlier. And reviewing the completed work in 1881, Herbert New notes with satisfaction that for the first time the English public is able to evaluate Milton not as "two Miltons," the poet and the polemicist, but as a "whole man" (New 106).[15]

Most of the poems I discuss in this book were written before the publication of the majority of Masson's biography. The point then is not that Masson converted Victorian poets to a historicist perception of Milton, but rather that his biography reflects and makes explicit a growing tendency, visible in the poetry of the period, to view Milton as part of a wider context, as one power among many. By contrast, Masson did very likely exert a direct influence upon George Eliot, especially upon her presentation of Milton in *Middlemarch* as a figure whose life and works were largely subject to circumstance. His biography is thus appropriately both symptom and source of a new, peculiarly Victorian perception of Milton. Although Masson presented Milton as the outstanding, often heroic embodiment of the most stirring period of English history, nevertheless the contextualization of the poet also led to an unprecedented sense of his circumscription. Or rather, the effect was one of *concentration;* Milton appeared paradoxically more sublime and more localized, greater and smaller at once. The old tradition that Milton, at least by the time he was writing *Paradise Lost,* was sequestered from all but heavenly influence has its source in the poem itself, and it continues in full

---

15. Joseph Wittreich suggests that the Romantics, too, perceived Milton as "whole"—that is, engaged with history as well as with transcendent sublimity—because they interpreted his poetry as prophecy, "read[ing] it in the future tense, so that poems emerging from one moment of crisis could reflect upon, and explain, another crisis in history when, once again, tyranny and terror ruled" (Wittreich, *Why Milton Matters,* 141; see also 172–76). Yet the Victorians far outdid the Romantics in integrating what had long been perceived as conflicting dichotomies within Milton's life and writings. In this they anticipated the work of recent critics of Milton who have sought to reconcile deeply entrenched and opposing camps of Milton criticism; see, for instance, William Kolbrener, who seeks to balance "satanic" and "angelic" readings: "Milton's poetics mediate between the claims of a hermeneutic guided by a commitment to contingency … and a hermeneutic guided by a commitment to the Absolute" (Kolbrener 5).

force through the Romantics. Even as late as 1860 W. B. Donne, reviewing Masson's first volume in the *Edinburgh Review,* could still assert that Milton's great periods of poetic composition were unaffected by outward affairs: "For the first thirty years of his life he was a secluded scholar: for the last portion he dwelt in deep retirement, his only companions a faithful few"; hence Milton's poetry, "being for all time, is...independent of the causes and circumstances of the great Rebellion" (Donne 312–13). But by the time Donne published his review, this traditional view was quickly changing. The Victorians were repeatedly struck by those aspects of Milton's work that revealed him as the product of a certain time and situation—less a source than an object of influence. Yet Milton seemed in some sense all the greater for being thus circumscribed: his poetry was no longer viewed as ahistorical but as actively transcending the circumstances of its composition, the "evil times" that compassed Milton round.

Masson and other critics paid particular attention not only to the historical contexts of Milton's poems but to their literary background, noting especially his imitation of earlier models in *Paradise Lost.* Milton came to be seen as above all a *learned* poet, a respondent (Masson, *Poetical Works* [1874], 1:54; Palgrave 401). "Original as it is," writes Masson, "original in its entire conception, and in every portion and passage, the poem is yet full of *flakes*—we can express it no otherwise—full of flakes from all that is greatest in preceding literature, ancient or modern" (*Poetical Works* [1874] 1:56). This perception was not new: eighteenth-century editors had carefully noted Milton's many borrowings and allusions, and Augustan poets, as Griffin points out, reassured themselves with the reminder that "the greatest writers are re-writers" (Griffin 237). But the renewed insistence on Milton's mundane sources of inspiration significantly revised Romantic notions of his unpremeditated genius. Yet the revision is ambiguous: Milton's learning is both his glory and his limitation.[16] Masson's odd comment about "flakes" (perfect snowflakes? or mere flecks?) hovers between apology and exaltation. J. C. Shairp, writing in 1875, notes that Milton's allusive style is both appealing (especially to young poets) and alienating: "[O]ur younger poets seem bent on choosing learned subjects and adopting the learned style, so cutting themselves off from that freer range and wider sympathy, which comes more from contact with man and outward nature than with books and classical models" (Shairp 559). In this Shairp foreshadows the animadversions of

---

16. The same praise and the same objection belong to Masson's *Milton;* Palgrave recognizes the biography's "great value," but asserts, "Its 'too much learning' encumbers it" (Palgrave 397). The subconscious equation of Milton and Masson is common in reviews of the biography.

T. S. Eliot: when Eliot calls Milton "inimitable," it is both a compliment and a warning (Eliot, *On Poetry and Poets,* 182).

Milton's style, being inimitable, is even more absolutely untranslatable; once again, this quality makes Milton at once grander and more limited. As Tulloch writes,

> Whenever his wonderful march of noble words flags . . . the chief charm of his poetry is gone; hence there never was another poet of Milton's rank whose poetry could so ill bear the test of translation. Translations of Paradise Lost, literal or otherwise, are absolutely unreadable, [whereas] the poorest rendering of Shakespeare . . . preserves the original interest in its most vital elements. (Tulloch 281–82)

The contrast between Milton and Shakespeare, a commonplace of Romantic criticism, remained frequent throughout the Victorian period (Nelson 13–15); what is new in Victorian criticism is the perception of Milton's parochialism that emerges from the comparison. The Germans and French, writes J. R. Seeley, are always astonished to "hear Milton's—the almost unknown Milton's—name familiarly coupled by Englishmen with that of the prodigy of literature" (Seeley, "Milton's Poetry," 420). Where Shakespeare was permitted to be a universal possession, Milton came to be seen, despite his biblical subject matter, as a peculiarly English poet, and the Victorians frequently commented upon this qualification. Arthur Henry Hallam, writing favorably of an Italian translation, nevertheless remarks that "As Englishmen, we cannot but feel that any transposition of Milton, however excellent, would seem to us like a discord in some favourite tune" (Hallam 510).

Matthew Arnold, writing about "A French Critic on Milton," notes the same phenomenon, considering it at once a limitation and a recommendation:

> [Milton] is our great artist in style, our one first-rate master in the grand style. He is as truly a master in this style as the great Greeks are, or Virgil, or Dante. The number of such masters is so limited, that a man acquires a world-rank in poetry and art, instead of a mere local rank, by being counted among them. But Milton's importance to us Englishmen, by virtue of this distinction of his, is incalculable. The charm of a master's unfailing touch in diction and in rhythm, no one, after all, can feel so intimately, so profoundly, as his own countrymen. Invention, plan, wit, pathos, thought, all of them are in great measure capable of being detached from the original work itself, and of being exported for admiration abroad. Diction and rhythm are not. (CPA 9:183)

Milton's style paradoxically assures him a "world-rank" at the same time that it limits a true appreciation of his greatness to his "countrymen." Milton's magnanimous choice described in *The Reason of Church-Government*—"not caring to be once nam'd abroad, though perhaps I could attaine to that, but content with these British Ilands as my world" (Prose 1:812)—appeared to the Victorians to have come true. Yet once again, this limitation appears in Arnold to be a source not of regret but of pride. The same quality that prevents Milton from being a universal possession renders him of "incalculable" value to those who truly appreciate him.

Another way of framing the same paradox would be to say that Milton seemed to the Victorians both more familiar and more alien than he had to previous eras. Masson's biography humanized its subject: Milton was no longer the timeless, inimitable bard of *Paradise Lost* but a more approachable and recognizable seventeenth-century writer in various genres. Yet as the canon of his works expanded in the early Victorian period, its contemporary relevance was perceived to contract. His divorce pamphlets were a case in point: "It is a notable fact, that Milton's works on Divorce, did not, as far as we remember, afford a single illustration to the great debate on the occasion of the recent Act [the Divorce Act of 1857]" (Tulloch 283). Donne (314) made the same point the following year, and yet another critic more broadly, though wrongly, predicts that Milton's views on divorce "have not only not been adopted, but they probably never will" (Allon 95). Bagehot declared categorically that the "present generation" (he was writing in 1859) constituted "a generation, almost more than any other, different from [Milton's] own" (Bagehot 148).[17]

In short, Milton, for all his imaginative wanderings through time and space, becomes in this period geographically and temporally localized. "Homer and Shakespeare claim universal homage without limitation or reserve. Milton is both a Puritan and a heretic, and draws from his countrymen a less complete, though perhaps an intenser, worship" (New 105). *Less universal, but more intense:* this is the basic contradiction of the Victorian Milton, although it follows naturally from what was already a critical commonplace. In Romantic criticism, as M. H. Abrams explains, Milton was consistently taken—usually

---

17. Masson, in a rare flash of irony, draws attention to the differences between Milton's ideal of humanity and the Victorians': "The great primitive father of our race did not walk in the garden of Eden inculcating on himself, as we moderns do, the duty of being earnest, firm, or specially true to this or that ideal; nor was his spouse a woman of highly intellectual tendencies" (Masson, "The Works of John Milton," 330). The irony is directed toward contemporary ideals, but the point remains that even ideals are historically determined, and that Milton's may seem alien to a Victorian reader.

in contrast to Shakespeare or Homer—to typify "subjective" poetry (Abrams 250–56). The subjective poet, as Robert Browning defines the term in his "Essay on Shelley," is in some sense all-encompassing:

> Not what man sees, but what God sees—the *Ideas* of Plato, seeds of creation lying burningly on the Divine Hand—it is toward these that he struggles. Not with the combination of humanity in action, but with the primal elements of humanity he has to do.

On the other hand, such poetry is not directly accessible; it constitutes a personal vision, fully comprehensible only with the aid of the poet's biography:

> Such a poet...does not paint pictures and hang them on the walls, but rather carries them on the retina of his own eyes: we must look deep into his human eyes, to see those pictures on them....Both for love's and understanding's sake we desire to know him, and as readers of his poetry must be readers of his biography also. (R. Browning 1:1002)

The first part of this definition—the universality of subjective poetry—had long been applied to Milton. Around the time of Masson's biography, the qualification too began to be applied: a subjective poet must be put in context in order to be fully understood. And to know Milton's biography is to feel him at once more familiar and more removed.

And yet Milton was all the more fascinating for this new separation. Seeley suggests, with regard to Milton's political writings, that their importance grows in inverse proportion to their direct applicability: because Milton "is removed from us by such a distance, and his direct influence has ceased, our curiosity to understand his views and enter into them may well increase" (Seeley, "Milton's Political Opinions," 300). An earlier critic in the *British Quarterly Review* makes the same point about Milton's writings more generally. Milton's visionariness is such that, like a prophet, his influence grows greater as he grows more distant: "We should be nearer the truth were we to say, that his influence was, and will yet be, all the greater that in his own day he was so little followed" (Anon., "Milton and the Commonwealth," 247). In the same way, Milton's poetry may have seemed a more indistinct presence to the Victorians than to their predecessors; but if so, it was all the more intriguing because its "direct influence had ceased."

When the angelic choir sings hymns to God in book 3 of *Paradise Lost,* they describe him in two different states.

Thee Father first they sung omnipotent,
Immutable, immortal, infinite,
Eternal king; thee author of all being,
Fountain of light, thyself invisible
Amidst the glorious brightness where thou sitst
Throned inaccessible . . .

This is one version of the Father: so luminous as to defy all access or approach. At other times, however, God seems to circumscribe his glory.

. . . but when thou shad'st
The full blaze of thy beams, and through a cloud
Drawn round about thee like a radiant shrine,
Dark with excessive bright thy skirts appear,
Yet dazzle heaven, that brightest seraphim
Approach not, but with both wings veil their eyes.
(PL 3.372–82)

At such moments, when God tempers the full force of his presence, he becomes paradoxically at once more accessible and more hidden. The outer skirts of his being begin to appear, and yet the angels now find him to be "dark with excessive bright"—a blind spot, rather than an unmistakable presence. The first version of God may be compared to the Romantic Milton conjured by Harold Bloom—the "author" who leaves no spot untouched by the blaze of his glory. The second version is the Victorian Milton, at once closer and more removed—still central and obvious, yet so much so as to seem obscure. Milton's presence did not fade in the latter part of the century but rather approached too near to be clearly distinguished. If for the Romantics Milton provides the very letters, the poetic alphabet, with which they compose, for the Victorians he is a purloined letter—something so patent as to go unnoticed, hidden in plain sight.

This passage from book 3 inspired two quite different poetic responses from Alfred Tennyson. In Tennyson's juvenile poem "Armageddon," which is practically a pastiche of different sublime passages in Milton, the visionary speaker encounters a seraph who

looked into my face
With his inutterable shining eyes,
So that with hasty motion I did veil
My vision with both hands, and saw before me

Such coloured spots as dance athwart the eyes
Of those that gaze upon the noonday sun.
("Armageddon" 2.4–9).[18]

Verbally, these lines imitate the second part of the passage from *Paradise Lost,* where the seraphim "with both wings veil their eyes." But in their method Tennyson's lines, like his whole poem, hew closer to the first model, that of direct, overwhelming influence. "Armageddon," written in 1827, is an archetypally Romantic poem, in which Milton is invoked in every other line as the speaker strives to achieve or even surpass the visionary powers of his predecessor.

The situation is entirely different, however, in Tennyson's next engagement with the same passage. Section 67 of *In Memoriam* was composed only about a decade after "Armageddon," but it provides a very different and recognizably Victorian response to Milton. Tennyson pictures the distant burial place of his lost friend Arthur Hallam:

When on my bed the moonlight falls,
    I know that in thy place of rest
    By that broad water of the west,
There comes a glory on the walls;

Thy marble bright in dark appears,
    As slowly steals a silver flame
    Along the letters of thy name,
And o'er the number of thy years.

The mystic glory swims away;
    From off my bed the moonlight dies;
    And closing eaves of wearied eyes
I sleep till dusk is dipt in gray:

And then I know the mist is drawn
    A lucid veil from coast to coast,
    And in the dark church like a ghost
Thy tablet glimmers to the dawn.

---

18. All quotations from Tennyson refer to *The Poems of Tennyson,* ed. Christopher Ricks.

This is not the most obviously Miltonic passage in *In Memoriam*. There are other, far more explicit echoes, especially of "Lycidas" and of Milton's sonnets, which are discussed in chapter 4. In section 67 the influence is quiet yet pervasive: not only the phrase "bright in dark" (line 5), but the repeated "glory," the mist that is "drawn" as God's cloud is "drawn," the "veil" that shields the speaker at the end—all recall the passage in *Paradise Lost*. The echo is apt and extremely moving. Tennyson, like the angels in book 3, is trying to approach a heavenly being (Hallam) whom he both loves and fears, who seems in his new state somehow closer and at the same time more mysterious than before—as Tennyson writes at the end of *In Memoriam*, "loved deeplier, darklier understood" (129.10). Milton provides him with the model he needs.

The point is not that Romantic allusions to Milton are all bald and obvious whereas Victorian echoes are muted and subtle.[19] Rather, the point is that we must understand how Milton can continue to exert a powerful influence while largely disappearing from view. In the case of the passage from *In Memoriam*, his influence is partly hidden by the existence of an earlier source: both Milton and Tennyson draw inspiration for their images of "bright in dark" and "dark with...bright" from Shakespeare's Sonnet 43 ("in dreams [my eyes] look on thee,/And, darkly bright, are bright in dark directed"). In "Armageddon," as in many Romantic poems, Milton stands out from all other predecessors; in *In Memoriam*, by contrast, Milton's voice blends with others, and as we shall see such blending is typical of Victorian poetry. This suggests one reason why Milton, despite his ubiquity, seems less manifest than in Romantic poetry: the purloined letter is all the more undetectable for being mixed up with other letters on the mantelpiece. But it is only one reason. There are many ways in which a cynosure or beloved object can become dark with the very excess of brightness, and these are what the following chapters explore.

---

19. On the complexities of allusion in Romantic poetry, see James Chandler, "Romantic Allusiveness." Chandler distinguishes between the intentionality of allusion in Augustan writing and its associative quality among the Romantics.

❧ CHAPTER 2

Milton as Classic, Milton as Bible

The differences between the Romantic and the Victorian Milton are due, as we have seen, not to any decline in awareness of Milton on the part of the Victorians, but quite the contrary. The very fact that Romantic poets so frequently and self-consciously invoked Milton rendered it unnecessary for Victorian poets to do the same, and various other external factors, such as David Masson's biography, contributed to make Milton "dark with excessive bright." But it is important to recognize as well the internal features of Milton's poetry that render it inherently so familiar as to escape mention. In this chapter I focus on *Paradise Lost* and discuss how by its very nature it constitutes a classic—that is, a work that goes without saying. In both its structure and its plot, *Paradise Lost* offers numerous examples of things that are left unsaid or are mentioned only in passing, not because they are unimportant, but because they are assumed to be obvious. This may serve as one model for the place of *Paradise Lost* itself in Victorian literature—for instance, in the poetry and criticism of Elizabeth Barrett Browning, who pays her greatest tributes to Milton when she speaks of him the least. A slightly different model applies in the case of Christina Rossetti, for whom *Paradise Lost* functions not just as any classic, but specifically like the Bible—a work that is influential not only when unmentioned but even when unread. The influence of *Paradise Lost* on Rossetti's "Goblin Market," which has long

been taken for granted, is more oblique and surprising than critics have usually recognized. The chapter concludes with a brief look at Gerard Manley
Hopkins, who offers a variation on both of these models.

Milton as Classic

The year 1825, which saw the publication of Milton's treatise *Christian Doctrine,* marks a watershed in the history of the poet's reception; it therefore
seems a natural point from which to date the beginning of the new, Victorian perception of Milton. The manuscript of the treatise (written in Latin)
was discovered in 1823, whereupon George IV ordered his royal librarian,
Charles Sumner, to translate it into English. The new book was immediately
reviewed in the *Quarterly Review* and the *New Monthly Magazine* and, most
notably, in the *Edinburgh Review,* where it was the subject of a long essay by
Thomas Babington Macaulay. "Milton" was Macaulay's first published article; it won him instant acclaim, launching his career as a critic and historian.
It also became a reference point for subsequent critics, often set in coun-
terpoise to Samuel Johnson's "Life of Milton": where Johnson expressed
a strong distaste for Milton the man and the politician, Macaulay served as
Milton's apologist.

The article spends only the obligatory page or two discussing the actual
volume being reviewed; the majority of the essay is dedicated to a defense of
Milton and the Parliamentary cause in the Civil War. But Macaulay also provides a number of keen literary insights. One of his most intriguing points
concerns the long lists or catalogues of proper names that mark certain books
of *Paradise Lost* (and, to a lesser extent, *Paradise Regained*):

> [W]e may remark, that scarcely any passages in the poems of Milton
> are more generally known, or more frequently repeated, than those
> which are little more than muster-rolls of names. They are not always
> more appropriate or more melodious than other names. But they are
> charmed names. Every one of them is the first link in a long chain of
> associated ideas. Like the dwelling-place of our infancy revisited in
> manhood, like the song of our country heard in a strange land, they
> produce upon us an effect wholly independent of their intrinsic value.
> One transports us back to a remote period of history. Another places
> us among the moral scenery and manners of a distant country. A third
> evokes all the dear classical recollections of childhood, the school-room,
> the dog-eared Virgil, the holiday, and the prize. (Macaulay 312)

Macaulay is right to say that Milton's "muster-rolls" were admired. Leigh Hunt published an article just a few months after Macaulay's, praising "Milton's harmonious use of proper names" and defending Milton's lists against the criticisms of Johnson, who in *Rambler* 88 had disparaged them as mere interruptions. Hunt by contrast finds them apt and well-deployed: "It is not that the names are merely beautiful or sounding in themselves, but that they are so grand and full of variety in their collocation" (Hunt 389).

Macaulay's assessment is rather different: "They are not always more appropriate or more melodious than other names. But they are charmed names. Every one of them is the first link in a long chain of associated ideas." Every exotic name that Milton pronounces seems vaguely familiar to Macaulay ("like the dwelling-place of our infancy revisited in manhood"); it conjures up associations. This peculiarity attaches not only to Milton's catalogues but to his poetry more generally: "The most striking characteristic of the poetry of Milton, is the extreme remoteness of the associations by means of which it acts on the reader" (Macaulay 311). Other Victorian critics also commented on the strange familiarity of Milton's names and offered various explanations. According to one rather circular argument, although Milton may have intended the names to be exotic and unfamiliar, the poem itself educated readers to recognize them: Milton "made, by means of this very *Paradise Lost,* the ordinary reading public familiarly acquainted with many a matter which, in the days of Charles the Second, had not penetrated very much deeper than the upper circle of scholars" (Maginn and Wilson 697–98). Frederick Pollock, writing in 1890, points out the effect of empire on a modern reader of Milton's poem: "It is curious for the modern Englishman to think how much nearer many of Milton's names, to him semi-fabulous, have come to our daily knowledge and concerns. The cliffs of Caucasus are explored by English mountaineers, and Agra and Lahore are no longer even under a puppet Great Mogul" (Pollock 519).

Yet neither of these arguments—the suggestions that Milton's allusions are familiar because we have read Milton, or because the world has shrunk— explains why Macaulay felt that every name in Milton came fraught with associations. Macaulay is referring to such densely allusive passages as the much-admired first description of Eden:

> Not that fair field
> Of Enna, where Proserpin gathering flowers
> Herself a fairer flower by gloomy Dis
> Was gathered, which cost Ceres all that pain
> To seek her through the world; nor that sweet grove

Of Daphne by Orontes, and the inspired
Castalian spring, might with this Paradise
Of Eden strive; nor that Nyseian isle
Girt with the river Triton, where old Cham,
Whom Gentiles Ammon call and Libyan Jove,
Hid Amalthea and her florid son
Young Bacchus from his stepdame Rhea's eye;
Nor where Abassin kings their issue guard,
Mount Amara, though this by some supposed
True Paradise under the Ethiop line.

(PL 4.268–82)

Some of these stories are familiar to the educated reader, but not all: do "Nyseian" and "old Cham" really call up for Macaulay a "long chain of associated ideas"? And even if we could grant that Macaulay himself was as learned as Milton, how could we explain that many readers, even those who presumably have never heard of "Orontes" and "the river Triton," find Milton's lists of names strangely suggestive?

Christopher Ricks remarks of this passage, "It is, I believe, the very fact that Milton's gaze is *not* directly on Paradise which makes these lines among the most haunting he ever wrote" (Ricks 148). Ricks's observation forms part of an important strain of Milton criticism, concentrating on his negative constructions: Milton is at his most suggestive when he tells us that we cannot know.[1] As Stanley Fish puts it, "Paradoxically, our awareness of the inadequacy of what is described and what we can apprehend provides, if only negatively, a sense of what cannot be described and what we cannot apprehend. Thus Milton is able to suggest a reality beyond this one by forcing us to feel, dramatically, its unavailability" (Fish, *Surprised by Sin*, 27). The same reasoning was used by Thomas De Quincey as long ago as 1839 to explain the presence of proper names in paradise. Arguing, like Hunt, against the strictures of Samuel Johnson, De Quincey explains that Eden can only be understood as the contrast or negation of what we know. "Out of this one principle of subtle and lurking antagonism, may be explained every thing which has been denounced under the idea of pedantry in Milton. . . . Paradise could not, in any other way, or by any artifice less profound, have been made to give up its essential and differential characteristics in a form palpable to the imagination" (De Quincey 11:439).

---

1. On the possible relation between Milton's negatives and his blindness, see Patterson, "Milton's Negativity," 86–92.

De Quincey, Ricks, and Fish all offer explanations of how the negated list of names in the simile quoted above helps the reader to conceive of paradise; but none of them explores the effect of the negative construction on the names themselves, which Macaulay and others have found so strangely resonant. Most of us have no previous knowledge of the names and places to which Milton refers, yet Milton *attributes* such knowledge to us by his "not." "Not that fair field... nor that Nyseian isle": these imply perfect familiarity, as if the reader had probably pictured Eden as resembling the Nyseian isle, and needed to be corrected. The reader seems to have associations with "the river Triton" and "old Cham" (though even Macaulay might be hard put to name what associations), because these names have been invoked dismissively. Just as, in describing Satan's spear, Milton introduces the image of a pine tree—*not* because it is really comparable in size (not even close), but because a reader might well think so at first—so the Nyseian isle, though woefully inadequate to describe paradise, is nevertheless offered to us as a concession.

Similarly, to help us conceive of the army of devils, Milton names other armies more familiar to us (for of armies we have heard), but again negates them:

> [N]ever since created man,
> Met such embodied force, as named with these
> Could merit more than that small infantry
> Warred on by cranes: though all the Giant brood
> Of Phlegra with the heroic race were joined
> That fought at Thebes and Ilium...
> And all who since, baptized or infidel
> Jousted in Aspramont or Montalban,
> Damasco, or Marocco, or Trebisond,
> Or whom Biserta sent from Afric shore
> When Charlemain with all his peerage fell
> By Fontarabbia.
>
> (*PL* 1.573–87)

Once again, Macaulay seems to have associations with all these names: he is probably thinking of this passage when he remarks that one of Milton's lists "brings before us the splendid phantoms of chivalrous romance, the trophied lists, the embroidered housings, the quaint devices, the haunted forests, the enchanted gardens, the achievements of enamoured knights, and the smiles of rescued princesses" (Macaulay 312). Milton's passage is indeed evocative— so much so that it is easy to overlook the crux in the concluding word,

"Fontarabbia." As Alastair Fowler points out in a note to this passage, such a place does exist, but it is scarcely famous. Nobody fell there, and certainly not Charlemagne, who never fell in battle at all; technically then, "Fontarabbia" should have no power to conjure up "the splendid phantoms of chivalrous romance."[2] But as Barbara Everett explains, the name is allusive without being denotative; it sounds "a note that by its emptiness holds enormous power of connotation: all courage, all romance, all arrogance, all delusion—the pastness of the dead past recalled in a voice of brass: *Fontarabbia*" (Everett 260). Even once we learn that "Fontarabbia" is an almost empty signifier its evocativeness does not diminish, since its connotative power is not inherent but derives from its placement. It is offered as a parallel to the utterly unimaginable troops of Satan, in comparison to which Fontarabbia is as much a part of our ken as Charlemagne. Or rather, not a parallel but what De Quincey calls a "differential"; to know that not even "Fontarabbia" can compare is to know all the characteristics that Macaulay and Everett both describe.

The same implicit familiarity attaches not only to names that are negated but to all allusions in the poem. *Paradise Lost* is set at the most remote possible time from the present and in a mostly prelapsarian state that is scarcely conceivable to our fallen minds. Hence every illustrative allusion is a contemporary allusion; it necessarily refers to something closer to us than the world of the poem is, and therefore implicitly more familiar. When Satan flying through the infernal landscape is compared to a fleet "Close sailing from Bengala, or the isles / Of Ternate and Tidore" (*PL* 2.638–39), the reader receives these names as proximate points of reference, familiar landmarks. Exotic as they are, the allusions are nevertheless accommodations, like anachronistic references that a speaker might use to put an audience at ease—and which tend to get an appreciative nod even from those who do not actually recognize what is being referred to. Johnson, or T. S. Eliot, might object that "Ternate and Tidore" are mystifying and grandiloquent words, introduced to inflate the image.[3] But the opposite is true: they are part of the mortal world,

---

2. To be exact, Fowler notes that there was one Spanish writer (Mariana) who put the fall of Roland at Fontarabbia, rather than Roncesvalles; but even in this version Charlemagne did not fall together with his peerage. Fowler suggests that Milton may have intended this line to contain a covert allusion to Charles II.

3. In "Milton I" Eliot asserts that some of Milton's roll calls are "not serious poetry, not poetry fully occupied about its business, but rather a solemn game"; and even when "Milton uses proper names in moderation," the "single effect" is "grandeur of sound" (Eliot, *On Poetry and Poets*, 163–64). Barbara Everett considers Eliot's critique seriously and turns it into a provocative critical challenge: "Any reader who appreciates Milton's verse should be able to answer Eliot: to say why he finds this Book XI catalogue [*PL* 11.385–411] *good,* without having recourse to the word 'music,' or its equivalent" (Everett 256).

as Satan is not, and even if we have never heard of them before, we recognize them as concessions to our knowledge. This is a wrinkle on the principle of accommodation as it is usually understood. As Raphael explains—and practices—it, accommodation involves representing the unknowable in terms of the familiar.[4] But Milton's more daring tactic is to represent what we cannot know (Eden, Satan) in terms of what we do not know (Orontes, Ternate, Tidore). The result is that the reader achieves not only a sublime, negatively defined understanding of one side of the equation, as De Quincey, Ricks, and Fish describe, but also an uncanny sense of familiarity with the other.

This effect applies even to passages in the poem that do not contain any muster roll of proper names. Consider the moment in book 9 when Satan is compared to

> one who long in populous city pent,
> Where houses thick and sewers annoy the air,
> Forth issuing on a summer's morn to breathe
> Among the pleasant villages and farms.
>
> (*PL* 9.445–48)

We might think that this metaphor seems familiar because it was so often admired and imitated by later poets, particularly the Romantics.[5] So we might think, erring. The image seemed familiar to readers long before the Romantics, because once again it is presented as something that everybody knows well, and which can therefore serve to explain the satanic state of mind. One could argue that the same is true of all similes: every simile assumes the familiarity of its vehicle, which can fulfill its illustrative purpose only if it is recognized. But Milton's simile has an effect that the same comparison would not have in Homer, or Spenser, or Wordsworth. Every simile in *Paradise Lost* is implicitly negated in advance, both by being necessarily inadequate—to compare Satan to a city dweller is to compare great things to small—and also by its temporal impossibility: "Satan was like a city dweller (if there had been such a thing as cities)." Milton, we are conscious, strays far outside the world

---

4. Raphael tells Adam that "what surmounts the reach / Of human sense, I shall delineate so, / By likening spiritual to corporal forms, / As may express them best" (*PL* 5.571–74). Milton gives further thoughts about accommodation in *Christian Doctrine* book 1, chapter 2 (Prose 6:133–36). See *M.Enc* under "Accommodation" for a brief account of the history of this concept in the Renaissance.

5. Coleridge echoes Milton's simile in "This Lime-tree Bower my Prison," 30, and in "Frost at Midnight," 52. Wordsworth in turn echoes these two passages, and Milton's more obliquely, in the peroration to the second book of *The Prelude*. Keats has a sonnet titled "To one who has been long in city pent."

of his poem, and far below its register, just to find a parallel with which we can sympathize. Hence the "populous city," like Ternate or Tidore, becomes part of our implied experience. Milton ascribes to the reader a knowledge of the whole postlapsarian world, and as a result every illustrative name or image seems familiar, even if unknown before.

Because of this attributed knowledge *Paradise Lost* is, by its very nature, a "classic." Mark Twain defined the classic as "a book which people praise but don't read" (Twain 241); a less cynical definition might be that a classic is a work that seems to be known even before it is read. A great book can be read; a classic can only be reread, since the first-time reader finds it already familiar. In Milton's poetry, characters repeatedly have the experience of reporting news that turns out not to be new at all, since the hearers seem to know it all already. Abdiel flies all night from Satan's camp to give word of the rebellion, only to arrive among the faithful angels where he "found / Already known what he for news had thought / To have reported" (*PL* 6.19–21). Meanwhile, the angel Nisroc stands up at the rebel council to propose that some new form of arms should be sought out, to which Satan coolly replies, "Not uninvented that, which thou aright / Believ'st so main to our success, I bring" (6.470–71). In book 7 Raphael frequently concedes that he is telling Adam what he already knows: "Needless to thee repeated"; "as thou knowst"; "thou rememberst, for thou heardst" (7.494, 536, 561). At the end of the poem, when Adam runs ahead of Michael to waken Eve and share the knowledge of his visions, he finds a reception similar to Abdiel's; Eve is already awake and tells him, "Whence thou returnst, and whither wentst, I know" (12.610). In *Paradise Regained* the Son displays the same disarming foreknowledge, to Satan's discomfiture: "Think not but that I know these things," he replies after Satan's long harangue about Athens (*PR* 4.286). Most notably, foreknowledge is, of course, an attribute of God. Even when the Father expresses delight at the Son's proffered intercession, that intercession cannot come as a surprise: "All hast thou spoken as my thoughts are, all / As my eternal purpose hath decreed"; and again, "all thy request was my decree" (*PL* 3.171–72; 11.47). The same applies to God's negotiation with Adam: "I, ere thou spak'st, / Knew it not good for man to be alone" (8.444–45). This sense of foreknowledge, repeatedly experienced by the characters of *Paradise Lost,* is shared by the reader of *Paradise Lost* and is inherent to the classic: a work of literature is classic if it seems already known.

Even according to this definition, classics can be made as well as born. A work can achieve classic status by becoming part of the cultural unconscious; those critics were not wrong who suggested that the proper names of *Paradise Lost* seemed familiar because the poem itself had made them familiar.

Certainly by late in the nineteenth century, *Paradise Lost* had become a school text, and hence not only familiar but overfamiliar. John Dennis, writing in 1880, notes (not wholly with approval),

> The great poets of England are now constantly served up in textbooks, in order that boys may win prizes, and students pass examinations. Every allusion is explained, every sentence has to be parsed, every grammatical peculiarity studied.... Every poem of Milton's has been thus placed in the hands of the dissector, and many poems of Wordsworth have felt also the scalpel of the grammarians. In this way it has come to pass that these poets are better known to young readers than they were twenty years ago. (Dennis 111)

But if, as Dennis suggests, some works achieve classic status or have it thrust upon them, others are born so. Their structure makes them seem familiar, as if their words and images were always known in advance. Long before it became a school text, *Paradise Lost* had already joined the list of natural classics.

The great exemplar of the natural classic is Virgil's *Aeneid*. Macaulay, trying to explain the unplaceable familiarity of Milton's muster rolls, suggests that they summon up "all the dear classical recollections of childhood, the school-room, the dog-eared Virgil." The Virgil is "dog-eared" because even to the schoolboy he appears to be already commonplace; Macaulay seems never to have encountered Virgil for the first time. This is because the *Aeneid* employs the same overarching time scheme as *Paradise Lost*. What Milton does for all of world history, Virgil does for Rome, focusing on the most distant part of its history in a manner that simply assumes the familiarity of the rest.[6] But an even closer analogue to *Paradise Lost* can be found in yet another natural classic, *Hamlet*. According to T. S. Eliot, Shakespeare's play can be fully understood only if "we perceive his *Hamlet* to be superposed upon much cruder material [i.e., an earlier play by Thomas Kyd] which persists even in the final form" (Eliot, *Selected Essays,* 142). In concentrating his attention on a lost older version of the tragedy, Eliot extends to the textual level a temporal layering that characterizes the entire play. The court of Claudius seems familiar to us, not only because *Hamlet* is a great work

---

6. For more on Virgil and his relation to this definition of a classic, especially as elucidated by T. S. Eliot in his essay "What is a Classic?" see Gray, "Nostalgia, the Classics, and the Intimations Ode." For the best account of this trope of overarching or overleaping, known as "metalepsis" or "transumption," see John Hollander, *The Figure of Echo,* 113–49.

that has become part of our cultural heritage, but because no other play of Shakespeare's so vividly conjures up the past. The world of Yorick and of old Hamlet forms a principal object of the characters' attention; there are few other plays in which one of the most memorable characters dies twenty-three years before the action begins. *Hamlet,* though in fact sketchy on many significant details (Claudius's election, Ophelia's mother), nevertheless makes the whole of Denmark's recent history seem familiar, by constantly looking back beyond it. This characteristic obliqueness—there is no need to focus our gaze directly on the action, since it is already so well known—is picked up and brilliantly exploited in Tom Stoppard's *Rosencrantz and Guildenstern Are Dead.*

That is why, if there were no external evidence of the existence of an ur-*Hamlet,* it would have to be invented; how else to explain that the play already seems so familiar? Like Eliot, William Empson traces this effect back to a predecessor play. Empson claims that Shakespeare was revamping an old but formerly popular play he had found "in the ice-box"; hence, even at the first performance, the audience felt it had seen all this before (Empson, *Essays on Shakespeare,* 80). Empson's criticism is intended to elucidate such a reaction as that of William Hazlitt, who begins his essay on *Hamlet* as follows:

> This is that Hamlet the Dane, whom we read of in our youth, and whom we may be said almost to remember in our after-years; he who made that famous soliloquy on life, who gave the advice to the players, . . . who talked with the grave-diggers, and moralised on Yorick's skull; the school-fellow of Rosencraus and Guildenstern at Wittenberg; the friend of Horatio; the lover of Ophelia; he that was mad and sent to England; the slow avenger of his father's death; who lived at the court of Horwendillus five hundred years before we were born, but all whose thoughts we seem to know as well as we do our own, because we have read them in Shakespear. (Hazlitt 4:232)

Hazlitt attributes the familiarity of these events to the fact that "we have read them in Shakespear," but they seem to have been known to him since before he was born. They are so familiar as to seem strange: "We have been so used to this tragedy that we hardly know how to criticise it any more than we should know how to describe our own faces" (4:233). This is another way of saying that *Hamlet* is a classic: too close to our own faces to be distinctly visible.

Walter Bagehot, in his review of volume 1 of Masson's *Milton,* runs through the whole of Milton's biography in a passage rhetorically reminiscent of Hazlitt's potted biography of Hamlet. Bagehot's criticism suggests to what extent Milton too was a classic, someone or something which we have all known "from our boyhood":

> The bare outline of Milton's life is very well known. We have all heard that he was born in the later years of King James, just when Puritanism was collecting its strength for the approaching struggle; that his father and mother were good quiet people, inclined, but not immoderately, to that persuasion; that he went up to Cambridge early, and had some kind of dissension with the authorities there ...

—and so on (Bagehot's biographical outline, like Hazlitt's, is a single long sentence) until—

> that after the Restoration he was naturally in a position of some danger and much difficulty; that in the midst of that difficulty he wrote *Paradise Lost;* that he did not fail in heart or hope, but lived for fourteen years after the destruction of all for which he had laboured, in serene retirement, 'though fallen on evil days, though fallen on evil times;' —all this we have heard from our boyhood. (Bagehot 2:113)

Bagehot's abstract is all the more convincing for beginning with misinformation and ending with a misquotation. The year of Milton's birth, 1608, is not one of the "later years of King James" but near the beginning of his reign. As for the quotation at the end, it seems almost purposefully inexact, since Bagehot quotes the line correctly—"On evil days though fallen, and evil tongues"—just twenty pages later. The point of the carelessness is that one does not look up Milton's dates, or quotations from the famous passages of *Paradise Lost,* as one would for a minor poet; they are already "very well known." This is even more true of the poem than of the poet. Masson himself, in an early essay, uses the same Hazlittean rhetoric of familiarity about Satan:

> And is this the Satan of the *Paradise Lost?* Is this the archangel ruined? this the being who warred against the Almighty, who lay floating many a rood, who shot upwards like a pyramid of fire, who navigated space wherever he chose, speeding on his errands from star to star ... ? Yes, it is he; but oh, how changed! (Masson, "Three Devils," 659)

My point is that to the Victorians, Milton, like *Hamlet,* had become a classic. To Hazlitt, although Hamlet "lived ... five hundred years before we were born," he is someone "we seem to know as well as we do" ourselves. To Macaulay, when Milton's book "lies on our table, we seem to be contemporaries of the great poet" (Macaulay 345).

Such a sentiment helps us understand the peculiarities of the Victorian Milton, as described in chapter 1. If the Romantics seem to be always reading and alluding to Milton, whereas the Victorians do not, this does not necessarily imply a falling-off but quite the contrary. Milton is not unfamiliar to the Victorians, but overfamiliar; not unread, but already read. This paradox was noted in the *New Monthly Magazine* in 1834: "Of John Milton, what can be now said which may not be familiarly known by all who possess even a superficial acquaintance with the literature of their country? Yet, perhaps, there is no illustrious writer who is so partially read or so little understood" (Anon., Milton's Prose Writings," 39). "Partially read": both because critics are not impartial, and because nobody bothers to read the whole of *Paradise Lost* anymore since it is "familiarly known by all" English readers simply by virtue of their literacy.[7] James Nelson, in an odd but pregnant aside suggests that such was the case of Tennyson: "Tennyson probably never knew when he first became aware of Milton" (Nelson 108). That familiarity from the womb that Tennyson claimed for himself with regard to Virgil—"I that loved thee since my day began" ("To Virgil," 19)—Nelson assigns also to the dog-eared Milton.

It is impossible, of course, to draw an absolute line at 1825, to claim that at that moment Milton suddenly began to be treated as a classic. But if we grant that attitudes shifted in the nineteenth century, that poets in particular became less apt to engage self-consciously with Miltonic precedents, it is far easier to believe that they thought of Milton simply as a given than that they forgot about him. The real anomaly in this case lies not with the Victorian poets' reaction to Milton but with that of the Romantics. Rather than rereading Milton together with Shakespeare and Virgil, the Romantics read *Paradise Lost* as something novel and demanding a response. Such a reading is by no means "wrong"; it is, in a sense, the satanic reading. If the characteristic of God, and of most of Milton's characters, is to know already what seems like news, Satan's way is to treat as news what everyone else seems already to know. "Strange point and new!" he exclaims when Abdiel reminds him of the Son's agency in creation (*PL* 5.855). Whereas Abdiel considers the

---

7. The claim or complaint that nobody actually reads all the way through *Paradise Lost* anymore continued throughout the Victorian era. Writing in 1922, R. D. Havens recalls, "A well-known orator won the smiling approval of a large audience some twenty-five years since, when he referred to Milton's epic as 'a poem that every one talks about and no one reads'"(Havens 3).

precedence of the Son over the angels to be logically obvious, Satan claims to find it so surprising that all of heaven now strikes him as suddenly unfamiliar: "New laws... new minds... new counsels... new commands" (5.680–91). This half-conscious repression of what is obvious continues after his fall. "Who knew?" becomes his refrain in hell (1.93). By the same token, the influence of Milton on the Romantics seems remarkable because it seemed remarkable to them: like the Satan of *Paradise Regained,* amazed afresh each time he recognizes the Son, the Romantic poets encountered Milton and his precedence with ever-renewed surprise. But if the Romantic reading is satanic, the Victorian reading is angelic—more in the manner of Abdiel, who takes God's precedence for granted and does not bother to articulate news that is already known. To the Victorians, Milton was not so much the giver of poetic tradition as the given.

Elizabeth Barrett Browning sometimes thought of Milton as too obvious to mention. In her review essay "The Book of the Poets" (1842), which offers a chronological survey from Chaucer to Wordsworth, she concludes the "third era" of English poetry with Cowley, then follows with this.

And then came "glorious John," with the whole fourth era in his arms;—and eloquent above the sons of men, to talk down, thunder down poetry as if it were an exhalation. Do we speak as if he were not a poet? nay, but we speak of the character of his influences; nay, but he was a poet—an excellent poet—in marble: and Phidias, with the sculpturesque ideal separated from his working tool, might have carved him. He was a poet without passion, just as Cowley was: but, then, Cowley lived by fancy, and that would have been poor living for John Dryden. (E. B. Browning 6:285)

A reader familiar with Johnson's *Lives of the Poets,* or even anyone familiar with the chronology of English poetry, would expect this paragraph to name not Dryden but Milton, who has yet to be discussed in the essay. Browning seems actively to court confusion by not naming Dryden until the end of the third sentence. The epithet "glorious John" usually refers to Dryden, but not always: an article in *Blackwood's* in 1838 referred to Milton as "Glorious John" (White 303). In any case, the ambiguity of the name seems deliberate, since Browning also describes Dryden in particularly Miltonic language ("thunder"; "exhalation"). For at least a sentence or two, she appears to be disparaging Milton, or at least damning him with faint praise; and the result, when the reader realizes that she is not referring to Milton at

all, is an exaltation greater than could have been achieved by outright pan-
egyric. Milton is apparently so integral to the history of English poetry, and
so unexceptionable, that one can with confidence overleap him in this way
without risk of serious misunderstanding. The effect is reminiscent of the
end of *Paradise Regained:*

> So Satan fell and straight a fiery globe
> Of angels on full sail of wing flew nigh,
> Who on their plumy vans received him soft
> From his uneasy station.
>
> (*PR* 4.581–84)

Grammatically, "him" and "his" should refer to Satan; but angelic wings do
not receive the devil, and no explanation is necessary. Chronologically, "John"
should refer to Milton; but Milton was not a passionless semipoet, so Browning goes on without stopping to clarify. Later she does "return upon [her]
steps" to "pause before Milton," but her appraisal has the feel of being almost
superfluous: Milton has already won "an eternal future of reminiscence" and
need not be named to be remembered (E. B. Browning 6:286–88).

Dustin Griffin notes a similar treatment of Milton in the eighteenth century, when *Paradise Lost* was often referred to as a "classic"—"In the latter part
of the century the accolade became a commonplace" (Griffin 35). Although
Griffin takes this to mean that Milton's poem was considered the equivalent
of the great works of antiquity, or else that it was a work of national literature, the term also applies in the sense I have been describing. Griffin points
out that in eighteenth-century literary histories, "Milton is nearly forgotten,
and appears only as an afterthought"; for instance, "in the epistle 'To My
Dear Friend Mr. Congreve,' Dryden omits Milton completely" (38). The
fact that Augustan critics foreshadowed the Victorians in treating Milton as
someone whom it is not necessary to mention corroborates the idea that he
is naturally a classic. Such literary histories draw attention to an important
aspect of Milton's work that we are apt to overlook if we concentrate too
exclusively on the Romantic Milton—its tendency, not to be striking, but
rather to strike one as obvious.

The same attitude reappears in Browning's poetry. Her 1844 collection contains two poems deeply influenced by Milton, but one displays
what seems to be a typically Romantic reaction to his influence, whereas
the other is Victorian in its response. *A Drama of Exile,* the longest and
most ambitious work in the collection, picks up the story of Adam and
Eve from the moment Milton left them at the end of *Paradise Lost.* The
poem, as its title indicates, takes the form of a closet drama, and Browning

acknowledges in her preface that Milton, too, considered writing *Paradise Lost* as a "drama" and even drew up "a rough ground-plan" for a play about the Fall (E. B. Browning 2:146). Throughout the preface she displays not just a consciousness but an uncomfortable consciousness of Milton's precedent haunting every aspect of her poem.

> But when all was done, I felt afraid, as I said before, of my position. I had promised my own prudence to shut close the gates of Eden between Milton and myself, so that none might say I dared to walk in his footsteps.... It would not do. The subject, and his glory covering it, swept through the gates, and I stood full in it, against my will, and contrary to my vow,—till I shrank back fearing, almost desponding; hesitating to venture even a passing association with our great poet before the face of the public. (2:144)

It would be difficult to describe a more Bloomian anxiety. The poet feels in the presence of Milton as naked and ashamed as Adam and Eve before God.

The case is altogether different in "The Lost Bower," one of the most successful (if not most popular) poems in the 1844 collection. The speaker of the poem describes discovering in her childhood an enchanting space in a forest: a natural garden or *hortus conclusus,* protected from the world by a wild wood. She leaves the bower, vowing to return, but is never able to find it again however much she searches. This loss is explicitly figured as a fall from innocence:

> For this loss it did prefigure
> Other loss of better good,
> When my soul, in spirit-vigour
> And in ripened womanood,
> Fell from visions of more beauty than an arbour in a wood.
> I have lost—oh, many a pleasure,
> Many a hope and many a power—
> Studious health and merry leisure,
> The first dew on the first flower!
> But the first of all my losses was the losing of the bower.[8]

This bower is a type of paradise: the poem concludes by claiming that the bower is not wholly lost, since there will "another open for me / In God's

---

8. Lines 291–300; all quotations from Browning's poetry refer to *The Complete Works,* ed. Porter and Clarke.

Eden-land unknown" (366–67). Moreover, it appears to be a specifically
Miltonic paradise. This is clear from the very title, since not only "Lost" but
"Bower" carries Miltonic associations: Eve's last tie to Eden, the space she
reserves for her final farewell after she is sentenced to exile, is her "nuptial
bower" (*PL* 11.280). Miltonic overtones likewise mark the speaker's first
entrance into the garden. She describes herself "overleaping /Thorns that
prick and boughs that bear" until she "stood suddenly astonied" ("Bower"
83–85); the lines echo Satan's first entrance into Eden ("overleaped"), and
Adam's last "astonied" view of it before his fall (*PL* 4.181, 9.890).

And yet Milton goes egregiously unmentioned in "The Lost Bower," even
while Barrett Browning pays tribute to her poetic predecessors. When the
speaker first catches sight of the bower, she immediately "thought of the old
singers /And took courage from their song" (76–77). The setting puts her
in mind of Wiliam Langland: the surrounding "Malvern hills" seem to her
the "Keepers of Piers Plowman's vision" (43–45). The space in the forest
reminds her of the poet who sang of "Bold Rinaldo's lovely lady," and also
of "Chaucer," who "marvelled /At those ladies fair" in just such a forest
bower (68–74). Later she hears a bird and finds that it too sounds "Most like
Chaucer's" (202). Elsewhere she casts her mind back further; this bower is
like "Oedipus's grave-place 'mid Colonos' olives swart" (280). Or perhaps

> could this same bower (I fancied)
> Be the work of Dryad strong,
> Who, surviving all that chancèd
> In the world's old pagan wrong,
> Lay hid, feeding in the woodland on the last true poet's song?
>
> (161–65)

The "last true" pagan poet, or Sophocles, or Ariosto—but Milton is never
mentioned as offering a possible analogue for this Edenic garden.[9]

It would be too easy, of course, to declare that every apparent absence
is a sign of presence; sometimes absence is simply absence. But "The Lost

---

9. John Guillory notes the importance of not naming in Milton's own poetry: "Milton defers
to the authority of Spenser... without recourse to the *name* of Spenser, an omission that can be con-
strued as itself a more complex form of deference" (Guillory 94). Spenser, incidentally, is the other
major poetic predecessor to go unnamed in "The Lost Bower," even though Browning refers to "the
bower of my romance" and at one point declares, "Henceforth, I will be the fairy /Of this bower"
(259, 241–42). Yet the omission of Milton is more striking, since her bower is far more Miltonic
than Spenserian. Unlike the Bower of Bliss in book 2 of *The Faerie Queene,* Browning's bower is not
destroyed but lost, together with childhood innocence; and in her bower nature imitates art, rather
than the opposite.

Bower" is a helpfully clear-cut example. Browning was consciously treading on Milton's turf in *A Drama of Exile;* she acknowledges the infringement in her preface to the 1844 *Poems*—at the same time incidentally displaying a deep familiarity with Milton's work, including the Trinity manuscript. Later in the same collection, however, her own personal drama of exile owes obvious debts to Milton, yet she feels no need to mention him among the "old singers." In its use of Milton, "The Lost Bower" contrasts not only with *A Drama of Exile* but with such Romantic poems as Wordsworth's Intimations Ode, which "The Lost Bower" resembles and sometimes echoes directly.[10] Wordsworth's poem never mentions Milton, but Milton's poetry insistently underlies the ode's meditations on loss, as many critics have noted.[11] The thought of "that fair field," for instance, intrudes on Wordsworth in a moment of "joy" and disrupts his communion with nature: "But there's a Tree, of many, one, / A single Field which I have looked upon, / Both of them speak of something that is gone" ("Ode" 50–53; Wordsworth 1:524). The "Tree" in these lines is biblical as well as Miltonic; the "Field," on the other hand, is pure Milton. In Wordsworth's poem, then, Miltonic language and imagery assume an obvious importance. In Browning's, their obvious importance is simply assumed. If Milton never seems to intrude on "The Lost Bower," that is because he is already there. This is due partly to Wordsworth himself: poems like the Intimations Ode helped ensure that Milton was in such common poetic circulation that his presence did not need to be signaled. But it is due more essentially to a Victorian reticence about Milton that is itself Miltonic, a willingness to "overleap" Milton, looking beyond him to Chaucer and Langland; yet such overleaping only underscores his obvious centrality.

Milton as Bible

If a classic is a book that is familiar even before it is read, then there is one quintessential example: the Bible. Many people who have never read the Bible believe that they must have done so at some point. It is possible to refer to, discuss, and even disagree with the Bible without ever having opened it. English speakers will frequently quote the Authorized Version not just

---

10. The very opening of the poem—"In the pleasant orchard closes, /'God bless all our gains,' say we; / But 'May God bless all our losses,' / Better suits with our degree" (1 4) imitates the Intimations Ode, in which Wordsworth offers a "song of thanks and praise" for "Fallings from us, vanishings" (141–44; Wordsworth 1:528).

11. See, for instance, Abbie Findlay Potts (612–16) and Gene W. Ruoff (54–56), both of whom note particularly the influence of book 11 of *Paradise Lost* on the Ode.

without having read it but without knowing that they are doing so. The Bible can be particularly useful in helping us understand Milton's legacy, not only because it is a classic and hence provides another model of the particular form of influence I have been discussing, but because Milton and the Bible naturally go together. Even experienced scholars frequently confuse them, crediting *Paradise Lost* for motifs and images that derive directly from the Bible (and vice versa). This conflation of the two texts is not new: already a century and a half ago, Masson observed that "now it is Milton's story of the origin and first events of the universe, rather than the biblical outline which suggested it to him, that has taken possession of the British mind" (Masson, *Poetical Works of John Milton* [1866], 1:lxviii).[12] But the confusion can be instructive, as in the case of Christina Rossetti's "Goblin Market," a poem that does reveal Miltonic influence, but only in a peculiar form that resembles biblical influence—that is, that does not depend upon actual contact.

As Kathleen Vejvoda has observed, "much critical discussion has been devoted to the influence of *Paradise Lost* on Rossetti's work, particularly on her most famous narrative poem, *Goblin Market*" (Vejvoda 555). This line of mostly feminist criticism derives from Sandra Gilbert and Susan Gubar's reading of Rossetti as one of "Milton's daughters" in *The Madwoman in the Attic* (1979). Critics had previously recognized that "Goblin Market" offers a foreshortened version of the overarching narrative of the Bible: beginning with two beings living in innocence, the story moves through a temptation and fall to a self-sacrificial redemption and restoration. In Gilbert and Gubar's reading, this biblical narrative becomes a "Miltonic" one: the answers to questions raised by the poem "may be embedded in the very Miltonic imagery Rossetti exploits" (Gilbert and Gubar 567). They point out, for example, that the fruit-eating scene in "Goblin Market" parallels the *Paradise Lost* scene in that both Eve and Laura gorge themselves on the fruit—a detail not found in Genesis (568). Yet they also admit that Laura's motivation is very different from that of Milton's Eve, and they do not cite other evidence of direct influence. Later critics, however, have often taken the Miltonic model for granted: Sylvia Bailey Shurbutt, for instance, claims, "The biblical and Miltonic overtones in Rossetti's poem are obvious as the story of the Eve-like Laura's fall is unfolded" (Shurbutt 41). Shurbutt repeatedly pairs "biblical" and "Miltonic" without distinguishing between them; she notes for instance that goblin fruit is "like Milton's biblical fruit" (41). Aspects of Genesis are

---

12. For a discussion of the influence of *Samson Agonistes* on Victorian perceptions of the Book of Judges, see Wittreich, *Why Milton Matters,* 180–86.

attributed to Milton, just as Masson described: "Milton's God feared Adam and Eve's gaining knowledge after tasting the fruit" (Shurbutt 42).

Others are more careful in distinguishing between the Bible and Milton as sources for "Goblin Market." Vejvoda remarks,

> The opening line of *Goblin Market* ("Morning and evening") echoes inversely the biblical account of the creation in the King James Bible: "And the evening and the morning were the first day" (Genesis 1:5). From the outset, Rossetti invites comparison with Genesis, and thus also with *Paradise Lost.* (Vejvoda 567)

Yet Vejvoda argues that it is easy to overestimate the influence of *Paradise Lost*. Although she grants it as a corollary ("Genesis, and thus also *Paradise Lost*"), she claims that Milton's epic offers few independent parallels, and argues instead that *Comus* serves as a major model for Rossetti's poem. Sarah Fiona Winters, writing a year later (2001), disagrees: "Most critics, in focussing on the biblical story, have neglected to see how closely Rossetti follows Milton and how radically she departs from him" (Winters 15). She notes several elements in "Goblin Market" that are more reminiscent of *Paradise Lost* than of the Bible: the trouble begins when the two protagonists separate for the first time; the second to accept the fruit does so only out of love for the first; and this second tasting of the fruit is followed by a moment of eroticism (15–18).

Notably few of the critics who make this comparison ask whether Rossetti would have had cause or inclination to study *Paradise Lost* in the first place.[13] The exception is Vejvoda, who examines the evidence and finds that the answer is no: there is no reason to think that Rossetti spent much time reading Milton's poem. Direct evidence is limited; as David Kent observes, "Any study of influence on Rossetti...must first acknowledge special difficulties," since she was particularly reserved on the subject of her reading and her literary opinions (Kent 251). But Vejvoda points out that both Anglo-Catholics (Rossetti was staunchly Anglo-Catholic) and the Pre-Raphaelite Brotherhood (by whom she was surrounded) tended to "despise Milton" (Vejvoda 557). Moreover, "from the only scrap of direct evidence we have

---

13. As George Eliot remarks (in "The Wasp Credited with the Honeycomb," from *The Impressions of Theophrastus Such*): "No premises require closer scrutiny than those which lead to the constantly echoed conclusion, 'He must have known,' or 'He must have read.' I marvel that this facility of belief on the side of knowledge can subsist under the daily demonstration that the easiest of all things to the human mind is *not* to know and *not* to read." (Eliot, *Impressions,* 92)

regarding Rossetti's opinion of Milton—a brief mention that appears in an unpublished letter—we might dismiss Milton as an influence on her altogether. In this reference, Rossetti suggests that Milton's work was generally unpalatable to her: 'Milton I cannot warm towards, even let alone all the theological questions' " (561). One might also add the account of her brother, William Michael Rossetti; describing her preferred reading, he specifically singles out Milton's epic as antipathetic: a "great thing which she disliked was Milton's *Paradise Lost:* the only poems of his which she seems to me to have seriously loved were the sonnets" (Rossetti, *Poetical Works,* lxx). D. M. R. Bentley takes this antipathy as itself an indication of likely influence: "Given Rossetti's apparent dislike of *Paradise Lost*... it is tempting to see in both 'Eve' and *Goblin Market* a residue of the Romantic penchant for rewriting Milton" (Bentley 73, n. 35). But Bentley's comment reveals the perspective of a professional teacher and critic, someone who is required to reread works he does not like. Since Rossetti, by contrast, was reading for pleasure and instruction, there is no particular reason to suppose that she ever reread the poem, or even read it all the way through; the evidence we have specifically informs us that she "disliked" *Paradise Lost* and objected to it on "theological" grounds. If the author in question were almost anyone else—if the parallel were being drawn to Dryden, for instance—then any critical argument assuming that Rossetti was familiar with his work, and sufficiently familiar not only to draw upon it but to take care to "rewrite" it, would require some special pleading.

Yet the question of Milton's influence is not like the question of Dryden's influence. Early readers and critics of "Goblin Market" seem never to have remarked any parallel to *Paradise Lost*. B. Ifor Evans, in "The Sources of Christina Rossetti's 'Goblin Market'" (1933), does not mention Milton; on the other hand, he does not mention the Bible either, and this omission is worth contemplating. Evans asserts that the idea of "temptation... linked with the proffering of rich fruits" would have occurred to Rossetti on account of her childhood reading of Thomas Keightley's *The Fairy Mythology;* he is confident enough about this claim to repeat it, referring to "the motive of tempting fruits found in Keightley" (Evans 158–59). To attribute "the motive of tempting fruits" to a collection of fairy tales without mentioning the book of Genesis may seem odd, but we should be wary about blaming Evans for this apparent oversight, since the Bible is not a "source" like any other. It may be that the analogy with Genesis was too obvious for Evans to have to say it; or it may have been too obvious for him even to see it. It is the nature of biblical influence to be so ubiquitous as to be invisible.

The same peculiarity attaches to Miltonic influence. Vejvoda, after conceding that Rossetti did not appreciate Milton, offers reasons for thinking that "Goblin Market" nevertheless represents a response to his poetry. In the first place, "Rossetti's grandfather, Gaetano Polidori, was an Italian emigrant and scholar who loved Milton and who translated Milton's work...into his native language," and hence Rossetti would have known about Milton from her childhood (Vejvoda 558). Later, Rossetti would again be associated obliquely with Milton through her "friendship with David Masson," who was "Rossetti's editor at *Macmillan's Magazine*" (559). One might also name Thomas Keightley, who "was a friend of the [Rossetti] household" (Evans 157) and was, like Masson, a leading Victorian Miltonist. What this circumstantial evidence points to, however, is not direct literary influence, but an early and constant familiarity. Rossetti's one recorded comment suggests the same thing. "Milton I cannot warm towards": this implies that Milton, though constantly unappealing, is constantly present, like a member of the extended family or a disagreeable lodger. Many Romantic poets were so steeped in Milton through their repeated reading of his works that they responded to him, even unconsciously, in their own work; it is unlikely that this was the case with Rossetti. It is very likely, however, that *Paradise Lost,* like a poetic Bible, helped shape "Goblin Market" without being read or reread.

In short, I am saying that the critics I have cited, beginning with Gilbert and Gubar, are entirely right in naming Rossetti as one of Milton's daughters; their claim is not only legitimate, but true. By "legitimate" I mean that their claim easily passes the unspoken standards by which we tend to judge the credibility of claims of influence. If a work is of sufficient magnitude, then it is fair to assert that every later work not only may be but necessarily is to some degree influenced by it.[14] Catherine Maxwell, discussing intertextuality in "Goblin Market" and responding to Gilbert and Gubar's analysis, carefully distinguishes such diffuse forms of influence from direct influence. "The most fundamental references [in "Goblin Market"] are biblical," she writes. "But Rossetti is also trading on the associations formed by the male

---

14. It is possible to distinguish at least three levels of influence that criticism regularly recognizes. At some untraceable level, every text that is or has been in circulation exerts influence on later texts. This is what Jerome McGann alludes to (though he is considering influence on a reader, not a writer of a text) when he claims that a work's textual history "is always *present* to a person's critical activity despite his ignorance of that history, and even his ignorance *of* his ignorance. It is simply that the history is *not* present to his *individual* consciousness" (McGann 25). The second level is what I describe in this paragraph: certain major works so shape literary tradition that anyone writing in that tradition will necessarily be influenced, if only indirectly. The third level of influence is direct influence: a critic will claim, and give evidence to support, that a later writer had first-hand knowledge of an earlier writer's work. What I describe in the case of Rossetti is a fourth kind of influence that combines the last two: a work so influential that it not only influences those who have not read it, but acts on them in the same way as if they had read it.

poetic tradition. Milton, often seen as the father of modern poetry, launches the figure of potent fruitfulness into English verse when he retells the story of the Fall in *Paradise Lost*" (Maxwell, "Tasting the 'Fruit Forbidden,' " 81). Writing as she was in an English as well as a male poetic tradition, Rossetti could not help but refer to Milton, since her very words inevitably carry Miltonic associations as well as biblical ones. By these standards, it is impossible for a post-Miltonic English-language poet to refer to x without also referring to Milton, where x includes (but is not limited to): angels, devils, Satan, sin, snakes, spirits, fruit, Tree, temptation, rebellion, hell, heaven, God, creation, wandering, tasting, or falling.

Yet Rossetti's relationship to Milton goes beyond this necessary debt. In the case of certain special works, like the Bible, the indebtedness of later authors will often be not just unconscious but inadvertent. If the classic provides a sense of unaccountable knowledge, the Bible provides something that shows more like ignorance. An example of this phenomenon appears in F. Scott Fitzgerald's *This Side of Paradise,* when one of the characters writes a careless article for the university newspaper.

"Well, you say here—let me see." Burne opened the paper and read: " '*He who is not with me is against me,* as that gentleman said who was notoriously capable of only coarse distinctions and puerile generalities.' "

"What of it?" Ferrenby began to look alarmed. "Oliver Cromwell said it, didn't he? or was it Washington, or one of the saints? Good Lord, I've forgotten."

Burne roared with laughter.

"Oh Jesse, oh good, kind Jesse."

"Who said it, for Pete's sake?"

"Well," said Burne, recovering his voice, "St. Matthew attributes it to Christ."

"My God!" cried Jesse, and collapsed backward into the wastebasket. (Fitzgerald 127)

The young journalist no more intended to quote St. Matthew than he intended to pray to God while falling into the wastebasket, but such language simply forms part of his natural discourse. What the Bible is to Jesse Ferrenby and his highly secular social set, Milton is to the Anglo-Catholic Christina Rossetti. In what follows I offer an example of how Rossetti, consciously adopting a biblical idiom, in fact adopts more of a Miltonic idiom. I then compare Rossetti's relationship to Milton with that of Percy Shelley, whose more conscious tussles with Milton represent a debt in some ways greater and in some ways smaller than that of his Victorian successor.

One of the most striking features of "Goblin Market" is its lists of similes. Five times in the poem, the heroines—Laura (thrice), Lizzie (once), and on one occasion both girls together—are described in a rapid string of comparisons. The first instance is the most succinct:

Laura stretched her gleaming neck
Like a rush-imbedded swan,
Like a lily from the beck,
Like a moonlit poplar branch,
Like a vessel at the launch
When its last restraint is gone.[15]

Other times the anaphora is slightly more varied:

Golden head by golden head,
Like two pigeons in one nest
Folded in each other's wings,
They lay down in their curtained bed:
Like two blossoms on one stem,
Like two flakes of new-fall'n snow,
Like two wands of ivory
Tipped with gold for awful kings.
                    (184–91)

In these passages Rossetti appears to be imitating a number of literary precedents, the most obvious being Petrarch. It is no accident that the first girl in "Goblin Market" to be blazoned in a rush of metaphors is named "Laura": Rossetti was very familiar with Petrarch's poetry and frequently invokes it in her sonnets. She even claimed on one occasion that she could prove her direct descent from Petrarch's Laura (Marsh 212). As in the Petrarchan blazon, the lists of similes in "Goblin Market" apply exclusively to the female characters and have a tendency to freeze or objectify them. Rossetti's reminiscence of Petrarch may well be ironic; it is in any case clearly conscious.

---

15. Lines 81–86; all quotations from Rossetti's poetry refer to *The Complete Poems,* ed. Crump and Flowers.

But behind Petrarch's use of this device, which was imitated by so many later sonneteers in English as well as Italian,[16] lies the original locus classicus for the trope, the biblical Song of Solomon. In some ways the Song of Solomon furnishes an even closer precedent than Petrarch for the lists of similes in "Goblin Market," since such lists form a recurrent feature of the Song's narrative and are shared between two different characters. On at least three occasions they describe the woman: "Thy hair is as a flock of goats...Thy teeth are like a flock of sheep...Thy lips are like a thread of scarlet...thy temples are like a piece of pomegranate within thy locks" (Song 4:1–3). In one case they describe the man: "His head is as the most fine gold...His eyes are as the eyes of doves...His cheeks are as a bed of spices...His hands are as gold rings set with the beryl: his belly is as bright ivory overlaid with sapphires" (Song 5:11–14). As Nilda Jiménez notes, the Song of Solomon is the single book of the Bible to which Rossetti refers most frequently in her poetry (Jiménez x). Mary Arseneau points out that "The Prince's Progress," the title poem of Rossetti's second collection of verse, closely imitates the Song: "[T]hrough plot and image, the Princess is associated with the bride of the Song of Solomon, a book of the Bible which Rossetti alludes to often" (Arseneau 280). It is no surprise, then, that like "Goblin Market," "The Prince's Progress" features a list of similes:

> she languisheth
> As a lily drooping to death,
> As a drought-worn bird with failing breath,
> As a lovely vine without a stay,
> As a tree whereof the owner saith,
> "Hew it down today"
>
>   (385–90).

Similarly, "A Birthday," which closely follows "Goblin Market" in Rossetti's 1862 volume, points toward the same source:

> My heart is like a singing bird
>   Whose nest is in a watered shoot;
> My heart is like an apple tree
>   Whose boughs are bent with thickset fruit;

---

16. Although the blazon, offering comparisons for each part of the beloved's body, does occur in Petrarch (e.g. "Quel sempre acerbo et onorato giorno," Durling 303), it is more common in the later Petrarchan tradition than in the original.

My heart is like a rainbow shell
That paddles in a halcyon sea;
My heart is gladder than all these
Because my love is come to me.
("A Birthday" 1–8)

The second simile alludes directly to the Song of Solomon: "As the apple tree among the trees of the wood, so is my beloved among the sons. I sat down under his shadow with great delight, and his fruit was sweet to my taste" (Song 2:3). The motif of the beloved's approach allies "A Birthday" and its string of similes more closely to the Bible than to the Petrarchan tradition.

Yet although the idiom Rossetti adopts in these poems is consciously biblical, her use of the trope displays a marked divergence from her apparent source. In the Song of Solomon, or in the Petrarchan blazon, every verse introduces a new tenor and a new vehicle (hair like goats, teeth like sheep, etc.). In "Goblin Market," on the other hand, there is a single tenor (usually Laura), who is then heaped with a flurry of competing images.[17] Although this may seem like a minor distinction, it produces a radically different effect. Whereas the blazon conveys a sense of richness, each additional simile in Rossetti's list is impoverishing. Typically, a simile aims to illustrate, to provide an insight into one or both of the elements of which it consists. But when Laura is compared in quick succession to a swan, a lily, a branch, a boat, the effect is rather self-defeating. As Katherine Mayberry writes, these lists of similes "suggest uncertainty or incompletion.... [They] serve, not as an enriching descriptive method, but as a desperate and hopeless means for defining an essence that is not known" (Mayberry 99). The similes do not accumulate, as they would if each pertained to a different tenor. Rather, they displace each other, and Laura, far from becoming more clearly defined to the reader through this series of descriptions, is drowned in a surfeit of superimposed images. This failure is purposeful: at this moment in the poem, Laura *seems* to be asserting her individuality, but in fact she is on the brink of losing herself. Elsewhere Rossetti consistently uses the same device in poems about vanity (including "Days of Vanity" and "As froth on the face of the deep") and self-destruction ("A Vain Shadow," which she put under the general heading "The World: Self-Destruction"). In each case the trope undermines itself: after the first or second comparison, each additional simile renders

17. The terms *tenor* and *vehicle,* which were introduced by I. A. Richards in *The Philosophy of Rhetoric,* have been shown to be problematic; but I retain them, despite their possible inadequacies, for what Richards calls their "immense convenience" (Richards 96).

the assertion of likeness more questionable, not more certain. In the Song of
Solomon, the lists of similes are luxuriant; in "Goblin Market," where each
list stands on a single slender base, they are unstable, deceptive.

The two major poetic precedents in English for this trope of listing multiple vehicles for a single tenor are Percy Shelley and, even more funda-
mentally, Milton. There do exist other possible models. In the traditional
Catholic litany of the Virgin, for instance, Mary is given a series of names
(Tower of Ivory, House of Gold, Star of the Morning), and Rossetti imitates
this practice in several of her devotional poems.[18] But these titles are rather
symbolic than metaphoric: we are not actually invited to find a physical resemblance between the Virgin and a house of gold, as we are in the similes
describing Laura and Lizzie. Other religious poets, particularly Metaphysical
poets, also tend to pile up metaphors, but each one is usually given the space
to be individually elaborated.[19] Epic poetry sometimes provides two comparisons in quick succession: one of the first epic similes in the *Iliad* is actually
a double simile, comparing Agamemnon's assembly both to the ocean and to
a wheat field (*Iliad* 2.144–49). But it is very rare to find four, five, or even
more similes all strung rapidly together, as we find in Rossetti.[20] The effect
is consistently one of precariousness, as in the example from "The Prince's
Progress" above, where the Princess is hovering between life and death, or
as in the final list of similes in "Goblin Market," where Laura is in the same
plight.[21] Once she begins to list, Laura soon topples completely:

Sense failed in the mortal strife:
Like the watch-tower of a town
Which an earthquake shatters down,

18. Although Rossetti was "firmly opposed to anything savouring of Mariolatry" (Rossetti
[1904] li), the listing of Marian symbols occurs in the two poems grouped under the heading "Feast
of the Annunciation": "Whereto shall we liken this Blessed Mary Virgin" and "Herself a rose, who
bore the Rose."

19. George Herbert's "Prayer (I)," like the Marian litany, is a series of metonyms or names rather
than actual metaphors. Rossetti has several poems inspired by Herbert that give a single extended
simile per stanza, including "A Better Resurrection" and "Confluents."

20. There is one brief biblical precedent for piling vehicles onto a single tenor, but it is apoc-
ryphal: the description of the high priest in Ecclesiasticus 50:6–10. Of this passage Edmund Burke
writes that it succeeds specifically because the individual images become confused: "the mind is so
dazzled as to make it impossible to attend to that exact coherence and agreement of the allusions,
which we should require on every other occasion" (Burke 119, part 2, section 13). Jiménez does not
note allusions to the apocrypha in Rossetti's poetry. Other nineteenth-century poets whose verse is
thickly metaphorical, including the Spasmodics and Swinburne (see Tucker, "Swinburne's *Tristram*,"
76–82), have no real equivalent to the anaphoric lists of similes found in Shelley and Rossetti.

21. The exception is "A Birthday," which does not convey the same sense of danger or desysra-
tion. Rather, as Mayberry points out, it provides one of the few examples of sensual gratification in

Like a lightning-stricken mast,
Like a wind-uprooted tree
Spun about,
Like a foam-topped waterspout
Cast down headlong in the sea,
She fell at last;
　Pleasure past and anguish past,
Is it death or is it life?

(513–23)

The bewildering similes intervene between "strife" and "life," so that the justifying rhyme is only barely audible. All of the lists of similes in "Goblin Market" come at similar moments, when the innocence or safety of Laura and Lizzie is being threatened. The sense of confusion is reinforced by the unstable rhetorical trope.

The closest precedent, as I have said, is neither Petrarch nor the Bible, but Milton. Consider the description of Eve when she makes the fateful decision to separate from Adam:

Thus saying, from her husband's hand her hand
Soft she withdrew, and like a wood nymph light
Oread or dryad, or of Delia's train,
Betook her to the groves, but Delia's self
In gait surpassed and goddess-like deport....
To Pales, or Pomona, thus adorned,
Likeliest she seemed, Pomona when she fled
Vertumnus, or to Ceres in her prime,
Yet virgin of Proserpina from Jove.[22]

"Likeliest" is one of the unlikeliest words for an epic simile, outside of Milton. Far from being a confident assertion of similarity, it confesses the insufficiency of the previous comparisons (oread, dryad, Delia); it seems to apply equally to two quite different comparisons (Pales or Pomona); and despite its superlative form, it is not the last but is followed (and superseded?) by the

---

the Rossetti canon (Mayberry 87); it thus stays close to its source in the Song of Solomon. Other Rossetti poems featuring a list of similes, however, tend to balance on a perilous edge; these include not only "Goblin Market" and "The Prince's Progress" but such lyrics as "Mirrors of Life and Death."

　22. *PL* 9.385–96; in line 394 I cite the 1674 reading ("Likeliest") rather than the 1667 reading ("Likest") retained by Fowler, though the meaning is identical.

comparison to Ceres in the following line. Eve is here the exact counterpart of Laura being subjected to a similar barrage of comparisons in "Goblin Market"; she is not merely half-hidden, like the subject of a sonnet blazon, but is nearly erased. The peculiar effect of the rhetoric, which seems to leave its subject suspended while the poet searches for the perfect likeness (and does not find it), allies Milton with Rossetti.

The habit of piling up lists of comparisons until they collapse is typical of Milton. It begins with the first simile in *Paradise Lost:* Satan is "as huge / As whom the fables name of monstrous size, / Titanian, or Earth-born, that warred on Jove, / Briareos or Typhon . . . or that sea-beast / Leviathan" (*PL* 1.196–201). Many of the muster rolls of proper names are actually lists of similes, including the "Fontarabbia" passage described above: each item in the catalogue (giants, Thebans, Trojans, Paladins) is intended as a comparison, but a failed comparison—yet another army that does not really compare with Satan's host of devils. The listing of possible vehicles becomes practically a rhetorical tic for Milton, especially when he is describing things infernal: hell is like "Pelorus, or . . . Aetna" (1.232–33); Satan stands "Like Teneriff or Atlas" (4.987). Unlike the fully developed double similes of Homer, Milton in these cases produces a stutter of alternatives, as if in self-correction.[23] This practice continues in *Paradise Regained:* Satan's perpetual frustration appropriately calls forth a list of vehicles.

> But as a man who had been matchless held
> In cunning, over-reached where least he thought,
> To salve his credit, and for very spite
> Still will be tempting him who foils him still,
> And never cease, though to his shame the more;
> Or as a swarm of flies in vintage-time,
> About the wine-press where sweet must is poured,
> Beat off, returns as oft with humming sound;
> Or surging waves against a solid rock,
> Though all to shivers dashed, the assault renew,
> Vain battery, and in froth or bubbles end.
>
> (*PR* 4.10–20)

The passage both describes vanity and illustrates it; the third simile paradoxically succeeds by being "Vain" and literally superfluous. Once again this is

---

23. On the ambiguity of Milton's similes, and on his use of the word *or,* see Peter Herman, *Destabilizing Milton,* chapters 1 and 2, respectively.

echoed by Rossetti, most notably in the passage describing the goblins' failed
temptation of Lizzie.

> White and golden Lizzie stood,
> Like a lily in a flood,—
> Like a rock of blue-veined stone
> Lashed by tides obstreperously,—
> Like a beacon left alone
> In a hoary roaring sea,
> Sending up a golden fire,—
> Like a fruit-crowned orange-tree
> White with blossoms honey-sweet
> Sore beset by wasp and bee,—
> Like a royal virgin town
> Topped with gilded dome and spire
> Close beleaguered by a fleet
> Mad to tug her standard down.
> ("Goblin Market" 408–21)

As critics have noticed, this passage shows a conscious imitation of traditional
prayers to the Virgin (D'Amico 74–75; Grass 367). Its siege imagery deliberately recalls Petrarch, while the fruit tree is biblical. *Paradise Regained,* on the
other hand, was almost certainly not in Rossetti's mind when she composed
this passage; yet once again not only its individual similes (waves, insects) but
its rhetoric and its effect of vain striving are far nearer to Milton than to any
of the other precedents. It is the sign of a powerful book, or a powerful discourse, that one picks it up while consciously reaching for something quite
different. Rossetti may not have known Milton's poetry well, but she knew
it in the biblical sense.

It is useful to compare Rossetti's use of Miltonic rhetoric to that of Shelley.
Almost alone of major English poets, Shelley shares with Milton and Rossetti the habit of listing similes. He does so at the beginning of "Hymn to
Intellectual Beauty" and then at greater length in "To a Sky-Lark"; these are
the two instances with which Rossetti is likely to have been familiar.[24] Shelley also uses the device in briefer lyrics ("To Sophia," "Remembrance") and

---

24. William Michael Rossetti asserts that Shelley was one of his sister's favorite poets, although
"she can have known little beyond his lyrics; most of the long poems, as being 'impious,' remained
unscanned" (Rossetti, *Poetical Works,* lxx; see also Gelpi 151). The "impious" poetry presumably

in political poems ("Similes for two Political Characters of 1819," *Swellfoot the Tyrant*). The example closest to "Goblin Market," however, is "Epipsychidion," in which the speaker repeatedly lavishes strings of metaphors upon his beloved Emily. The first time he apostrophizes her with a Marian litany of names:

> Sweet Benediction in the eternal Curse!
> Veiled Glory of this lampless Universe!
> Thou Moon beyond the clouds! Thou living Form
> Among the Dead! Thou Star above the Storm!
> Thou Wonder, and thou Beauty, and thou Terror![25]

The second time he employs a series of more tentative metaphors, reminiscent of the Song of Solomon:

> Art thou not...
> A well of sealed and secret happiness,
> Whose waters like blithe light and music are,
> Vanquishing dissonance and gloom? A Star
> Which moves not in the moving Heavens, alone?
> A smile amid dark frowns? a gentle tone
> Amid rude voices? a beloved light?
> A Solitude, a Refuge, a Delight?
>
> (56–64)

Finally he tries to capture her essence in a series of meta-metaphors; Emily is

> An image of some bright Eternity;
> A shadow of some golden dream; a Splendour
> Leaving the third sphere pilotless; a tender
> Reflection of the eternal Moon of Love
> ... A Metaphor of Spring and Youth and Morning.
>
> (115–20)

These rapid lists of comparisons resemble those in Milton and Rossetti, not only because each applies to a single tenor but because each is admittedly

---

included "Epipsychidion." For a more complete discussion of this aspect of Shelley and of the use of the trope elsewhere, see Gray, "Faithful Likenesses."

25. Lines 25–29; all quotations from Shelley's poetry refer to *Shelley's Poetry and Prose,* ed. Reiman and Fraistat.

self-defeating. Thrice the speaker attempts to put his conception into words, and thrice (like Satan) he fails. After the first list he finds that all these images are but "dim words which obscure thee" (33). The second attempt ends in a similar concession: "I measure / The world of fancies, seeking one like thee, / And find—alas! mine own infirmity" (69–71). The third time the speaker recognizes his own shortcomings in a particularly Miltonic lament: "Ah, woe is me! / What have I dared? where am I lifted? how / Shall I descend, and perish not?" (123–25; cf. *PL* 7.12–20). Shelley's use of Miltonic rhetoric in these passages is not just incidental. The lists of similes in "Epipsychidion," although they may all eventually collapse, epitomize the ideal of questing after something unattainable—an ideal that is central to Shelley's self-conception as a poet and that he consistently identifies with Milton.

According to Shelley's *A Defence of Poetry,* all poetry consists of a striving after a perfect but unattainable likeness: when a poet begins to compose, "inspiration is already on the decline, and the most glorious poetry that has ever been communicated to the world is probably a feeble shadow of the original conception of the poet" (Shelley 531). Appropriately, then, Shelley concludes the *Defence* with a flurry of metaphors—poets are mirrors, words, trumpets—in a peroration that simultaneously displays the author's imagination and his failure to light upon a single, perfect image. The strings of similes in "Epipsychidion" are merely explicit manifestations of the essence of poetry, since all poems continually strive—vainly—to produce a likeness of "the original conception of the poet." But Shelley's figure in the *Defence* for the true quester, who continues to seek despite the acknowledged futility of seeking, is Milton's Satan, "who perseveres in some purpose which he has conceived to be excellent in spite of adversity and torture" (526). This description fits the speaker of "Epipsychidion" (composed, like *A Defence of Poetry,* in early 1821), who according to the "Advertisement" pursued "a scheme of life, suited perhaps to that happier and better world... but hardly practicable in this" (392). Unlike Rossetti, Shelley was clearly conscious of Milton's precedent in compiling his catalogues of similes.

According to Shelley love too, like poetry, depends upon a futile quest for similitude. In "On Love" Shelley writes, "We are born into the world and there is something within us which from the instant that we live and move thirsts after its likeness" (504). Once again, the reference is to Milton—not to Satan in this case, but Adam, whose first request of God after he begins to "move and live" is for a "likeness" (*PL* 8.281, 450). When Shelley thirsts after the perfect likeness in "Epipsychidion," therefore, he engages in a pursuit and in a rhetorical trope that he explicitly associates with Milton, whose example he both imitates and resists. This form of influence has long been familiar to critics. Rossetti's relationship to Milton, on the other hand, is more unusual: the affinity is inadvertent and almost invisible, because Rossetti's conscious imitation of the Bible camouflages the presence of the Miltonic idiom. Yet the manifestation of Milton's influence in "Goblin Market" is at least as powerful as it is in "Epipsychidion." Whereas Shelley seeks to overcome and overwrite Milton, Milton simply underwrites Rossetti, and his influence is all the more extraordinary for being understated.

A concluding example is furnished by Gerard Manley Hopkins, in whose work these models assume a slightly different aspect. If Milton was someone whom Christina Rossetti "could not warm towards, even let alone all the theological questions," Hopkins had a rather more heated and decided opinion. "I think he was a very bad man," Hopkins wrote to Robert Bridges in 1877; Milton's views on divorce are alone sufficient to damn him eternally: "those who contrary to our Lord's command both break themselves and, as St. Paul says, consent to those who break the sacred bond of marriage, like Luther and Milton, fall with eyes open into the terrible judgment of God" (HSL 88). Hopkins here puts Milton in dangerous company. In "The Wreck of the Deutschland," the first poem that Hopkins permitted himself to write after he renounced poetic composition upon becoming a Jesuit, Luther is a type of Antichrist. He is paired with St. Gertrude (who shared the same hometown in Germany) to show how great good and great evil can be neighbors: "But Gertrude, lily, and Luther, are two of a town, / Christ's lily, and beast of the waste wood."[26] It is to this "beast of the waste wood" that Hopkins links Milton. Milton was of the devil's party, and Hopkins knew it.

Considering Milton's position as a Puritan reprobate, one would scarcely expect his poetry to serve as a model for "The Wreck of the Deutschland," nor for any of Hopkins's poems in his newly developed, Jesuit-suited strain. And yet Milton serves not only as a model but, on one level at least, as the primary model. In the same letter in which he condemns Milton together with Luther "to the terrible judgment of God," Hopkins writes, "I have paid much attention to Milton's rhythm. . . . His achievements are quite beyond any other English poet's, perhaps any modern poet's" (HSL 87). "In fact," he later tells Bridges, "all English verse, except Milton's, almost, offends me as 'licentious'" (HSL 90). This is Hopkins's repeated assessment throughout

---

26. "The Wreck of the Deutschland," 157–58; all quotations from Hopkins's poetry refer to *The Poetical Works of Gerard Manley Hopkins,* ed. MacKenzie.

his life: to R. W. Dixon he writes, "Milton's art is incomparable, not only in English literature but, I shd. think, almost in any" (HSL 107). In developing a new style of poetry appropriate to his calling, Hopkins settled upon an un- usual rhythm he called "counterpoint"; and his exemplar, "the great master" (as he says in the preface to his poems), "the great standard in the use of coun- terpoint," is Milton (Hopkins 116; HSL 108). Apparently Hopkins was able to maintain a mental reservation, condemning the spirit of Milton's poetry while exalting and imitating the form. As he comments to Dixon, "His verse as one reads it seems something necessary and eternal (so to me does Purcell's music)" (HSL 106). But this approbation applies only to Milton's style, the "music" of his verse. The parenthetical comment about Purcell is peculiarly indicative, since Hopkins, in his sonnet "Henry Purcell," submits a special plea to God on behalf of the soul of the Protestant composer. For Milton, on the other hand, he makes no such allowance. Quite the opposite: in response to Bridges's own sonnet about Milton, Hopkins declares that to admire Milton's life or thought is "wicked" and "impious" (HSL 88).

In contrast to Christina Rossetti, then, Hopkins knew Milton's poetry ex- tremely well, and his imitation of Milton's rhythms and structures (Hopkins's caudated sonnets are based on Milton's)[27] was perfectly deliberate. Yet at the same time Hopkins, even more than Rossetti, repudiated the content of Milton's writings. Although Hopkins in his letters frequently admires Mil- ton's prosody, he never so much as mentions the actual subjects of Milton's poetry. Nevertheless, critics who have written about Hopkins's relation to Milton have seen it as a relatively straightforward case, treating Hopkins as if he were Shelley—deeply admiring of Milton, but also anxious and resistant. John J. Glavin, for instance, argues that "The Wreck of the Deutschland" is a rebuttal of Milton's "Lycidas," and Dennis Sobolev has recently made a similar argument about "The Loss of the Eurydice."[28] The evidence these critics adduce is circumstantial, though in almost any other case it might be sufficient; they argue that Hopkins was deeply conversant with Milton's poetry and therefore could not help but reply to "Lycidas" when writing

---

27. Hopkins's caudated sonnets—fourteen lines plus two or more codas or tails—include "Tom's Garland" and "That Nature is a Heraclitean Fire." In their correspondence concerning the form, Bridges confirmed Hopkins's impression that Milton's "On the New Forcers of Conscience" is the archetype for all such poems in English (HSL 263–64).

28. Other critics have also assumed a connection, particularly with "The Wreck of the Deutsch- land." Robert Boyle finds that in "The Wreck" Hopkins "set out to be a Catholic Milton" (Boyle 106); Walter J. Ong, meanwhile, seconds Glavin's conclusions: "Hopkins knew that there was no way to deal with his heroic death-by-drowning theme without confronting Milton's poem" (Ong 47).

about shipwreck in a religious context.[29] Yet Hopkins's case is not like any other: he was a Jesuit, writing for an audience (if any at all) of Jesuits; he does not need to rebut Milton, any more than he needs to rebut Luther. It is no more possible to "prove" that Hopkins was *not* responding to "Lycidas" than it is possible to prove that he was. (In any case, the real core of both Glavin's and Sobolev's articles—the contrast between the two poets—does not depend upon Hopkins's conscious or unconscious response; the insights that emerge from their antithetical criticism remain valid either way.) But in the absence of any verbal echoes or other clear indication that Hopkins is responding to the ideological content of Milton's poems—and very few such echoes or allusions have been detected anywhere in Hopkins's mature poetry[30]—it seems probable that Hopkins's relation to Milton is more anomalous than these critics suggest.

For Hopkins, Milton is both too bad and too good to be rebutted. Most aspects of Milton's writing do not require active resistance on Hopkins's part, because they are too antipathetic to present a temptation. In the matter of verse form, meanwhile, Milton rises above antipathy or resistance; he is simply inevitable, as Hopkins explains to Dixon: "Milton is the great master of sequence of phrase," which may be defined as "a dramatic quality by which what goes before seems to necessitate and beget what comes after, at least after you have heard it it does" (HSL 103). Milton's phrasing always seems already familiar to the reader—"His verse as one reads it seems something necessary and eternal" (HSL 106). In other words, Milton is a classic: his meter and phrasing are so familiar, so standard, that their influence requires no special apology, or even acknowledgment. Even more pertinent is the model of Milton as Bible of poetic form. The imitation in this case is not inadvertent, since Hopkins openly acknowledges that he is continually seeking a "more Miltonic" style (HSL 117, 128). But Hopkins's admiration is that of the nonbeliever who quotes bits of Scripture ("He who is not with me is

29. Glavin cites as evidence of influence, in addition to Hopkins's admiration for Milton's prosody, the following parallels: "genre; the personal situations of the poets at the time of composition; the poems' titles [i.e., subtitles]; the historical background of each work; narrative progress; and, finally, formal arrangement" (Glavin 523). Sobolev asserts that based on earlier criticism, "the close relation between Milton and Hopkins can be considered as demonstrated," but he does not distinguish between a prosodic influence (the subject of most such criticism) and influence of the sort he describes (Sobolev 533). Both Glavin and Sobolev invoke Bloom, though Sobolev notes that Bloom does not consider Hopkins a "strong" poet—i.e., one who would feel the need to wrestle with the works of a major poetic precursor (Sobolev 531–32).

30. MacKenzie's edition notes a few scattered echoes. But the only mature poem by Hopkins that seems to echo Milton in a more than accidental way is "The Shepherd's Brow"; see Mariani 305–311, and Boyle 102–105, the latter of which gives a number of useful bibliographical references.

against me") for the way they sound, wholly ignoring their original meaning or context.[31] By consciously divorcing sound from sense, Hopkins, in a peculiar twist on the models of relationship presented in this chapter, allows Milton to be both everywhere and nowhere an influence on his poetry.

---

31. Hopkins's treatment of Milton thus resembles Matthew Arnold's treatment of the Bible. In *On Translating Homer* Arnold prescribes "one English book and one only" as an infallible stylistic guide—the King James Version of the Bible: "The Bible . . . is undoubtedly the grand mine of diction for the translator of Homer" (CPA 1:155–56). In making this prescription Arnold refers only to the form of the Bible, not to its content: had Arnold become a Jesuit (or a Hindu), he would presumably have continued to recommend the King James Version and no other as a model for translators. By the same token, when Hopkins takes Milton as his model, he does so without particular reference to the meaning of the poetry.

❧ CHAPTER 3

Milton, Arnold, and the Might of Weakness

First, an example from Anthony Trollope. *The Warden* and *Barchester Towers,* which make up the first two installments of Trollope's *Chronicles of Barsetshire* and together form a single, near-continuous narrative, are among the most prelatical novels in the English language. Their sympathies seem entirely un-Miltonic. All of the admirable characters (the male ones at least) are members and defenders of the ecclesiastical hierarchy—bishops, deans, archdeacons, some of them holding multiple benefices; they are the very princes of the church against whom Milton fulminated, beginning with his first political pamphlet, *Of Reformation.* The villains, meanwhile, are reformers: in *The Warden,* the opponent is the *Jupiter,* a journal that self-righteously denounces those who seek to enrich themselves by church livings; in *Barchester Towers,* it is Mr. Slope, a low-church minister who offends the Barchester clergy by preaching against embellishments to the church service. Both are "villains" rather for their hypocrisy than for their views on reform; and their high-church opponents also come in for their share of ridicule. Still, the sympathy of the reader is engaged almost entirely on the side of the conservative Barchester hierarchs.

And yet the novels are in another sense highly Miltonic. In the first place, they are crammed with references to *Paradise Lost,* especially *Barchester Towers,* as U. C. Knoepflmacher has noticed. Knoepflmacher points out that Mr. Slope is repeatedly equated to Milton's Satan, both in his devious rhetoric and in his manner of exerting power over men by flattering women (Knoepflmacher 31–32). On the other hand, Slope's opponent, Archdeacon Grantly, is also equated with Satan, since his meetings with the dean and chapter form a "superb parody" of the hellish conclave in book 2 of *Paradise Lost* (32–33). The same episode is parodied again later in the novel, during Miss Thorne's famous party at Ullathorne: while the potentates gather inside the house to debate, the lower ranks amuse themselves outdoors with mock-epic jousts; and the whole scene is introduced by a bathetic version of Milton's epic catalogue of demons: "Then the Grantlys came; the archdeacon and Mrs. Grantly and the two girls, and Dr. Gwynne and Mr. Harding..." (Trollope, *Barchester Towers,* 342; vol. 3, ch. 2). The parallel is reinforced by the reference to "pandemonium" later at the same party (377; vol. 3, ch. 5).

But the most sustained allusion to *Paradise Lost* comes in the figure of Madeline Neroni, to whose temptations Mr. Slope succumbs. Beautiful and enticing from the waist up, unmentionably deformed from the waist down, she is a Victorian version of Milton's Sin. She has her father's eyes, which are "bright as Lucifer's" (67; vol. 1, ch. 9); more significantly, she has his name. Madeline Neroni inexplicably adopts as part of her married name her father's first name, Vesey: "Madeline Vesey Neroni" her card reads, as if, like Sin, she were married to her own father (68). This onomastic incest is further deformed by the Bishop of Barchester. " 'La Signora Madeline Vicineroni!' muttered, to himself, the bewildered prelate" (79; vol. 1, ch. 10), unwittingly highlighting the "Vice" that Madeline represents; his conflation also cements in place the "sin" that lurks in the small space that separates her father's name from her husband's.

Yet these allusions do not in themselves reveal much about this pair of novels. Trollope's novels are filled with incidental allusions and quotations from Milton, although he usually favors "Lycidas" to *Paradise Lost;* the line from Milton that appears with the most frequency in his work is "the last infirmity of noble mind" (Terry 367). The line is quoted, for instance, near the end of the first chapter of *Barchester Towers.* But the more revealing sentence, the one that suggests the novel's true affinity to Milton, comes in the previous paragraph. Defending Dr. Grantly's quite natural ambition to become bishop, Trollope questions the church's traditional manner of making bishops: "The *nolo episcopari,* though still in use, is so directly at variance with the tendency of all human wishes, that it cannot be thought to express the true aspirations of rising priests in the Church of England" (Trollope

Barchester Towers, 8; vol. 1, ch. 1). Compare Milton's less sympathetic observation on bishop-making in *Of Reformation:*

> But when [a man] steps up into the Chayre of *Pontificall* Pride, and
> changes a moderate and exemplary House, for a mis-govern'd and
> haughty *Palace, spirituall Dignity* for carnall *Precedence,* and *secular high
> Office* and *employment* for the *high Negotiations* of his Heavenly *Embas-
> sage,* Then he *degrades,* then hee *un-Bishops* himselfe; hee that makes
> him *Bishop* makes him no *Bishop.* (Prose 1:537–38)

Trollope is not alluding to this passage in Milton; rather, both Trollope and
Milton are puzzling over the same phenomenon, that the only way to become a bishop in the Church of England is to refuse to become a bishop.
"Nolo episcopari" (I do not wish to become bishop): from Milton's day
down to Trollope's, this was the formula by which a man was supposed to
reply to the offer of a bishopric. Trollope's narrative imitates Milton most
closely in its fascination with this paradox: that the way to achieve power is
to refuse it.

As has often been noted, with the exception of the divine chariot that
overwhelms the rebel angels in book 6 of *Paradise Lost,* all of Milton's heroes overcome their enemies not by confrontation but by refusing combat.
The most notable instance is the Son in *Paradise Regained,* who sums up the
tendencies of the earlier protagonists, beginning with the Lady in *Comus.*
The Son has willingly abdicated godhead to be incarnated, and he begins
the poem by retreating from his place among his disciples to expose himself
alone in the wilderness. Having thus doubly resigned, he then further resigns
himself to suffer Satan's punishments and temptations without putting forth
his power. The result is a nearly plotless poem consisting of a series of refusals
but ending, nevertheless, with triumph.

The Warden stands out among mid-Victorian novels much as *Paradise Regained* does among epic poems. It is surprisingly devoid of plot, and the
grand action with which it concludes is an abdication. For the first third of
the novel, there is not even a single clear protagonist, until the title character,
Mr. Harding, the warden of the almshouse known as Hiram's Hospital, first
contemplates resignation: "As he paced up and down the room he resolved
in his misery and enthusiasm that he could with pleasure, if he were allowed,
give up his place" (Trollope, *The Warden,* 118; ch. 9). In the end, this power of
refusing proves irresistible. Mr. Harding first retreats from Barchester, the seat
of the controversy, to London, a retreat that lasts (with biblical resonances)
three days. His abdication utterly confounds the most powerful figure in

the book, Archdeacon Grantly, who is left spluttering and helpless. "'But I shall resign,' said the warden, very, very meekly"—a meekness that baffles his son-in-law "beyond all endurance" (244–45; ch. 18). At the end of three days, Mr. Harding returns to Barchester triumphing in his descent: "Had he not cause for triumph? Had he not been supremely successful? Had he not for the first time in his life held his own purpose against that of his son-in-law[?]" (256; ch. 19).

Mr. Harding's narrative continues in *Barchester Towers* along the same lines, and the overarching narrative of the two books is purely Miltonic, a tale of paradise not only lost but also regained by means of a fall. Mr. Harding and his daughter Eleanor both dream of returning to their beloved former home, Hiram's Hospital. "Eleanor...sauntered forth with her father to revisit the old hospital. It had been forbidden ground to her as well as to him since the day on which they had walked forth together from its walls" (Trollope, *Barchester Towers*, 60; vol. 1, ch. 8). Yet having refused this Eden in the earlier novel, Mr. Harding turns down the wardenship again in the sequel, only to be rewarded for this abdication by the offer of a deanship, a far more lucrative and powerful position. This too he refuses (once again confounding Dr. Grantly), and his refusal again works out for the best. The deanship is offered to his other son-in-law, Mr. Arabin, who insists that Mr. Harding should live with him and serve as "co-dean," with all of the benefits and none of the responsibilities. "Pressed by such arguments as these, what could a weak old man do but yield?" asks the narrator, relishing the irony (491; vol. 3, ch. 18). Mr. Harding has moved from the Eden of the hospital to the New Jerusalem of the deanery without having committed a single action over the course of two novels except the "weak" one of perpetually yielding his rightful claim.

The general principle that Mr. Harding illustrates—that the meek shall inherit the earth—is Christian, not specifically Miltonic. But as a literary device and a method of constructing narrative, the Mr. Harding Principle— that the best way to win is to lose, or seem to lose—is very much Miltonic. Once Trollope's overt allusions have directed our attention to Milton, it is possible to detect the much larger congruence between their narratives. The same applies to Matthew Arnold, who forms the main subject of this chapter. Arnold's poetry and prose are both littered with references to Milton, and as in Trollope these incidental references suggest Arnold's greater underlying debt. Much of Arnold's writing depends upon the idea that the best policy is to stand and wait, or even to withdraw; and this principle is most clearly illustrated in works that attest to Milton's influence.

The Miltonic paradox of powerful resignation or retreat, moreover, not only influences Arnold but provides a way of understanding the relationship

between the two writers. Although Milton looms large in Arnold's acknowledged pantheon of great predecessors, he does not exert the same obvious
influence as he does on Wordsworth, for instance, or as Wordsworth does
on Arnold. Milton almost never forms the subject or the primary model of
Arnold's writing but rather exerts his sway from the margins or the background; the same applies to other Victorian writers as well. If the influence
of Milton on Romantic writers was direct and overwhelming—a chariot
scattering their forces, or (in Harold Bloom's image) a cherub with a sword
preventing their access to the source of original inspiration—Milton's influence over Victorian writers, particularly poets, is more oblique. Yet Milton's
own writings train us to recognize that such influence, though less apparent, is none the less real. It possesses the power of restraint, the power that is
demonstrated by refusing to put forth all one's power. I begin by tracing at
some length the might of weakness in Milton's prose and poetry, and then
show how it serves as both an influence on Matthew Arnold and a model
of that influence.

Milton himself points out that his model of heroic action differs from
that of all previous epic poets. Whereas others write of combats and direct
assaults—"Wars, hitherto the only argument/Heroic deemed"—he sings of
"the better fortitude/Of patience and heroic martyrdom" (*PL* 9.28–32).
Nor is this an empty distinction. Many critics have discussed the unusual
quality shared by the heroes and heroines of Milton's narrative poems, the
most notable and insistent of these critics being Stanley Fish. In *Surprised by
Sin: The Reader in* Paradise Lost (1967), Fish defines "Christian Heroism"
as consisting of one thing: remaining obedient to God, a duty that more
often requires one to stand still than to take action (Fish, *Surprised by Sin,*
158–207). In *How Milton Works* (2001), Fish applies this same principle not
only to *Paradise Lost* but to all of Milton.[1] To do nothing—or rather, to do
one thing (be obedient), which usually means to stand and wait, or to sit
in order serviceable—is the key to everything. Milton works by apparently
refusing to work.

Fish finds this principle already in effect as early as the Nativity Ode, in
which God manages to rout the forces of evil by perfect passivity.

---

1. One notable precursor of Fish on this topic is Edward Dowden, writing in 1872: "There is
a victory, which is God's, not ours; it is our part to cleave to the Eternal One, his part to achieve the
triumph on our behalf. Here we possess the dominant idea which governed the inner life of Milton,
and the dominant idea around which revolves the cycle of his poetical works" (Dowden 202). Earlier
epic heroes—Achilles, Odysseus, Aeneas—also employ tactical retreat and self-restraint; but Milton
makes these virtues the very basis of heroism.

The climax of this plot coincides with the entrance, so often heralded, of the hero, who, when we finally meet him, turns out to be the least active figure in the landscape. Indeed, no sooner has he appeared than he lays his head on a pillow and falls asleep. And yet this inactivity, rather than once again blocking the exercise of power, somehow releases it; for as stanza XXV declares, "Our Babe, to show his Godhead true,/Can in his swaddling bands control the damned crew" (227–8). "Control" is a very strong verb, especially in this poem, and its assertiveness is in direct contrast to the babe's posture. How can there be an exertion of power without any exertion? (Fish, *How Milton Works,* 320)

This paradox is absolutely typical of Milton: "This moment in the *Nativity Ode* establishes a pattern that will appear in almost everything that Milton writes" (321). Some version of the Mr. Harding Principle is at work not only in the ode and in *Paradise Lost,* but in all the major poems: "[T]ypically in Milton's poetry the important thing is either never said or said in a manner addressed only to initiates (as when the Lady [in *Comus*] declines to explain the 'sage and serious doctrine of virginity'); the climactic act either occurs offstage (as in *Samson Agonistes*) or in silence (as in all of the things the Son *doesn't* say in *Paradise Regained*) or in a declaration that remains mysterious in relation to everything that precedes it (as when the speaker in *Lycidas* declares, 'Henceforth thou art the Genius of the shore' [183])" (59).[2]

Milton's four major poems show a definite progression, or rather a recession: victory is obtained first by sitting still, then by tactical retreat, and finally by losing outright. But the same sequence of poems also displays an ever greater anxiety about the difficulties and dangers attending the Mr. Harding Principle. To begin with the earliest: the triumphant action in *Comus* is a non-action, a refusal. First the Lady refuses to drink; yet this action by itself does not win the day, since it merely arouses Comus to renewed attempts and higher rhetoric. It is afterwards, when the Lady refuses to engage in debate at all, even to defend her own position, that the enchanter first feels himself

---

2. Stanley Fish is not the only critic to have remarked on this pattern, but he is the only one to have declared it the central motif of all of Milton's poetry. In the following survey of Milton I have not cluttered my discussion with footnotes referring to similar observations in Fish's work and distinguishing our points of view; my indebtedness must simply be understood. But although many of our examples may overlap, I am making a quite different point from Fish's. I argue that the phenomenon of mighty weakness was one that fascinated and sometimes frustrated Milton, but was in any case an actual, active principle. For Fish, this apparent phenomenon is in the end little more than a by-product of the one true principle, obedience; weakness is not only no mightier than might, but no more surprising or interesting. To treat it as an independent phenomenon, as I do, is to fall prey to an idolatrous temptation, according to Fish.

overcome. "Thou art not fit to hear thyself convinced," she tells Comus, and this abstention overwhelms him: "She fables not, I feel that I do fear/Her words set off by some superior power; /And though not mortal, yet a cold shuddering dew/Dips me all o'er" (*Comus* 791, 799–802).

As if to illustrate this point—that Comus can be defeated only by refusing to fight or debate with him directly—the Lady's two brothers blunder in at this moment, brandishing their swords and putting the whole evil crew to rout, and yet by their action leaving their sister in sorrier plight than before. The secret is not fight, but flight; hence the day is saved only by Sabrina, a goddess who achieved her apotheosis not by combating evil but by fleeing it: "The guiltless damsel flying the mad pursuit/Of her enraged stepdame Guendolen, / Commended her fair innocence to the flood/That stayed her flight with his cross-flowing course" (828–31). Appropriately, therefore, Thyrsis concludes the masque by recommending another retreat—"Come Lady while heaven lends us grace,/Let us fly this cursed place" (937–38)—and the performance ends without further confrontation.

Victory through abjection, the paradox that underpins Sabrina's power, also constitutes the basis of the Incarnation and hence underlies the whole action of Milton's two epics. We have already seen how the hero of the Nativity Ode exerts his power by relinquishing it: the "dreaded infant" controls the band of devils simply by falling asleep. The paradox is formulated concisely by the Father in book 3 of *Paradise Lost,* after the Son has offered to put off godhead and become mortal: "[T]hy humiliation shall exalt/With thee thy manhood also to this throne" (*PL* 3.313–14). This exaltation by humiliation, begun at the Nativity, is completed at the Crucifixion. Milton struggled to represent the Crucifixion in his two early poems "The Passion" and "Upon the Circumcision"; he eventually summed up its mystery in Michael's pointed description to Adam: although Christ is "nailed to the cross," yet by that act, paradoxically, "to the cross he nails thy enemies,/The law that is against thee, and the sins/Of all mankind, with him there crucified" (*PL* 12.413–17). Nor is this method restricted to the Incarnation; *Paradise Lost* suggests that God always works by relinquishing his power. Just as the Son's offered "humiliation" in book 3 turns out to be an exaltation, so his earlier exaltation, described in book 5, turns out to be another form of humiliation. Abdiel explains to Satan that the Son's assumption of command over the angels is really a form of abasement, "since he the head/One of our number thus reduced becomes" (5.842–43). For God, glory is always achieved through self-reduction.

Even the war in heaven, which with its old-fashioned heroic battles and confrontations appears to be the exception to this pattern, is won by a diminishment of full strength. In order that the war may accomplish its true aim, his greater glory, God tempers the power of both armies ("the eternal king omnipotent/From his stronghold of heaven high overruled/And limited their might" [6.227–29]) and "suffer[s]" a prolonged battle that he could have won outright at any moment (6.701). Even at the end, when the Son in his divine chariot chases the rebels out of heaven and threatens to obliterate them utterly, "Yet half his strength he put not forth, but checked/His thunder" (6.853–54). The policy of not putting forth full power does not end when God refrains from destruction, but governs Creation as well. Chaos exists in the first place because, by God's own choice, "I uncircumscribed myself retire,/And put not forth my goodness," and it continues to exist after the world's creation because God chooses "to circumscribe" this created universe, rather than bringing all space to order (7.170–71, 226). Self-limitation thus precedes and creates all things, just as it eventually redeems them.

Paradise Regained furnishes the most constant demonstration of this principle, as it consists wholly of a series of successful non-combats and retreats. God sends his Son explicitly "To conquer Sin and Death the two grand foes,/By humiliation and strong sufferance:/His weakness shall o'ercome Satanic strength" (*PR* 1.159–61). The Son intuitively understands this method: when he realizes that "I no more should live obscure,/But openly begin" the work of salvation, he does not burst forth but instead promptly withdraws from the world he is meant to redeem and rule, retiring into the wilderness (1.287–88). This is repeated at the conclusion of the poem, when the angels instruct him, "Now enter, and begin to save mankind," and he responds by going privately "Home to his mother's house" (4.635–39). Such an ending, apparently so anticlimactic, is only natural, since every victory the Son has achieved throughout the poem has come through retreat. For this he has good precedent, not only in the heavenly self-circumscriptions described in *Paradise Lost* (actions of which the Son in *Paradise Regained* has no memory), but in the Bible. He remembers, for instance, the example of Elijah: "He saw the prophet also how he fled/Into the desert" (2.270–71). The story of Elijah's flight from Jezebel is told in the first book of Kings, where it is followed by the spectacular diminuendo that describes, as well as any passage in the Bible, how God's greatness is often conveyed in little: "And behold, the Lord passed by, and a great and strong wind rent the mountains, and brake in pieces the rocks before the Lord; but the Lord was not in the wind: and after the wind an earthquake; but the Lord was not in the earthquake: And after the earthquake a fire; but the Lord was not in the fire: and after the fire a still small voice" (1 Kings 19:11–12).

And yet *Paradise Regained* reveals a keen awareness of the danger lurking in this policy of restraining one's power, a twofold danger. In the first place, weakness can be a temptation—can be treated as something good in itself, and so a specious excuse for not performing one's duty and fighting the good fight when necessary. (The Son, aware of this possibility, hastens to explain to Satan that his rejection of worldly power does not spring from indolence or irresponsibility: "What if with like aversion I reject/Riches and realms;/yet not for that a crown,/Golden in show, is but a wreath of thorns,/Brings dangers, troubles, cares, and sleepless nights/To him who wears the regal diadem,/When on his shoulders each man's burden lies" [2.457–62].) Secondly, the Mr. Harding Principle can just as easily be used by evil people as by good—not merely as an excuse, but as a conscious and powerful tool for doing ill. Both possibilities cause tensions in *Paradise Regained* and throughout Milton's writings.

Almost all of the later temptations with which Satan tries the Son show that Satan has understood the Son's tactics and is using them in return; he offers not the opportunity to seize power, but the temptation to retreat from it. The Athenian temptation is an offer not so much of immediate knowledge as of perpetual preparation and cloistered study; the city's academies are described as retreats, "sweet recess," "studious walks and shades," "Plato's retirement" (4.242–45). The Son could even work from home, as he will eventually decide to do: "These here revolve, or, as thou lik'st, at home,/Till time mature thee to a kingdom's weight" (4.281–82). Milton makes clear just how enticing such a temptation is, not only by using the language of "home" that reappears at the end of the poem, but by echoing the discourse of maturation that haunts his own early works. The conviction that one must not enter prematurely onto a great work, which Milton expresses at the beginning of "Lycidas" and in the seventh Prolusion, and the corresponding desire to remain in retirement at home, "revolving" plans until the time is ripe—these are the impulses to which Satan appeals, even more than to the love of classical learning.

In other words, the Son is being tempted to rely too much on his own best principle. A suggestion of this comes already in book 3, when Satan offers the Son rule over the Parthians before he offers him Rome. Even before they are named, the Parthians are easily identifiable by their actions: "How quick they wheeled, and flying behind them shot/Sharp sleet of arrowy showers against the face/Of their pursuers, and overcame by flight" (3.323–25). In Latin literature, overcoming by flight is the distinguishing mark of Parthian warriors; Milton notes the same characteristic the only other time in his poetry he mentions them, in Elegia VII.[3] The Parthians emblematize the

---

3. "Qui post terga solet vincere Parthus eques" (line 36: the Parthian horseman, who conquers by turning his back).

principle of mighty weakness, and the Parthian temptation thus foreshadows the more subtle temptations to come, culminating in the last and most insidious, the pinnacle. When Satan suggests, "Cast thyself down," he is challenging the Son once again to choose weakness (4.555). Instead the Son stands still, and the brilliance of this climax rests in how the refusal, apparently so similar to his others, actually represents a reversal of the established pattern. When Satan, now finally toppled, is compared to Antaeus—"As when Earth's son Antaeus... oft foiled still rose,/Receiving from his mother Earth new strength,/Fresh from his fall, and fiercer grapple joined" (4.563–67)—the reader must do a double take to understand to which character the epic simile applies. At the beginning of the poem, when God ordained that "His weakness shall o'ercome Satanic strength," and the Son's best policy was to lose as often as necessary, Antaeus would have been an exemplum of good. That he becomes a figure for Satan suggests the danger of the principle of weakness, how easy it is to rely too much on evasion and delay.

Parthian tactics are a double-edged sword, not only able to tempt the well-meaning into shirking their responsibilities, but available to evildoers, and just as powerful in their hands as in others'. The Son reasons to himself that his inaction is a form of action: "Who best/ Can suffer, best can do" (3.194–95). But Belial can make the same argument in *Paradise Lost* ("To suffer, as to do,/Our strength is equal") and stand accused by Milton of having thus "Counselled ignoble ease, and peaceful sloth" (*PL* 2.199–200, 227). Belial turns to the same tactics in *Paradise Regained,* when the devils debate how to corrupt the Son. He suggests using women, the weaker vessel, a tactic that had worked with both Adam and Solomon, and he describes his proposed temptresses in the language of retreat: "Skilled to retire, and in retiring draw/Hearts after them tangled in amorous nets" (*PR* 2.161–62). Neither of Belial's proposals happens to find favor with his captain, but such tactics are frequently employed by bad men. Even kings sometimes exercise their tyranny in retirement, as Milton well knew, and as he illustrates in the figure of Tiberius.

In *Paradise Regained* the kingdom of Israel "Obeys Tiberius," even though he has already "from Rome retired/To Capreae" (3.159; 4.91–92). That Tiberius exerted power by retreating is a commonplace. In Ben Jonson's *Sejanus: His Fall,* the emperor retires from Rome to Capreae at the end of act 3 and does not reappear in the play; yet it is only by this retreat that he is able to overthrow Sejanus, who was apparently too powerful to confront directly. Tiberius moreover became emperor only by first suffering exile, as Gilbert Burnet points out in his *History of My Own Time* (1724), which concludes by drawing a parallel between Tiberius and Charles II.

[Charles's] person and temper, his vices as well as his fortunes, did resemble the character that we have given us of Tiberius so much, that
it were easy to draw the parallel between them. Tiberius his banish-
ment, and his coming afterwards to reign, makes the comparison in
that respect come pretty near.... [H]is art of covering deep designs,
particularly of revenge, with an appearance of softness, brings them so
near a likeness, that I did not wonder much to observe the resemblance
of their face and person. At Rome I saw one of the last statues made
for Tiberius, after he had lost his teeth; but bating the alteration which
that made, it was so like king Charles, that prince Borghese and signior
Domenico to whom it belonged, did agree with me in thinking that it
looked like a statue made for him. (Burnet 2:470)

Milton would not of course have read Burnet's account, but his portrait of
the "retired" and "lascivious" emperor in *Paradise Regained* suggests that he,
too, was conscious of a parallel between the two rulers. Milton had long been
painfully aware that the use of Parthian tactics was not restricted to nymphs
and gods and devils, but was of pressing contemporary relevance.

Already in *Of Reformation* (1641), the same pamphlet in which he alludes to the *nolo episcopari,* Milton voices tortured animadversions on the
subject of willing weakness. The pamphlet opens by comparing the history of the Church to the life of Christ: just as Christ "suffer[ed] to the
lowest bent of weaknesse, in the *Flesh,* and presently triumph[ed] to the
highest pitch of *glory,* in the *Spirit,*" so the Reformation was the glorious
result of the abjection into which the Church had fallen (Prose 1:519).
Yet by the end of the first paragraph, Milton is anxiously denouncing those
unreformed churchmen who make a show of weakness, whose "Slav-
ish approach" and "Servile crouching" go "under the name of *humility*"
(1:522). The accusation is all the more shrill for the way in which high-
church ceremony dangerously resembles the true humility of Reformation;
but in this case, Milton insists, "their humility... indeed, is fleshly pride"
(1:523). The glorious abasement of Christ, he points out, can be falsely
and wrongly imitated.

Such was *Peters* unseasonable Humilitie, as then his Knowledge was
small, when *Christ* came to wash his feet; who at an impertinent time
would needs straine courtesy with his Master, and falling trouble-
somly upon the lowly, alwise, and unexaminable intention of *Christ* in
what he went with resolution to doe, so provok't by his interruption
the meeke *Lord,* that he threat'nd to exclude him from his heavenly

Portion, unlesse he could be content to be lesse arrogant, and stiff neckt in his humility. (1:523–24)

The church of St. Peter, by its endless but inappropriate humility, would try even the meekness of Christ.

Having thus finished "characterizing the *Depravities* of the *Church,*" Milton turns back to the "bright and blissfull *Reformation*" (1:524). Yet he immediately falls into difficulty again, since among the greatest strengths of the Reformation he lists "the *Martyrs,* with the unresistable *might* of *Weaknesse,* shaking the *Powers* of *Darknesse*" (1:525). Again, this is Christlike—"His weakness shall o'ercome Satanic strength"—but again it is open to false imitation; even unjust causes have their martyrs, and Milton next spends considerable effort discrediting the martyrdom of Bishops Cranmer, Ridley, and Latimer. These men, he claims, "prostituted" themselves to "every Politick Fetch" during the reign of Edward VI, to the detriment of true Reformation (1:531); their execution under Mary is therefore moot. "But it will be said, These men were *Martyrs:* What then? Though every true Christian will be a *Martyr* when he is called to it; not presently does it follow that every one suffering for Religion, is without exception" (1:533). The might of weakness is "unresistable," but it is not always right.

Whenever possible, Milton enlists the might of weakness on his own side, both for himself and for the republican cause in general. In the *Second Defence,* for instance, on the subject of his blindness: "There is a certain road which leads through weakness, as the apostle teaches, to the greatest strength. May I be entirely helpless, provided that in my weakness there may arise all the more powerfully this immortal and more perfect strength; provided that in my shadows the light of the divine countenance may shine forth all the more clearly" (4:589–90). The irony, however, is that the same glorious weakness characterized Milton's chief opponents. Charles I enjoyed a resurgence of power by dying, and it is easy to hear the bitter frustration in Milton's tone when he complains in *Eikonoklastes* that the people now "bring him that honour, that affection, and by consequence, that revenge to his dead Corps, which hee himself living could never gain to his Person" (3:342). More frustrating still was Charles II, who while living in exile subjected his conquerors. The reference in *Paradise Lost* to the devil Rimmon and "Ahaz his sottish conqueror," who began to "adore the gods/Whom he had vanquished," alludes glancingly to this irony (*PL* 1.472–76). The same "sottishness" is denounced more directly in *The Readie and Easie Way,* Milton's 1660 pamphlet arguing against the Restoration: "basely and besottedly to run thir necks again into the yoke which they have broken, and prostrate all the fruits of thir victorie for nothing at the feet of the vanquishd, besides our loss of glorie, will be an ignominie, if it befall us, that never yet befell any nation possessd of thir libertie" (Prose 7:363). The same pattern is repeated throughout Milton's prose: the "unresistable *might* of *Weaknesse,*" which is the principle of the Incarnation and also, Milton would like to think, of his own life, is constantly being turned back against Milton by his enemies.

The mingled triumph and tragedy of this principle comes out finally and most strongly in *Samson Agonistes.* Samson, through most of his life at least, would seem to be a counterexample, since he is a warrior who confronts his enemies head on. But like the angelic war in heaven, Samson's early career is rather a demonstration of the futility of direct fight, and the benefit of not putting forth all one's power. Samson's heroism, according to the chorus, lay in redefining heroism; he "Made arms ridiculous, useless the forgery/Of brazen shield and spear, the hammered cuirass,/ Chalybean-tempered steel, and frock of mail/Adamantean proof;/But safest he who stood aloof" (*SA* 131–35). By making arms and armor ridiculous, just as the angelic warriors do in heaven, Samson reveals the insufficiency of direct force. As the last line suggests, "standing aloof" is not a bad tactic, and Samson is very willing to use apparent weakness to gain his victories. His greatest military triumph comes when he chooses at first not to put forth all his power, and having "retired" to "the rock of Etham" allows himself to be taken by the "men of Judah" (253–56):

> and they as gladly yield me
> To the uncircumcised a welcome prey,
> Bound with two cords; but cords to me were threads
> Touched with the flame: on their whole host I flew
> Unarmed, and with a trivial weapon felled
> Their choicest youth; they only lived who fled.
>
> (259–64)

Again weapons have been proved "trivial." They only survive who flee, and tactical retirement wins the day.

The plot of the play as it unfolds reveals the same pattern, beginning with Samson's "Retiring from the popular noise" (16). Although he is in despair, he soon recalls other times when his apparent failures led to greater glory. Not only the battle by the rock of Etham, but Samson's disastrous first marriage to the woman of Timna fits this description, since although she was the "daughter of infidel" and proved faithless, yet "I knew/From intimate impulse, and therefore urged/The marriage on; that by occasion hence/I might begin Israel's deliverance,/The work to which I was divinely called" (221–26).

Samson yields to a similar, seemingly sacrilegious impulse at the end of the play, and the catastrophe unfolds as a series of willing surrenders. First he decides no longer to resist the Philistine demand that he perform at the feast of Dagon, but to submit: "I am content to go" (1403). Having performed he retreats again, "As over-tired" and weakened from his exploits, to lean against the pillars of the theater (1632). But with his final act of self-sacrifice he brings ruin on his enemies, and the chorus compares him to the Phoenix, whose apparent loss is actually a glorious resurrection—"then vigorous most/When most unactive deemed" (1704–5).

Yet the comparison to the Phoenix suspiciously resembles the comparison to Antaeus, another being who "oft foiled still rose," and the suspicion is justified. *Samson Agonistes* demonstrates as much as any of Milton's works the difficulties attendant upon weakness. It must not be deliberately chosen, since purposeful failure is an act of pride, not humility, and self-destruction is a sin, as Manoa tells Samson: "Be penitent and for thy fault contrite,/But act not in thy own affliction, son,/... Which argues over-just, and self-displeased/For self-offence, more than for God offended" (502–15). Moreover, as in *Paradise Regained*, winning by weakness in *Samson Agonistes* is an attribute as much of the evil characters as the good, and of none more than Dalila, about whom the word *weakness* hovers like a charm. She is first mentioned by Samson, who recalls being "vanquished with a peal of words (O weakness!)" (235). The parenthetical exclamation is ambiguous: it seems at first to refer to Samson's own weakness in being "vanquished," but it could refer just as well to the means of his defeat, mere words and tears.

In fact, it refers equally to both, as Dalila makes clear when she sails in, requesting, "Let weakness then with weakness come to parle" (785). There is no clear way to distinguish good weakness from bad. "All wickedness is weakness," as Samson reminds Dalila when she pleads it in her own defense (834); hers differs from his only in its aims. During their interview, she tries to tempt him with retreat, offering a place "At home in leisure and domestic ease" (917)—a feebler version of Satan's Athenian temptation in *Paradise Regained*. When this fails, Dalila reveals herself to have been a Parthian all along, triumphing over Samson's fall as she exits, which causes the chorus to exclaim, "She's gone, a manifest serpent by her sting/Discovered in the end, till now concealed" (997–98). Nowhere is Milton more acutely conscious that Parthian tactics are available to all and must be used with care. Yet *Samson Agonistes* still concurs with Milton's other poems: victory is achieved not by putting forth all one's power and smiting blindly with the jawbone of an ass; rather, one must "stand aloof" and retreat when necessary.

★ ★ ★

One would not usually think of Matthew Arnold, the refined prophet of culture, as much resembling Milton's Samson. But both made it their life's work to rid their land of Philistines; and both found that Philistinism was best overcome, not by furious activity, but by tactical retreat and cultivated inaction.[4] "Safest he who stood aloof" could serve as the epigraph to all of Arnold's prose and poetry, including *Culture and Anarchy,* his most extended defense of the Mr. Harding Principle. As Stefan Collini writes, Arnold's chief weapon in *Culture and Anarchy,* as in his other works of criticism, is his irony, which "can conjure up the suggestion of much wisdom and judgement held in reserve" (Arnold, *Culture and Anarchy,* xii). Such a suggestion is appropriate, since the book's central argument concerns the need to store up reserves of wisdom and judgment (or "sweetness and light") rather than immediately exerting all one's energy. Arnold declares that "the best way" to counter the ills of Victorian society is "not so much by lending a hand to our friends and countrymen in their actual operations for the removal of certain definite evils, but rather in getting our friends and countrymen to seek culture, to let their consciousness play freely round their present operations and the stock notions on which they are founded" (CPA 5:191). To charge blunderingly ahead, even in a good cause, is a sign of Philistinism—that is, an excess of what Arnold calls "Hebraism," the principle of action and self-righteousness. This must be tempered by a balance of "Hellenism," the principle of cultivation and patient self-perfection.

Given this premise, it is no surprise that *Culture and Anarchy* has distinctly Miltonic overtones. Arnold refuses wholeheartedly to lend his support to the policy of free trade, despite its beneficial effects (such as the repeal of the Corn Laws): "This policy, as having enabled the poor man to eat untaxed bread, and as having wonderfully augmented trade, we are accustomed to speak of with a kind of thankful solemnity" (5:209). For this disinclination Arnold finds himself upbraided by the press:

It is because I say (to use the words which the *Daily Telegraph* puts in my mouth):—'You mustn't ... hold big meetings to agitate for reform bills and to repeal corn laws,—that is the height of vulgarity,'—it is for this reason that I am called ... a Jeremiah about the reality of whose mission the writer in the *Daily Telegraph* has his doubts. (5:88)

---

4. When Arnold introduces the term *Philistine* into his critical vocabulary in his essay on Heine, he does so with a Miltonic allusion: "[Heine's] counsel was for open war. ... It was a life and death battle with the Philistines" (CPA 3:111). It is ironic that Arnold should cite Moloch (*PL* 2.51), the most "Philistine" and single-minded participant in infernal debate.

The disagreement recapitulates the first confrontation in *Paradise Regained* between the Son and Satan. Satan also has his doubts about the reality of the Son's mission, and therefore asks him to turn stones into bread in order that he may "us relieve/With food, whereof we wretched seldom taste" (*PR* 1.344–45). The Son demurs, on the principle, not that feeding the hungry is wrong, but that even actions with evidently good results must be undertaken only for good reasons, rather than because Satan requests them, or because the middle class desires a more cheaply fed labor force.

Such a policy of "cultivated inaction, making its believer refuse to lend a hand at uprooting the definite evils on all sides of us," frustrates Arnold's critics much as it frustrates Satan. Arnold quotes one of these critics, who voices his objections in Miltonic terms: "Mr. Frederic Harrison . . . at last gets moved to an almost stern and moral impatience, to behold, as he says, 'Death, sin, cruelty stalk among us, filling their maws with innocence and youth,'" while Arnold retires to his study to revolve these problems at leisure (CPA 5:115–16).[5] The language of Sin, Death, "maw" (from *PL* 2.845–47) is only appropriate, since Arnold's position is essentially Miltonic. He too invokes the language of Milton and turns it right back on his critics. "[W]e all call ourselves, in the sublime and aspiring language of religion which I have before noticed, *children of God,*" writes Arnold (CPA 5:103); but like Satan making the same point ("All men are Sons of God"), he finds that the phrase "bears no single sense" (*PR* 4.517–20). Arnold agrees with Milton that divine filiation in its highest sense is revealed, not by "muscular Christianity" and other such "machinery," but more passively, by the "single-minded love of perfection" (CPA 5:104).

This parallel may seem unlikely, even somewhat forced, since Arnold and Milton differ in their most basic justifications for inaction. Arnold disbelieves in the notion of the "one thing needful" and therefore recommends a continual quest for wider knowledge, whereas Milton believes that precisely one thing is needful and no more. Milton, in other words, is apparently a representative of that "Puritanism" that for "more than two hundred years," according to Arnold, has been "crossing the central current [of civilized development] and checking it" (5:175). He would seem to be the patron of those dissenting Philistines, against whose unthinking, single-minded obedience Arnold directs his most biting irony. But even as Arnold denies that Puritanism and its modern descendants can ever help to "ennoble" English culture, he makes a special plea to exempt Milton from the roll of Puritans.

---

5. Harrison alludes not only to Milton but to Shakespeare: Arnold is pictured in the midst of death and cruelty "handing out [his] pouncet-box" (CPA 5:116; see *1 Henry IV,* act 1, scene 3).

> But a lover of perfection, who looks to inward ripeness for the true springs of conduct, will surely think that as Shakespeare has done more for the inward ripeness of our statesmen than Dr. Watts, and has, therefore, done more to moralise and ennoble them, so an Establishment which has produced Hooker, Barrow, Butler, has done more to moralise and ennoble English statesmen and their conduct than communities which have produced the Nonconformist divines. The fruitful men of English Puritanism and Nonconformity are men who were trained within the pale of the Establishment,—Milton, Baxter, Wesley. A generation or two outside the Establishment, and Puritanism produces men of national mark no more. With the same doctrine and discipline, men of national mark are produced in Scotland; but in an Establishment. With the same doctrine and discipline, men of national and even European mark are produced in Germany, Switzerland, France; but in Establishments. (5:237–38)

Milton the Puritan, thanks to his early training, is grandfathered into the established church, and hence into the list of the children of sweetness and light. This is lucky for Arnold, whose eloquence is suffused with Miltonisms: not only the repeated "doctrine and discipline" (which may perhaps be a stock collocation, though it was made famous by Milton), but more notably the insistently repeated "inward ripeness" of the first sentence, which comes from Sonnet 7 ("And inward ripeness doth much less appear," line 7). Arnold's language and thought are too pervasively Miltonic to allow him to classify Milton among the Philistines, where his beliefs would duly seem to place him.

Arnold had every reason to sympathize with Milton: Milton's sonnet about "inward ripeness" could apply almost as well to Arnold's early career as to Milton's. George Sand, meeting the young Arnold in France, was reminded of "*un Milton jeune et voyageant*" (Arnold, *Letters,* 4:330), and she was not alone in noting the resemblance.[6] The parallels are numerous: a vocation for poetry as a young man; defensiveness about this choice, particularly toward a more active and worldly father; a turn after the age of thirty from poetry to polemical prose and to laborious work on behalf of the state. Moreover Arnold, like Milton, continued to feel the pull of the Athenian temptation: he

---

6. J. R. Seeley compares their poetry on the ground of its Hellenism: Milton "is the founder of that school of classical revival which is represented in the present age by Mr. Matthew Arnold" (Seeley, "Milton's Poetry," 413). Similar sentiments were voiced by many of Arnold's reviewers, as Carl Dawson's *Critical Heritage* volume amply reveals.

never wholly repudiated a life of secluded study and self-preparation, of the sort that Milton enjoyed for seven years at Horton; to the contrary, *Culture and Anarchy* recommends precisely such a life as beneficial to the state as well as to the individual. Yet like Milton, Arnold was also aware of the Parthian temptation, the tendency to cultivate only oneself, to the neglect of real and worthwhile action. This is the flaw of the English aristocracy, whom Arnold designates the "Barbarians": they dedicate so much time to the acquisition of "graces" and "external culture" that they accomplish nothing worthwhile (CPA 5:141).

Arnold did not class himself among the "Barbarians," yet in many of his works he struggles like them against the temptation of inaction. Arnold's critical career begins with the "Preface" to his 1853 *Poems,* in which (like Belial, or the Son) he pairs the concepts of "suffering" and "doing"; surprisingly, though, he denounces works, such as his own *Empedocles on Etna,* that depend too wholly on the former. "What then are the situations, from the representation of which, though accurate, no poetical enjoyment can be derived? They are those in which the suffering finds no vent in action; ... in which there is everything to be endured, nothing to be done" (1:2–3). This is an unexpected beginning for a critic who more generally could be considered, like Samson, "then vigorous most when most unactive deemed"; and despite the strictures of the "Preface," most of the poems in the 1853 volume show a deep dedication to the Mr. Harding Principle, as we shall see. But Arnold's life and writings show the same anxious animadversions on the topic as Milton's.

Drawing such parallels can sometimes be more amusing than instructive. If one speaks in general enough terms, the lives and works of any two writers can seem similar; and the very idea of comparing Arnold's poetry to Milton's may seem presumptuous. But drawing an extended comparison in this case is more than just a game, because Milton is not just any English poet. Throughout Arnold's writings, Milton is a constant point of reference and comparison—a "touchstone," as Arnold designates him—and consistently used as such. In "On Translating Homer," Arnold's first extended work of criticism, Milton is quoted as an exemplar of the grand style along with Homer and Dante (1:137, 212); he is the most recent poet to be so honored, and also the only English poet. In his essay on Samuel Johnson, Arnold declares, "Milton, in whom our great poetic age expired, was the last of the immortals" (8:316). In "Maurice de Guérin" (3:15) Arnold praises Milton's prose style as well (though he was also sensitive to its faults—in "The Study of Poetry" he calls it "obsolete and inconvenient" [9:179]). Throughout his work he shows an extraordinary knowledge of Milton's entire corpus: he is able to toss off a reference to the *History of Britain* (Preface to *Discourses in America,* 10:240) as easily as he quotes from Milton's minor poetry. So familiar is Milton that when Arnold reaches the Renaissance in his critical survey of English poetry, like Elizabeth Barrett Browning he simply skips over Shakespeare and Milton; these two are "our poetic classics" and therefore require no discussion, being, like all classics, already familiar ("The Study of Poetry," 9:178). No more recent poet can compare to Milton in greatness and importance; in a letter composed shortly after completing his edition of Wordsworth, Arnold admits that "Milton belongs to a more puissant poetic order than Wordsworth, surely. I cannot say to myself a line like 'With dreadful faces throng'd, and firing arms' without feeling this" (Arnold, *Letters,* 5:62). The careless misquotation of his own touchstone ("firing" for "fiery") reinforces the point: Milton is a classic—always present, and always remembered, if only hazily.

Milton's life and opinions appealed to Arnold far less than his poetry; Arnold repeatedly laments that Puritan narrow-mindedness nearly ruined the poet. "Milton was a born humanist, but the Puritan temper, as we know, mastered him. There is nothing more unlovely and unamiable than Milton the Puritan disputant" (CPA 8:296). But in an essay of the same year Arnold is able to salvage the Puritan Milton, as he had in *Culture and Anarchy,* by again conscripting him into the Established church. Illustrating the difference between an Anglican prayer service and a Dissenting one, Arnold almost perversely compares the Anglican liturgy to a reading from Milton, whereas the other is like a passage from a popular poetaster; Arnold liked this twisted analogy sufficiently to repeat it (8:344–45; 9:156–57).[7] If "Milton the Puritan disputant" had an overabundance of Hebraism, he also had a compensating overabundance of Hellenism, a mixture that Arnold was quick to appreciate. In his "Preface to *Merope*" he asserts that "it is impossible to praise the *Samson Agonistes* too highly" (1:62); the play, in its structure and its very title, provides a quite literal mingling of Hebraic and Hellenic.

For this reason Arnold objected to criticism that concentrated too exclusively on the polemical aspect of Milton's writings. In "A French Critic on Milton" he disapproves of both Samuel Johnson and Thomas Babington Macaulay for allowing Milton's partisanship—and hence their own—to overshadow his "Hellenism." By contrast he praises the French critic of the

---

7. The essays cited are, respectively, "Equality" and "Irish Civilization and British Liberalism," both 1878, and "The Future of Liberalism" (1880), where the comparison of the Anglican service to a passage from Milton is repeated.

title, Edmond Scherer, for recognizing Milton the noncombatant: "From the first, two conflicting forces, two sources of inspiration, had contended with one another, says M. Scherer, for the possession of Milton—the Renascence and Puritanism" (8:178). Arnold sees in Milton not only "the last of the immortals" but the first man of modern culture: he represents the successful mingling of Renaissance and Puritanism, Hellenism and Hebraism, cultivated inaction and effort, that Arnold aspired to.

To sum up: Arnold repeatedly cites Milton as a touchstone, the great exemplar of style in English poetry. His works display a deep knowledge and constant awareness of Milton, whose language often pervades Arnold's own. Arnold also shares with Milton an urge for what Arnold calls "Quiet Work," a mixture of effective action and retired contemplation; and even where Milton would seem to be ideologically ranged among Arnold's ultra-Protestant opponents, Arnold manages to enlist him in his own cause. And yet, despite all these factors, Milton would not be considered by most standards a "strong" or major influence on Arnold. He is a constant presence in Arnold's prose and poetry, but never a central one. The piece called "Milton," published in *Essays in Criticism, Second Series,* is not really an essay at all, but merely a brief address that Arnold was asked to give upon the unveiling of a stained-glass window dedicated to Milton; and Arnold put himself at a further remove by treating the memorial as if it were in honor not of Milton, but of his wife.[8] Arnold's most sustained writing upon Milton comes in "A French Critic on Milton," but even there, as the title indicates, he does not address his subject directly: "I did not propose to write a criticism of my own upon Milton I proposed to recite and compare the criticisms on him by others" (8:186). Milton appears as a "classic" in "The Study of Poetry" and as a necessary touchstone in essays on Gray, Keats, Byron, and Wordsworth, but never as the topic of any essay of Arnold's. "Arnold's criticism," as Maurice O'Sullivan remarks, "tends either to disregard Milton's subjects or to approach them only obliquely" (O'Sullivan 82). The same obliqueness is evident in the poetry: Miltonic language and imagery constantly recur, yet Milton is almost never the single dominant influence on a poem of Arnold's. Invariably another writer (Homer, Wordsworth, Keats) provides the immediate inspiration, while Milton exerts his influence from the background, in a "strictly circumscribed" manner (O'Sullivan 82).

---

8. Lois W. Parker notes that this is wholly Arnold's own interpretation, since both the archdeacon who commissioned the window and the American donor who sponsored it considered it to be a tribute to Milton himself—although they do mention Catherine Woodcock, his second wife, who was buried in the church (Parker 50).

Yet the very principle that Milton and Arnold share suggests a way of describing their relation to each other. The connection is one of analogy, of course, not causality: Milton's influence on Arnold is oblique and circumscribed, but not because both writers happened to believe in the virtues of mighty weakness. There is no question, however, that the notion of mighty weakness was one of Milton's legacies to Arnold. Arnold is fascinated with the Mr. Harding Principle, and like Trollope, he tends to illustrate that principle in works that teem with overt, incidental allusions to Milton. Whenever Arnold considers the benefits of retiring from the fray rather than entering it, of overcoming difficulty by retreat, Milton can almost invariably be glimpsed, like the Scholar-Gipsy, just disappearing around the corner. The effect of the comparison then is twofold. First, by tracing Miltonic echoes in Arnold's poetry, we are drawn to observe the broader correspondence between the two poets—their ability to construct a poetry of retreat and avoidance. Secondly, and with greater repercussions for Victorian poetry in general, we can see how a poetic influence can be strong without ever being dominant, or even direct. Among the voices that echo through Arnold's poetry, Milton's is never the loudest, but it is no less influential for that.

The opening question of Arnold's early sonnet, "To a Friend"—"Who prop, thou ask'st, in these bad days, my mind?"—seems at first to be self-answering.[9] The author has apparently been reading Milton, whose sonnet "To Mr Cyriack Skinner Upon his Blindness" asks the same rhetorical question: "What supports me dost thou ask?" In response to his own question Arnold refers, in a roundabout way, to three authors. First the poet who "though blind" (line 4; cf. "though blind" in the final line of Milton's sonnet) nevertheless saw so much; but this, it turns out, means Homer. Next the philosopher driven into exile by the tyrant—Epictetus. And finally, he "whose even-balanced soul,/From first youth tested up to extreme old age,/Business could not make dull, nor passion wild;/Who saw life steadily, and saw it whole" (9–12). Again the description fits Milton, but does not apply to him; the poet who balanced business and passion is Sophocles. Although Milton apparently provides the impetus for the sonnet, he then disappears from view as Arnold looks beyond him to cite anterior examples.

---

9. All quotations from Arnold's poetry refer to *The Poems of Matthew Arnold*, ed. Kenneth Allott; 2nd ed., ed. Miriam Allott (London: Longman, 1979). I am frequently indebted to this excellent edition; many of the echoes I discuss are cited in the Allotts' annotations.

A similar overleaping occurs in another early poem, "Horatian Echo," which begins as follows:

Omit, omit, my simple friend,
Still to enquire how parties tend,
Or what we fix with foreign powers.
If France and we are really friends,
And what the Russian Czar intends,
    Is no concern of ours.

                (1–6)

This is indeed an echo of the beginning of Horace's Ode II, xi. But intervening between Horace and Arnold comes Milton's own imitation of the same ode, in his other sonnet to Cyriack Skinner ("Cyriack, whose grandsire"): "Let Euclid rest and Archimedes pause, / And what the Swede intend, and what the French" (7–8). It is typical of Arnold to have echoed one of the few Miltonic sonnets that turn away from politics to call for a balance of business with pleasure. Milton's sonnet "disapproves that care, though wise in show, / That with superfluous burden loads the day, / And when God sends a cheerful hour, refrains" (12–14)—displaying that mixture of "Puritan and Renascence" that Arnold noted with approval. It is equally typical of Arnold once again to have echoed Milton in a poem that acknowledges another, earlier author as its source.

The only poem of Arnold's that admits Milton as its prime influence is his late work, "Westminster Abbey" (1881), an elegy on A. P. Stanley. By this time Arnold had long since all but abandoned writing verse (the only other poems he published in the 1880s were two elegies for deceased dachshunds and one for a canary), and the result of his renewed attempt is embarrassing. "Westminster Abbey" reads like a pastiche of the Nativity Ode, of which it clumsily imitates the stanza form and the language—"But once, at midnight deep, / His mother woke from sleep, / And saw her babe amidst the fire, and screamed"—varied by a dash of "Lycidas"—"Though sunk be now this bright, this gracious head!" (91–93; 176). Aside from this one example, Milton appears in Arnold's poems glancingly, a figure always overshadowed by some other precursor. Yet he exerts a constant influence on Arnold's language and his sentiments: as both "To a Friend" and "Horatian Echo" demonstrate, verbal reminiscences of Milton occur most frequently in poems that also reveal a temperamental affinity with Milton, a desire to retreat from the world in order to "see it whole."

Like Samson and the Son, the central characters of Arnold's poems have often retired from the fray, at least temporarily, to gather strength. Even in "Alaric at Rome," Arnold's schoolboy prize poem, the Gothic warlord stands aloof, passively contemplating Rome from a hilltop (eliciting the Miltonic apostrophe "Yet once again, stern Chief, yet once again...Pour from a thousand hills thy warriors of the north!" [85, 96; cf. the opening of "Lycidas" and *PL* 1.351–52]). The Strayed Reveller, the title character of Arnold's first book of poems, retreats not from battle but from festivity; but he too has a Miltonic air about him, as he encounters Circe and drinks from her cup. The pattern continues with Mycerinus and Empedocles, although both of these figures retreat out of weakness rather than strength. Not so Aepytus in "Merope," whose Parthian tactic is to regain his kingdom by playing dead: "well I hope/Through that pretended death to live and reign" (49–50). But the most notable examples of the trope come in "Resignation," *Sohrab and Rustum* (and its pale twin, *Balder Dead*), and "The Scholar-Gipsy."

"Resignation" is Arnold's early, forthright declaration of the Mr. Harding Principle. True success, he asserts, goes not to those who strive for it—the Crusaders and Goths and Huns described in the poem's opening verse-paragraph. It belongs rather to the gipsies, whose life of perpetual retreat allows them to avoid the "Crowded and keen" struggles of the age (133). Yet the gipsies exaggerate in the opposite direction: they rely too much upon the principle of inaction. The golden mean is achieved by "the poet," who lives within view of the world but separated from it. Unlike the gipsies he does expend effort, but only in pursuit of greater knowledge: "The poet... Subdues that energy to scan/Not his own course, but that of man" (144–47). Arnold pictures the Poet retired from the bustling world to the top of a hill from which, like Sophocles in "To a Friend," he can see life steadily, and see it whole.

The acknowledged source for "Resignation" is not Sophocles, but Wordsworth: the poem is set in the Lake District, and its situation is modeled almost exactly on "Tintern Abbey." Yet the Poet of the poem bears very little resemblance to Wordsworth; he is too close to the gipsies (in Wordsworth, symbols of mere idleness) and too removed from sympathy with others to be Wordsworthian.[10] The Poet represents no single figure, of course; he seems

---

10. Numerous critics have compared and contrasted "Tintern Abbey" to "Resignation"; David Riede, for instance, writes that in the latter, "the un-Wordsworthian description of an eminently Wordsworthian situation leads Arnold eventually to a discussion of poets and poetry and to an implicit refutation of his predecessor" (Riede 58).

rather to be an amalgam of many of the authors Arnold admires: Sophocles, Horace, Lucretius, Senancour. But it is striking how consistently the language used to describe him is Miltonic. When describing first what the Poet is *not,* Arnold turns to book 1 of *Paradise Lost:*

Though he hath loosed a thousand chains,
Though he hath borne immortal pains,
Action and suffering though he know—
He hath not lived if he lives so.
He sees, in some great-historied land,
A ruler of the people stand,
Sees his strong thought in fiery flood
Roll through the heaving multitude;
Exults—yet for no moment's space
Envies the all-regarded place.

("Resignation" 150–59)

"Chains," "immortal," "roll" and "fiery" all come from the first description of Satan (*PL* 1.48–53), where they are shortly followed by the collocation of suffering and doing, of "rolling" and "flood" (1.158, 324). The reminiscence of Milton is natural, since Arnold's Poet is a poet by virtue of his active nonparticipation: "Arnold is explicit that the poet must give up all action" (Trilling 101). When Arnold goes on to describe what the Poet *is* (not what he does, since the Poet does very little), he likewise remembers Milton:

He leans upon a gate and sees
The pastures, and the quiet trees.
Low, woody hill, with gracious bound,
Folds the still valley almost round;
The cuckoo, loud on some high lawn,
Is answered from the depth of dawn;
In the hedge straggling to the stream,
Pale, dew-drenched, half-shut roses gleam;
But, where the farther side slopes down,
He sees the drowsy new-waked clown
In his white quaint-embroidered frock
Make, whistling, tow'rd his mist-wreathed flock—
Slowly, behind his heavy tread,
The wet, flowered grass heaves up its head.

("Resignation" 172–85)

"High lawn" derives from "Lycidas" (25), and "heaves up its head" recalls "L'Allegro" (145; see also the description of Satan at *PL* 1.211, a passage that contributes to the earlier description too). But more generally these lines ring with the language and the rhythms of both "L'Allegro" and "Il Penseroso." The octosyllabic couplets, the passive constructions ("The cuckoo... is answered") surrounding a figure who passes through the busy haunts of men, rejoicing in their activity but never sharing it—these are familiar from Milton's companion poems. Compare a passage from "L'Allegro":

From the side of some hoar hill,
Through the high wood echoing shrill.
Sometime walking not unseen
By hedgerow elms, on hillocks green,
Right against the eastern gate,
Where the great sun begins his state,
Robed in flames, and amber light,
The clouds in thousand liveries dight,
While the ploughman near at hand,
Whistles o'er the furrowed land.

(55–64)

Arnold borrows his "whistling" directly from this scene, but in general Milton's impact is indirect. He walks, at best, "not unseen" in the background of Arnold's poem, one of its presiding geniuses, but only rarely participating and never acknowledged. Late in "Resignation" the Poet is compared to Homer and Orpheus—again, two names with strong Miltonic associations. But Milton himself remains in the margins.

Sohrab and Rustum: An Episode also nods in the direction of Homer. Arnold derived the story of the poem from a Persian legend recounted by Charles Augustin Sainte-Beuve, but he chose the "episode" because it gave him an opportunity "to imitate the manner of Homer," as he acknowledged and as reviewers of the poem recognized (Riede 103). The combat between the two champions is Homeric in all its details and recalls particularly the slaying of Hector by Achilles. Rustum further resembles Achilles in his initial refusal to engage in the battle, preferring to linger in his tent; and his situation also recalls that of Odysseus: he has an old father living in reduced state at home and an unknown son who seeks him. Above all, the foregrounded and extended epic similes are conscious if sometimes clumsy Homeric imitations. And yet the poem seems ultimately Miltonic, both in meter and manner. Arnold would later declare that anyone wishing to capture the manner of Homer in

English translation would have to avoid blank verse, since "to [Homer's] rapidity the elaborate movement of Miltonic blank verse is alien" (CPA 1:104). Arnold's poem lays itself open to this very charge, yet the reminiscence of Milton is only appropriate, since the plot (and this probably formed part of its appeal for Arnold) concerns a highly Miltonic noncombative fight. *Sohrab and Rustum* features the retreatingest battle scene since *Samson Agonistes.*

Milton makes his presence felt from the beginning of *Sohrab and Rustum.* The opening line of the poem originally read "And the first rays of morning streaked the east," recalling "Tomorrow ere fresh morning streak the east" (*PL* 4.623); the echo was removed only in Arnold's fair copy. But the change could not suppress the Miltonic sound of the blank verse, as becomes evident when Arnold produces his first epic simile, comparing the Tartars to cranes (110–16). Although it can claim a legitimate Homeric precedent, even to Arnold's own ear the simile sounded Miltonic. Discussing *Sohrab and Rustum* in a letter to John Duke Coleridge, Arnold writes, "I think it is certainly true about the Miltonic air of part of it—but Milton is a sufficiently great master to imitate—the cranes are not taken directly from him, as far as I can remember, but the passage is no doubt an imitation of his Manner—so with many others" (Arnold, *Letters,* 1:279). The "many others" include the passage describing Rustum's club (408–16), which like Satan's spear is compared to a tree used in shipbuilding (*PL* 1.292–94). And like his similes, Arnold's frequent muster rolls of place names also carry a "Miltonic air."

This pervasive reminiscence draws attention to the fact that *Sohrab and Rustum,* although superficially a martial episode, resembles the battle in heaven or *Samson Agonistes* in making arms ridiculous. The episode begins with a battle being called off, to allow the two champions to fight. Rustum at first refuses to accept Sohrab's challenge, but when he is goaded by the messenger, his response turns into a *nolo episcopari,* a refusal that ends in acceptance:

> "O Gudurz, wherefore dost thou say such words?
> Thou knowest better words than this to say.
> What is one more, one less, obscure or famed,
> Valiant or craven, young or old, to me?
> Are not they mortal, am not I myself?
> But who for men of nought would do great deeds?
> Come, thou shalt see how Rustum hoards his fame!"
>
> (250–56)

The tactic of refusing combat then switches back and forth between the combatants. When they meet, Rustum proposes a truce; when Rustum falls the first time, Sohrab proposes a truce. This goads Rustum into forgetting his better strategy, and he strikes and blusters with all his might—to no avail, as he is twice again struck down. Yet these falls eventually end in victory for Rustum, though an odd victory: Sohrab's defeat, caused merely by his hearing Rustum's name pronounced, nearly kills his father, who falls down senseless. Sohrab is vanquished by a word (O weakness!), Rustum by a death. In other ways, too, Sohrab's defeat constitutes a victory, though tragic: it achieves the double purpose of preserving the Tartar army and of discovering the father and son to each other. Sohrab reveals both his merit and his birthright better in dying than he would have by conquering with sword and spear.

At the moment of Sohrab's successful fall, Arnold introduces one of his better epic similes:

> As when some hunter in the spring hath found
> A breeding eagle sitting on her nest,
> Upon the craggy isle of a hill-lake,
> And pierced her with an arrow as she rose,
> And followed her to find her where she fell
> Far off; anon her mate comes winging back
> From hunting, and a great way off descries
> His huddling young left sole; at that, he checks
> His pinion, and with short uneasy sweeps
> Circles above his eyry, with loud screams
> Chiding his mate back to her nest; but she
> Lies dying, with the arrow in her side,
> In some far stony gorge out of his ken,
> A heap of fluttering feathers....
>
> (556–69)

J. B. Broadbent remarks that "To Milton Arnold owes 'pinion' and the usage of 'sole,' and 'out of his ken' has its colloquial quality elevated by Miltonic reminiscence" (Broadbent 406). In a note to this passage, Kenneth and Miriam Allott add that "Far off" and "a great way off descries" come from Milton as well (*PL* 2.636–43). There are other reminiscences: "uneasy sweeps" recalls Satan's "uneasy steps," also occurring at the end of a line (*PL* 1.295). The Miltonic echoes cluster around the fallen Sohrab.

Yet Broadbent's aim is not to single out Milton as the chief source of the simile. Quite the contrary: he notes "the extraordinary confluence of imitations that makes the influence of Milton seem comparatively slight." He mentions Homer, Wordsworth, and the Authorized Version (he might also have added Tennyson, notably the "Morte d'Arthur"), and goes on to suggest that "this is a good example of the running together in Victorian poetry generally of the main literary currents of the Renaissance. . . . By 1853 the Renaissance had educated a really large audience which would appreciate both the Miltonic and Homeric echoes, and appreciate Biblical and colloquial tones" (Broadbent 406–7). Throughout his article Broadbent is rather dismissive of the indistinctness he associates with "Victorian poetry generally," but he rightly perceives that Milton's influence in this case manages to be at once pervasive and "comparatively slight." Milton is essential to Arnold's poem, to the effect of its plot structure as much as to its rhythms and rhetoric; yet at the same time he seems to retreat into the background, an authorized poetical bible, a reference rather than a source.

Many of the same patterns are evident in *Balder Dead,* Arnold's next attempt at a Homeric episode.[11] The action of the poem begins with Odin's words, "Enough of tears, ye Gods, enough of wail!" (1.18), an echo of Manoa's closing speech in *Samson Agonistes:* "Nothing is here for tears, nothing to wail" (*SA* 1721). The allusion is apt, as Odin is mourning a heroic son who has fallen through his one weakness, which he had foolishly revealed. The role of Samson in Arnold's poem is split between Balder and his unwitting murderer, the blind god Hoder, who laments his weakness and sense of being an outcast (*Balder Dead* 1.95–110) and later kills himself. Miltonic reminiscences continue throughout the poem: at one point, in a reversal of the hellish synod in *Paradise Lost,* the gods assemble in heaven and propose invading hell, only to conclude that there is no point in struggling against death's almighty power (3.225–94). Again, Milton is just one influence among many—the Eddas that provided the story; Homer; the "Morte d'Arthur" again. But the importance of the Miltonic influence becomes apparent at the end, when Balder suddenly reveals the significance of his death. He is happy, he declares, to have escaped from "too much of war and broils, which make / Life one perpetual fight" (3.505–6). He foresees that his fall will now be followed by that of all the other gods, and that through their death, and his own inaction, a happier paradise will be obtained, free of struggle:

Inactive therefore let me lie, in gloom,
Unarmed, inglorious; I attend the course
Of ages, and my late return to light,

---

11. As the Poet in "Resignation" is compared to Homer and Orpheus, so *Balder Dead* is both Homeric and Orphic. The middle section of the poem concerns Hermod's embassy to the underworld to win back Balder; like Orpheus, he narrowly fails to meet the conditions for the return of the dead. To enter the forbidden regions, Hermod is said to "o'erleap the grate that bars the wall" (2.185); compare Satan, who "o'erleaped" the "bar" of Eden (*PL* 4.583–85).

In times less alien to a spirit mild,
In new-recovered seats, the happier day.
(3.509–13)

This renewed world is described in language out of Milton as "an earth/More fresh, more verdant than the last, with fruits/Self-springing, and a seed of man preserved" (3.528–30; Allott compares Adam's assurance that after the devastation of the Flood "man shall live/With all the creatures, and their seed preserve" [*PL* 11.872–73]). Like Sohrab and Rustum and the Poet of "Resignation," and like all of Milton's heroes, Balder begins to triumph when he withdraws—then vigorous most when most "Inactive" deemed.

"The Scholar-Gipsy," Arnold's signature piece, is also his fullest exploration of the principle of retreat. What "Resignation" prescribes, "The Scholar-Gipsy" illustrates, and the central figure, more fugitive even than Arnold's other heroes, combines the characteristics of the Poet and the gipsies from the earlier poem. As usual, Arnold takes his story from one source (Joseph Glanvill) and his verse form from another (Keats), mingling with these a number of other clear influences—Tennyson again (the "Lotos-Eaters"), and Gray's elegy, among others. Milton seems lost in the mix, but as always he appears at crucial points. The "wattled cotes" in the second line of Arnold's poem come from *Comus,* at the moment where the two brothers are waiting for a spark from heaven to fall (*Comus* 343). Arnold's rhetorical self-correction after he thinks he sees the Scholar—"But what—I dream! Two hundred years are flown"—imitates the two-hundred year old "Lycidas": "Ay me, I fondly dream!" ("Scholar-Gipsy" 131; "Lycidas" 56).

According to David Riede these echoes serve to highlight a contrast between the two poets. Whereas "Milton stood, waiting for God[,] Arnold's speaker sits, waiting 'till sun-down' (l. 22) for the shepherd." He continues,

[Arnold] tries to invoke Milton as a powerful ally to justify the speaker's passivity, but in these latter days, as the later part of the poem makes clear, waiting for a "spark from heaven" (l. 171) is an exercise in futility and despair. The language that pointed, for Milton, to ultimate truth can only point, for Arnold, to Milton. (Riede 139)

This is a useful reminder: like Riede, nineteenth-century readers who noted Arnold's affinity to Milton also remarked upon the gap between them. As William Wilson observes, "To Swinburne, Arnold was disturbingly un-Miltonic, despite his intentions to be the Victorian avatar of Samson" (Wilson 382). But no one was more aware of this discrepancy than Arnold himself: the scholar-gipsy is such an elusive figure because the state of purposeful inaction he represents is so much rarer and more difficult to attain in the nineteenth century than it was "in days when wits ran fresh and clear." For the same reason Milton is an elusive figure in the poem: he continues to stand as an ideal even though he can no longer serve as a model.

Hence Milton is most important in the poem, not as a direct verbal influence, but as the presiding "Genius" ("Scholar-Gipsy" 149), and nowhere is this more evident than in the two final stanzas, the set-piece metaphor of the Tyrian trader. This coda is rife with echoes of earlier writers, among whom we once again find Milton. Arnold's description of the "intruder" on the Tyrian's "ancient home," found "Lifting the cool-haired creepers stealthily,/The fringes of a southward-facing brow," imitates the description of Eden first seen through Satan's eyes ("Scholar-Gipsy" 234–40; cf. *PL* 4.258–62). More notably, the retiring Iberian traders of the final lines are not Iberian at all, but Parthian. "There, where down cloudy cliffs, through sheets of foam,/Shy traffickers, the dark Iberians come": this echoes the description of the Parthians in *Paradise Regained,* who come from the "cliffs/Of Caucasus, and dark Iberian dales" ("Scholar-Gipsy" 248–49; *PR* 3.317–18). Again, the reminiscence is entirely appropriate: the concluding stanzas are Miltonic not only because of their diction, but because like all of Arnold's great endings, they are in retreat.

Herein lies the true significance of tracing Milton's peculiar form of influence on Arnold: it helps reveal the unexpected source of Arnold's poetic strength. Even warm admirers of Arnold's poetry—and there seem to be ever fewer—are happy for his poems to end. Nothing in Arnold's best poems becomes him like the leaving of them. Just as Dalila reveals her true nature only as she turns to go—"She's gone, a manifest serpent by her sting/Discovered in the end, till now concealed"—so Arnold reveals his true poetic character not in addressing his topic, but in turning away from it. The most successful part of *Tristram and Iseult,* for instance, is its coda, the seemingly unrelated episode of Merlin and Vivien. Most of Arnold's best-known lines come from the end of poems: the "unplumbed, salt, estranging sea" of "To Marguerite—Continued," or the wonderful diminuendo that concludes "The Buried Life": "And then he thinks he knows/The hills where his life rose,/And the sea where it goes." Many poems leave the reader with the impression that Arnold has not finished so much as given up, or simply changed the topic; but this giving up proves to be his most effective poetic weapon. What better way to end a poem on resignation than by turning away? "Resignation" seems to end at line 260 ("Whence, equally, the seas of life and death are fed"), which has an air of finality, being an alexandrine that communicates a familiar moral in the broadest terms ("life and death"). Yet the poem does not end there, but adds instead a far better and less conclusive conclusion.

> And even could the intemperate prayer
> Man iterates, while these forbear,
> For movement, for an ampler sphere,
> Pierce Fate's impenetrable ear;
> Not milder is the general lot
> Because our spirits have forgot,
> In action's dizzying eddy whirled,
> The something that infects the world.
>
> ("Resignation" 271–78)

"The something": it is the placeholder used by someone trying to remember the words to a poem and failing. This sense, or absence, is reinforced by the disappointingly perfect rhyme of "whirled" and "world": Arnold is emphasizing his inability as a poet either to name the world's problems or to harmonize with them. Yet this second ending, in illustrating the poet's weakness, illustrates also his strength, the poetry he achieves by throwing up his hands.

The same holds true for the description of the Oxus at the end of *Sohrab and Rustum* and the Tyrian trader in "The Scholar-Gipsy." Both codas turn away from the body of their respective poems, both describe a retreat, and both succeed despite their seeming irrelevance because they conclude poems that celebrate overcoming by flight. The ending of *Sohrab and Rustum* is Miltonic, not just because the floating "mist" of the Oxus echoes the final simile of *Paradise Lost* (*Sohrab and Rustum* 875; *PL* 12.629–30), but because it celebrates the Miltonic principle of victorious retreat. The ending of "Dover Beach" provides perhaps the most familiar example. "Dover Beach" names Sophocles yet once more, and it concludes with an episode from Thucydides, but it is haunted by Milton.

> Ah, love, let us be true
> To one another! for the world, which seems
> To lie before us like a land of dreams,
> So various, so beautiful, so new,
> Hath really neither joy, nor love, nor light,
> Nor certitude, nor peace, nor help for pain;
> And we are here as on a darkling plain
> Swept with confused alarms of struggle and flight,
> Where ignorant armies clash by night.
>
> (29–37)

"Neither joy, nor love" are Satan's words upon looking at lost paradise (*PL* 4.509); the "world which [lies] before us" echoes the prospect seen by Adam and Eve as they leave Eden ("The world was all before them," 12.646).[12] The two possible courses of action the speaker detects in the world—struggle and flight—are the same that always face both poets; far more often than not the former kicks the beam.

The self-divide in Milton between a strict adherence to duty and a love of ease or beauty has been a critical commonplace almost from the first. By the later Victorian period, when Arnold was established as perhaps the foremost critic in England, the latter inclination of Milton's was habitually called "culture." Peter Bayne in 1873 described Milton's self-conflict thus: "But above the hasty rebukes of friends, and deeper than the hints of conscience in moments of self-reproach, was the predominant conviction that he who, in his youth, addresses himself, with the whole energy of his soul, to culture, is in the path of duty, and need not shrink from 'the great Task-master's eye' " (Bayne 433). John Dennis, also on the subject of "culture," contrasts Milton to Goethe: "Most Englishmen . . . have the conviction, not altogether just, perhaps, that Goethe's devotion to self-culture[,] to the full development of his majestic intellect, detracts from his greatness, and may reasonably lessen our admiration of his character. Milton, although he too proposed, even in youthful days, to give his life to poetry, when a time of trial came, made a great sacrifice for England, and although called by Nature to another task, devoted to her the best years of his life" (Dennis 110). Neither critic mentions Arnold, yet Arnold's priorities hang over both statements—even though one holds culture to be self-justifying while the other demands a counterbalance of action. Arnold is the source of neither statement, yet the presiding genius of both. It is only appropriate that he should influence Milton criticism in the same way that Milton influenced his own poetry and criticism—definitely, yet glancingly, from the background.

---

12. The first echo is noted by Martin Bidney (86); the echo of the concluding lines of *Paradise Lost* is discussed by O'Sullivan (83–84), and later by Ronald Sharp (53).

❧ CHAPTER 4

Milton and Tennyson:
Diffusive Power

       The earliest extant piece of Alfred Tennyson's writing is a letter to his aunt, composed when he was twelve years old. Nearly the entire letter is devoted to the schoolboy's criticism of Milton. "Going into the library this morning," he writes, "I picked up 'Sampson Agonistes,' on which (as I think it is a play you like) I shall send you my remarks." Those remarks comprise a tissue of cross-reference: one passage "puts me in mind of that in Dante, which Lord Byron has prefixed to his 'Corsair' "; another passage, in which Samson is said to be "carelessly diffused," is illuminated by a quotation from Horace. As the commentary continues, Milton's work becomes enmeshed in an ever-expanding web of literary references:

> To an English reader the metre of the Chorus may seem unusual, but the difficulty will vanish when I inform him that it is taken from the Greek. In line 133 there is this expression, "Chalybean tempered steel." The Chalybes were a nation among the ancients very famous for the making of steel, hence the expression "Chalybean," or peculiar to the

---

The subtitle of this chapter is drawn from Tennyson's *In Memoriam* (henceforth IM): "But though I seem in star and flower/To feel thee some diffusive power,/I do not therefore love thee less" (130.6–8). All quotations from Tennyson's poetry refer to *The Poems of Tennyson,* ed. Christopher Ricks; throughout this chapter I am frequently indebted to Ricks's footnotes.

Chalybes: in line 147 "the Gates of Azzar"; this probably, as Bp. Newton observes, was to avoid too great an alliteration, which the "Gates of Gaza" would have caused, though (in my opinion) it would have rendered it more beautiful: and (though I do not affirm it as a fact) perhaps Milton gave it that name for the sake of novelty, as all the world knows he was a great pedant. (*Memoir* 1:7–9)

Coming at the end of such a letter, the accusation of pedantry is unintentionally humorous. As Henry Van Dyke, the author of one of the first critical monographs on Tennyson, observes concerning Tennyson's juvenile poetry, "The display of learning is so immense that it becomes amusing; but it is not without significance, for it distinctly marks Tennyson as one of those who, like Milton, were students before they were poets" (Van Dyke 10–11). Tennyson's letter confirms Van Dyke's assertion that Tennyson resembled Milton in precocious learning, and also shows how largely Milton figured in the young Tennyson's erudite imagination. Yet he figures, not alone, but at the center of a pantheon of great writers, first among equals.

Van Dyke's book, which was published in 1889 during the poet's lifetime, devotes an entire chapter to the relation between Tennyson and Milton, although he notes that the affinity is not immediately obvious.

Tennyson has been compared most frequently with Keats; sometimes, but falsely, with Shelley; and sometimes, more wisely, with Wordsworth. Our accomplished American critic, Mr. Edmund Clarence Stedman, who touches nothing that he does not adorn, has a chapter in his *Victorian Poets* on Tennyson and Theocritus. But the best comparison,—one which runs far below the outward appearance into the profound affinities of genius—yet remains to be carefully traced. Among all poets,—certainly among all English poets,—it seems to me that Tennyson's next of kin is Milton. (Van Dyke 49–50)

Comparison between the two poets, at least in terms of their stature, dates back all the way to 1833, when Arthur Henry Hallam wrote to Tennyson to inform him "that a question is put up at the Cambridge Union, 'Tennyson or Milton, which the greater poet?'" (*Memoir* 1:91).[1] Tennyson continued to admire and to imitate Milton throughout his life. In his bachelor days,

---

1. As Robert Bernard Martin points out, however, "since the Union's minutes apparently record no such debate Hallam's account may have been a kindly fiction" intended to cheer up his friend (Martin 173).

he used to amuse his friends by "enact[ing] with grim humour Milton's 'So started up in his foul shape the fiend,' from the crouching of the toad to the explosion" (*Memoir* 1:184). Many years later, with even grimmer humor, he seemed to suggest that he was unwittingly enacting Satan's later incarnation in the serpent: in 1889, apropos of his own bodily decrepitude, "He quoted Milton, the 'Imbodied and Imbruted' passage."[2] Imitation of Milton, willing or unwilling, likewise marks Tennyson's verse. According to W. David Shaw's rough calculation, allusions to Milton in Tennyson's poetry are outnumbered only by allusions to (what else?) the Bible, and far outdistance the other nearest competitor, Shakespeare (Shaw 27). And such direct verbal echoes tell only part of the story; as J. F. A. Pyre asserts, "So thoroughly is [Tennyson's] verse suffused with the colors of Milton's descriptive poetry that the phrases actually taken by him direct from Milton only feebly illustrate the extent to which he has submitted his technique to the Miltonic discipline" (Pyre 236).

Tennyson's "fixation on Milton," especially in his early poems, marks him, according to Herbert Tucker, "as a very junior scion of the Romantic line, half a generation behind Shelley and Keats" (Tucker, "Strange Comfort," 2). But there are at least two aspects of Tennyson's treatment of Milton that differ from that of his predecessors. In the first place, as we have already seen in the letter about Samson, Milton is preeminent without being predominant in Tennyson's imagination. Like Matthew Arnold, Tennyson frequently embeds allusions to Milton within allusions to other, often older writers.[3] This habit is not unique to the Victorians; Percy Shelley and John Keats occasionally

---

2. From Hallam Tennyson's "Diary of A.T.'s Illness" for May 13, 1889, reprinted in LT 3:392. As the editors note, this is a "pathetic revelation if (as seems likely) Tennyson was applying to himself Satan's words in *Paradise Lost,* ix, 163–7" about his "foul descent." It is not certain which passage of Milton Tennyson was quoting: "Embodies and imbrutes" occurs in *Comus* 467. But Lang and Shannon are probably right in suggesting that Tennyson was more likely citing Satan's apt complaint about being constrained "This essence to incarnate and imbrute" (*PL* 9.166).

3. For instance, in an early, unpublished poetic manifesto, "To Poesy" (1828), Tennyson speaks of the mind, "Whose trumpet-tongued, aërial melody/May blow alarum loud to every wind,/And startle the dull ears of human kind" (3–5). The sudden Miltonic allusion ("singing startle the dull night" ["L'Allegro" 42]) is itself startling, coming in the midst of a more complex allusion to Macbeth's soliloquy in act 1, scene 7 ("trumpet-tongued," "blow," "wind"). Tennyson further complicates the allusions, and displays the range of his knowledge, when he continues "Methinks I see the world's renewèd youth/A long day's dawn"—as Ricks notes, a reminiscence of *Areopagitica:* "Methinks I see her as an Eagle mueing her mighty youth…at the full midday beam."

Or consider Tennyson's 1880 translation of the Anglo-Saxon "The Battle of Brunanburh," in which Tennyson imports Milton's description of the Parthians—"numbers numberless" (*PR* 3.310)—into his translation: "Fell on the war-field, numberless numbers" (54). (The original half-line, "*unrim heriges,*" means "countless of the host.")

do the same. If one takes for example the two most Miltonic of their longer poems, *Prometheus Unbound* has an Aeschylean framework, and the story of *Hyperion* comes from Hesiod, via Lemprière. But in Keats and Shelley such classical ur-texts seem to be mere pretexts, whereas in Tennyson's imagination, as we shall see, Milton is far more truly integrated with other writers and myths.

The second difference is that whereas Romantic poets chiefly imitated Miltonic sublimity—as *Prometheus Unbound* and *Hyperion* both demonstrate—Tennyson was just as impressed by Milton's earth as he was by heaven and hell. His most Miltonic passages frequently fixate on the beautiful rather than the sublime: light rather than darkness, flowers rather than stars. Francis Turner Palgrave records that Tennyson was "like Keats, devoted to 'Miltonian storms, and more, Miltonian tenderness,'" and that he particularly admired "the great vision of Eden (Book IV. 205–311), which he read aloud…often" (*Memoir* 2:503). Palgrave here cites Keats's early poem, "To Charles Cowden Clarke," which admires "Miltonian storms, and more, Miltonian tenderness;/ Michael in arms, and more, meek Eve's fair slenderness" (58–59). These lines are a reminder that the Romantics, too, appreciated Milton's beauty together with his grandeur; but in Tennyson a significant shift of balance occurs, away from "giant forms" and toward "Eve's fair slenderness."

Two poems in which Tennyson refers to Milton by name illustrate these characteristics.[4] In "The Palace of Art" (1832, but much revised 1842), the Soul's throne room is hung round with "choice paintings of wise men":

> For there was Milton like a seraph strong,
>   Beside him Shakespeare bland and mild;
> And there the world-worn Dante grasped his song,
>   And somewhat grimly smiled.
>
>   (131; 133–36)

Milton comes first, described by his own coinage, "seraph" (a back-formation from the biblical plural "seraphim"; in the 1832 version Milton had been

---

4. Two other poems mention Milton directly. "Milton's Mulberry," a poem written at Cambridge but not published by Tennyson, celebrates the tree supposed to have been planted by Milton at Christ's College; it displays a Miltonic disdain for the pedantry of Cambridge dons. "Romney's Remorse," one of Tennyson's last dramatic monologues (1889), alludes to "Milton's amaranth" (106); the allusion is apt, since one of George Romney's most famous paintings depicts Milton dictating *Paradise Lost* to his daughters, and since Romney, like Milton, was accused of having been neglectful of both his wife and his child (hence the "remorse" of the title).

simply "an angel"). But Milton is not the sole presiding spirit in the palace; once again his name is joined with that of Dante and others.[5] Moreover, it is not clear exactly what the invocation of Milton may represent, since the Miltonic echoes in the poem point in different directions. The palace is described first in the language of Eden: "From those four jets four currents in one swell/Across the mountain streamed below/In misty folds," just like the four conjoining streams in Milton's paradise (33–35; *PL* 4.226–33).[6] On the other hand, the lighting—"light in wreaths and anadems,/And pure quintessences of precious oils/In hollowed moons of gems,/To mimic heaven" ("Palace" 186–89)— recalls the "God-like imitated state" of Pandemonium (especially the diabolical lamps of *PL* 1.726–30, a passage concerning which Tennyson commented, "I always like this, it is mystical" [*Memoir* 2:518]). Meanwhile, the bells that adorn the palace's towers—"Moved of themselves, with silver sound"—echo the very gates of heaven, "harmonious sound/On golden hinges moving" ("Palace" 130; *PL* 7.206–7). The Soul's habitation thus derives equally from Milton's earth, hell, and heaven, and everything in between: the ceiling decorated with "angels rising and descending" imitates the stairs of heaven, where Satan saw "Angels ascending and descending" ("Palace" 143; *PL* 3.511).

It is only natural that a space as morally debatable as the Palace of Art should draw from all different areas of Milton's moral universe. But the range of allusion in this relatively short poem suggests that Milton represented to Tennyson no one prevailing idea but could serve impartially as a source of imagery. This comes out clearly in the decoration of one of the rooms of the palace, which has an Arthurian theme:

> Or mythic Uther's deeply-wounded son
>> In some fair space of sloping greens
> Lay, dozing in the vale of Avalon,
>> And watched by weeping queens.
>>>> ("Palace" 105–8)

Foreshadowing a connection between Milton and the Arthurian legend that will become more pronounced later in his career, Tennyson here bases Avalon on Milton's Garden of Adonis, where Adonis slumbers to heal his "deep

---

5. On the association of Milton with Dante in the early nineteenth century, see Milbank 8–28.

6. The four rivers are found in Genesis (2:10), but Tennyson's and Milton's descriptions share vocabulary not found in the Bible's account, including "mountain," "current," "fell," and "streams." All these terms come from the particular passage (*PL* 4.205ff.) that Palgrave mentions as having been one of Tennyson's favorites. The "misty folds" recall the "dewy mist" that waters the earth in *Paradise Lost* (7.333).

wound," similarly overlooked by a "sad queen" (*Comus* 999–1001). Milton appears "carefully diffused" throughout "The Palace of Art"; he is just as evident in the "fair sloping greens" as in the descriptions of the guilty splendors of the palace.

A second direct mention of Milton in Tennyson's poetry comes in 1863. Among the "Attempts at Classical Metres in Quantity" published in that year is one entitled "Milton," written, as the subtitle informs us, in the "Alcaic" meter.

> O mighty-mouthed inventor of harmonies
> O skilled to sing of Time or Eternity,
> > God-gifted organ-voice of England,
> > > Milton, a name to resound for ages;
> Whose Titan angels, Gabriel, Abdiel,
> Starred from Jehovah's gorgeous armouries,
> > Tower, as the deep-domed empyrëan
> > > Rings to the roar of an angel onset—
> Me rather all that bowery loneliness,
> The brooks of Eden mazily murmuring,
> > And bloom profuse and cedar arches
> > > Charm, as a wanderer out in ocean,
> Where some refulgent sunset of India
> Streams o'er a rich ambrosial ocean isle,
> > And crimson-hued the stately palm-woods
> > > Whisper in odorous heights of even.

The first half of the poem picks out for admiration Milton's great vatic descriptions—heaven, eternity, the battle of mighty powers—only for the second half to express a preference for Milton's other voice. This is a preference of which Van Dyke wholly approves:

> Is it not true? True, not only that the organ voice has the twofold gift of beauty and grandeur; true, not only that Tennyson has more sympathy with the loveliness of Eden than with the mingled splendours and horrors of celestial battlefields; but true, also, that there is a more potent and lasting charm in Milton's description of the beautiful than in his description of the sublime.... We have forgotten this; we have thought so much of Milton's strength and sublimity that we have ceased to recognize what is also true, that he, of all English poets, is by nature the supreme lover of beauty. (Van Dyke 55)

Tennyson never forgot this aspect of Milton. Hallam Tennyson records, in an appendix to his *Memoir,* the commentary Tennyson gave on *Paradise Lost* when his son was a schoolboy; much of the praise is lavished on the description of Eden and its flowers (*Memoir* 2:519–20). In old age Tennyson continued to cherish these lines: Hallam records that in December of 1888 his father "quoted Milton's description of Paradise and with his usual emphasis, ended with 'Where the unpierced shade/Imbrown'd the noontide bowers' [4.245–46]" (LT 3:384).

Even in the first half of his tribute, where he praises Milton's sublime descriptions, Tennyson singles out the more modest elements of heaven. Among the "Titan angels" he names not Raphael and Michael, who between them govern nearly a third of *Paradise Lost,* but Gabriel and Abdiel. The oddity of this choice is underlined by Samuel Johnson's treatment of the four chief angelic characters in Milton's poem, which implies a clear difference in stature between them, naming Gabriel and Abdiel almost as an afterthought. "Among the angels the virtue of Raphael is mild and placid, of easy condescension and free communication; that of Michael is regal and lofty, and, as may seem, attentive to the dignity of his own nature. Abdiel and Gabriel appear occasionally, and act as every incident requires"—although Johnson does go on to add that "the solitary fidelity of Abdiel is very amiably painted" (Johnson 1:173). It is in keeping with Tennyson's attitude to notice the "occasional" or "incidental" angels.

This is not to say that Tennyson failed to admire Milton's heaven or hell, or the sublimity of which his "organ-voice" was capable. But it is to say that Tennyson savored "Miltonian tenderness" and sensuality to an even greater degree than his Romantic predecessors, even Keats. More specifically, Tennyson admired Milton's ability to connect the two voices, to leap so quickly and smoothly from universals to minute particulars—a facility for which Tennyson, too, strove throughout his career (Albright 10–11). This joining of the two voices is summed up in the one word "Charm" at the beginning of line 12 of "Milton," which suggests a reminiscence of the opening of book 8 of *Paradise Lost:*

> The angel ended, and in Adam's ear
> So charming left his voice, that he awhile
> Thought him still speaking, still stood fixed to hear.

Tennyson noted these three lines as being "beautifully expressed" (*Memoir* 2:523). Both here and in Tennyson's own poem, the word "charm" serves the same function: it forms a bridge between the angelic voice and the human, between the celestial magnificence of book 7 and the more earthy self-accounting of Adam in book 8, his "bowery loneliness."[7]

The joining of heaven with the visible diurnal sphere is characteristic of Tennyson. His poetic response to Milton can be divided into three parts. Among the shorter poems, Milton's influence is clearest in the earliest works, as has often been remarked (Nelson 108–14; Pyre 13–14; Van Dyke 71–72), although it continues to be noticeable even in such a late poem as "Demeter and Persephone (In Enna)" (1889).[8] The other two major responses come in Tennyson's two longest works, *In Memoriam* and *Idylls of the King*. Like the Romantics before him, Tennyson, perhaps conscious of the preemptive effect of "Lycidas" and *Paradise Lost* on subsequent English elegy and epic, eschews these traditional forms; instead he hybridizes them, producing an epic elegy and an idyllic epic. But in contrast to the Romantics, Tennyson's accommodation permits him, not to avoid Milton, but rather to engage with the whole of Milton's oeuvre in both of these longer poems. In this chapter I consider these three responses, beginning with the early poems, up to and including *The Princess*, then moving on to the two great "Arthur" poems. In the lyrics Tennyson's imitation of Milton is characterized by modesty: in such works as "Mariana" and "Tithonus," he borrows grand Miltonic abstractions and renders them simply material, while in other poems he imitates the more unregarded parts of Milton's poetry—its delicacy and occasional bathos. *In Memoriam* similarly draws from all parts of Milton's corpus ("Lycidas," *Paradise Lost*, the sonnets, *Comus, Samson Agonistes*) in order to emphasize a sense of physical presence; Tennyson either echoes Milton's images of material concretion or else deliberately reverses Miltonic moments of etherealization. *Idylls of the King* borrows not only a Miltonic

---

7. The phrase "bowery loneliness" anticipates Tennyson's later tribute "To Virgil," whose "charm" is to be found "often flowering in a lonely word" (6; see Tucker, *Tennyson and the Doom of Romanticism*, 438). James Nelson notes that Virgil and Milton were Tennyson's two great models (Nelson 106–7), and Tennyson repeatedly links their names. To his son he commented that "Milton had evidently studied Virgil's verse" (*Memoir* 2:384). In a letter to Samuel Edward Dawson, he admired both poets' ability to profit from their predecessors: "I am sure that I myself, and many others, find a peculiar charm in those passages of such great masters as Virgil or Milton where they adopt the creation of a bye-gone poet, and re-clothe it, more or less, according to their own fancy" (LT 3:240; note "charm" again as the point of connection between two voices).

8. The title recalls "that fair field/Of Enna, where Proserpin gathering flowers/Herself a fairer flower by gloomy Dis/Was gathered" (*PL* 4.268–71). The allusion is repeated in line 9, "When here thy hands let fall the gathered flower," which also calls to mind Adam's hand letting fall the garland gathered for Eve (*PL* 9.892). Tennyson continues the Miltonic allusion in line 16, "The shadow of a likeness to the king" (i.e., Dis; compare the description of Death, *PL* 2.669, 673). But Tennyson characteristically mingles these allusions with echoes of Keats, his predecessor in appreciating "Miltonic tenderness"; see especially lines 121–25, 129–30, and 145, and Ricks's notes thereto.

subject but also one of Milton's most subtle narrative ploys—omitting the originary event, the crucial moment that sets the plot in motion but remains unrecorded or unexplained; this serves as a model of Milton's own hidden influence on *Idylls of the King*. In all three cases Milton exerts an influence no less powerful for being unsublime and often inconspicuous.

Throughout his career Tennyson thus engages with Milton in ways that both illustrate and complicate the various forms of influence I have already discussed. His tendency to embed allusions to Milton among references to other poets recalls Arnold's practice, described in chapter 3. Tennyson's focus on the embodied particulars of Milton's verse reflects the Victorian tendency, outlined in chapter 1, to consider Milton in connection with a material, historical context, rather than viewing him as timeless or unearthly. *Idylls of the King*, meanwhile, presents another version of Milton as classic, as defined in chapter 2: its highly elliptical structure imitates (without directly acknowledging) similar ellipses in *Paradise Lost* and *Samson Agonistes*. What emerges from a close examination of this complex relationship is a surprising sense of both Tennyson and Milton as poets of understatement. There have been numerous important critical reconsiderations of Tennyson over the past twenty years, all of which have been particularly attuned to small details of his verse, to its subtle ironies and intricacies. Nevertheless, throughout these widely varied revaluations—among others, Tennyson as late-Romantic prophet; as subversive conservative; as poet of empire; as resounding verbalist[9]—what remains constant is a sense of Tennyson, like Milton, as a consciously "major" poet. Yet to examine the influence of Milton on Tennyson is to realize how often both poets deliberately narrow their scope and achieve their most powerful effects through what is left understated or unstated altogether.

Tennyson's earliest poems have titles like "Armageddon" and "The Coach of Death"; as one might expect, these works are filled with echoes from Milton's sublime descriptions of hell. The landscape in "Armageddon," for instance, is "shrouded in . . . darkness almost palpable" (1.124–25). "The Coach of Death" describes at some length "the marvellous bridge" between heaven and hell, which is built by "loathly Sin" and "Strong Death" (145–56); compare the infernal bridge constructed by Milton's Sin and Death (*PL* 10.293–305). Yet even here Tennyson's characteristic treatment of Milton begins to be apparent: as Tucker argues, Tennyson seems more fascinated with

9. See, respectively, Herbert Tucker, *Tennyson and the Doom of Romanticism* (1988); Isobel Armstrong, *Victorian Poetry* (1993), chapters 2 and 10; Matthew Reynolds, *The Realms of Verse 1830–1870* (2001), chapters 1 and 8–10; and Seamus Perry, *Alfred Tennyson* (2005).

the technical (physical and poetic) qualities of Milton's bridge than with its moral valence (Tucker, "Strange Comfort," 11). Already in these apocalyptic works, the allusions show an appreciation for Milton's material particulars as much as for his spiritual profundities. In "Armageddon," for instance, while the speaker witnesses a great universal vision from a mountain, like Adam at the end of *Paradise Lost* or like the Son in *Paradise Regained,* two echoes from "L'Allegro" unexpectedly intrude. First he hears "the hum of men/Or other things talking in unknown tongues,/And notes of busy Life" (2.36–38; cf. "the busy hum of men" in "L'Allegro" 118); next he sees a second earth, full of "protruded arms/Of hairy strength, and white and garish eyes" (4.13–14), recalling the goblin who "basks at the fire his hairy strength" ("L'Allegro" 112). In both cases the visionary sublimity is momentarily interrupted by a vivid, corporal detail—the hum of a crowd of voices, a single hairy arm; yet the physical details are just as Miltonic as the visions.

A similar insistence upon materiality marks the end of "Mariana" (1830): "but most she loathed the hour/When the thick-moted sunbeam lay/Athwart the chambers" (77–79). The "thick-moted sunbeam" derives from "Il Penseroso," where "vain deluding Joys" are said to possess the brain "As thick and numberless/As the gay motes that people the sunbeams" (1, 7–8; see Burnett 208). The allusion is apt in several ways: Mariana is a se-cluded *penserosa,* and also particularly liable to the vain delusions that dwell in "idle brain[s]" and "fancies fond" ("Il Penseroso" 5–6). But it is worth noting that Tennyson has once again invoked Milton to enrich not the moral but the material texture of his poetry. He echoes, not the paratactic and largely tactile body of Milton's poem, but its ten-line moral prelude; yet he divests the allusion of both its moral and its immateriality. Milton's "vain Joys" and "gay motes" become palpable clouds of dust, with enough physical presence to lie "athwart" Mariana's chamber (with the subliminal hint that Mariana senses herself to be not merely deluded by them, but thwarted).

In later poems the allusions become more complex but continue consis-tently to display Tennyson's two characteristic tendencies: an interest in the material and earthly (or edenic) aspects of Milton's verse, and a tendency to mingle Miltonic allusions with others. "Oenone" (1832, revised 1842) provides an example of the many different forms Milton's influence takes. Although it is taken from classical mythology, the story, as Dwight Culler notes, "has echoes of the temptation scenes in *Paradise Lost* and *Paradise Regained*" (79). Some of these echoes derive from the basic similarities be-tween the story of the Fall and the story of Paris (temptation, an apple), but Culler is right to notice that Tennyson's poem has a peculiarly, even assert-ively Miltonic cast. This is evident not only in the many local verbal echoes that Christopher Ricks records in his notes, but also in peculiar motifs. Paris, for instance, invites Oenone to retire before the goddesses arrive, that she may "unbeheld, unheard/Hear all" ("Oenone" 87–88); so Adam tells Eve to retire when Michael descends, where she "unseen/Yet all had heard" (*PL* 11.265–66). More notably still, the golden apple is always described in conjunction with a human hand, a detail derived from Milton: "So saying, her rash hand in evil hour/Forth reaching to the fruit, she plucked, she ate"; "She gave him of that fair enticing fruit/With liberal hand" (*PL* 9.780–81, 996–97). In "Oenone," Paris "opening out his milk-white palm/Disclosed a fruit of pure Hesperian gold,/That smelt ambrosially"; next he "held the costly fruit/Out at arm's-length," until finally at the crucial moment, "when I looked, Paris had raised his arm," the apple was gone, and the deed was done ("Oenone" 64–66, 133–34, 185).

More direct verbal echoes also take various forms. Consider Oenone's entrance into the poem:

> Hither came at noon
> Mournful Oenone, wandering forlorn
> Of Paris, once her playmate on the hills.
> Her cheek had lost the rose, and round her neck
> Floated her hair, or seemed to float in rest.
>
> (14–18)

"Wandering forlorn/Of Paris" derives most directly from "Erroneous there to wander and forlorn" (*PL* 7.20), but in essence seems closer to Eve's grief at being "forlorn of [Adam]" after their fall (10.921). Oenone is introduced into the poem by her hair, as Paris too will be: "his sunny hair/ Clustered about his temples like a God's" (58–59). This recalls the introduction of Adam and Eve, she distinguished by hair that "waved" (as Oenone's "floated"), he with hair that "hung/ Clustering" (*PL* 4.302–6). Most difficult of all to pin down are the rhythmic echoes. Shaw observes that "No other imitator, with the possible exception of Keats, catches so well as Tennyson Milton's majestic use of the sixth syllable caesura," and he quotes as an example the break in the line "Her cheek had lost the rose" (Shaw 311). Such similarities are far more difficult to demonstrate than verbal reminiscences, especially since their effect tends to be cumulative rather than dwelling in single instances. But Shaw's example seems well chosen; "Her cheek had lost the rose" carries a whiff of the enjambment that conveys Satan's changed appearance: "His form had not yet lost/All her original brightness" (*PL* 1.591–92). "Oenone" ends, however, with a more direct allusion: Tennyson recalls Milton's description of the war in heaven—"all air seemed then/ Conflicting fire" (6.244–45)—in the final line, with its foreshadowing of the Trojan War: "All earth and air seem only burning fire."

The same variety of reminiscence marks "Tithonus" (drafted 1833, published 1860). At line 33 Tithonus catches a "glimpse of that dark world" of men; the echo of Milton's "Ere half my days, in this dark world" (Sonnet 16, line 2) is poignant: Tithonus cannot so number his days, though he longs to. The other verbal parallel comes when Tithonus remembers "that strange song I heard Apollo sing,/ While Ilion like a mist rose into towers" (62–63), recalling Pandemonium, which "Rose like an exhalation, with the sound/ Of dulcet symphonies and voices sweet" (*PL* 1.711–12). As in "The Coach of Death," Tennyson fixates on a Miltonic moment of materialization, and once again he removes its moral connotations. Or rather he inverts them: in Tithonus's world, the backward sublimation—from spiritual to concrete—is not sinister but simply happy. As the Miltonic allusions remind us, Tithonus has reversed the course—and curse—of Adam; he has moved from mortal to eternal. His demand that the goddess should "take back thy gift" of immortality (27) recalls Adam's similar but opposite complaint to God: it was "thy perfect gift" that caused his fall into mortality (*PL* 10.138). Likewise, Tithonus's plea, "Release me, and restore me to the ground" (72), reverses Milton's redemptive vision: "Restore us, and regain the blissful seat" (*PL* 1.5). The gentlest echo of all comes in the bittersweet conclusion, when Tithonus fantasizes about reentering the world of death, just as Adam and Eve reluctantly do at the end of their poem—"I earth in earth," just as "They hand in hand":

They hand in hand with wandering steps and slow,
Through Eden took their solitary way.
(*PL* 12.648–49)

I earth in earth forget these empty courts,
And thee returning on thy silver wheels.
("Tithonus" 75–76)

"Thy silver wheels" follows in the trace of "their solitary way," but the resemblance is only there for one who, like Tithonus, wishes to perceive it. And even Tithonus is forced to replace the linear "way" with the cyclical repetitiveness of "wheels."

In the early 1830s Tennyson began composing idylls, poems with subjects more local and homely than the mythological subjects that dominated his earliest poetry. For inspiration he turned, understandably, to Milton's Eden, and above all to Eve—not the rebellious Eve imitated by Mary Shelley, but "Eve's fair slenderness," Eve the fairest of her daughters. In "The Miller's Daughter" (published in 1832 and thus not grouped with the 1842 "English Idyls" that it so much resembles), the title character is consistently equated with Milton's heroine. She first appears reflected in the "level flood" of the millpond (75), as Eve first sees herself in the "liquid plain" of a lake (*PL* 4.455); but Tennyson has carefully pruned away the narcissistic overtones of the episode in Milton, since in his poem only the speaker, and not the woman herself, gazes on the reflection. When the speaker first addresses her, she "Flushe[s] like the coming of the day" (132), just as Eve "blush[es] like the morn" on meeting Adam (*PL* 8.511). When the miller's daughter is "fearful," the "dews, that would have fallen in tears,/I kissed away before they fell" (148–52); similarly, when Eve "feared to have offended," Adam "ere they fell/Kissed" the "drops that ready stood" to fall (*PL* 5.132–35). The association grows even stronger in "The Gardener's Daughter" (written in 1833, published 1842), where the speaker refers directly to his beloved's home as "Eden" (187). When he first glimpses her, she is propping up an "Eastern rose" blown over in a gale and herself appears

> a Rose
> In roses, mingled with her fragrant toil,
> Nor heard us come, nor from her tendance turned
> Into the world without.
>
> (122, 141–44)

The passage recalls two separate moments in *Paradise Lost:* both the point when Eve "Rose" from listening to Adam and Raphael to turn her "tendance" to her flowers (8.44–47), and more notably the crucial moment when Satan in the serpent spies her

> Veiled in a cloud of fragrance, where she stood,
> Half spied, so thick the roses bushing round
> About her glowed, oft stooping to support
> Each flower of slender stalk, whose head though gay . . .
> Hung drooping unsustained.
>
> (9.425–30)[10]

---

10. The second passage itself recalls an earlier passage, in *Comus,* where the tempter tells the Lady, "Beauty is Nature's coin, must not be hoarded,/. . . Unsavoury in the enjoyment of itself/If you let slip time, like a neglected rose/It withers on the stalk with languished head" (*Comus* 738–43). This

The echo suggests the possibility that the speaker himself is a Satan figure, come to tempt or corrupt; but again, the poem discourages such an association. The descriptions of his courtship rather recall Adam and his account of the moment he led the blushing Eve to their "nuptial bower":

> Joyous the birds; fresh gales and gentle airs
> Whispered it to the woods, and from their wings
> Flung rose, flung odours from the spicy shrub,
> Disporting, till the amorous bird of night
> Sung spousal, and bid haste the evening star
> On his hilltop, to light the bridal lamp.
>
> (*PL* 8.510–20)

Compare the speaker of "The Gardener's Daughter":

> The lark could scarce get out his notes for joy
> But shook his song together as he neared
> His happy home, the ground. To left and right,
> The cuckoo told his name to all the hills;
> The mellow ouzel fluted in the elm;
> The redcap whistled; and the nightingale
> Sang loud, as though he were the bird of day.
>
> (89–95).

Milton's "amorous bird of night" here mistakes himself for "the bird of day"; there is even a sight rhyme of "spousal" and "ouzel," though Tennyson insisted that it was only a sight rhyme.[11] The more the Miltonic imagery accumulates, the more it becomes clear that even the title harkens back to Eden. Aside from Rose herself, there is no gardener in "The Gardener's Daughter"—unlike "The Miller's Daughter," which begins with a portrait of "the wealthy miller." The imagery suggests rather that Rose is "the gardener's daughter" in the sense that she embodies an ideal of womanhood, of all those daughters descended from the pair Tennyson elsewhere calls "The gardener Adam and his wife."[12]

---

in turn is echoed in Tennyson's description of "Rose, the Gardener's daughter" who lived "hoarded in herself" (48–51).

11. Tennyson complained that "some people are fools enough to prounce it ou*sel*: why, it ruins the whole line" (LT 3:333).

12. "Lady Clara Vere de Vere," 51. In an earlier reading of the same line, Adam was simply "the grand old gardener"—unnamed, as he is in "The Gardener's Daughter."

Finally, *The Princess* (1847), although it is the most ambitious of Tennyson's poems before *In Memoriam,* displays the same modest tendencies; only in this case, it is not the sublimity but the heroism of *Paradise Lost* that is recast in a lower tone. *The Princess* draws an uneasy line, what the narrator calls a "strange diagonal," between the heroic and the mock-heroic ("Conclusion" 27). Had the battle of the sexes been intended as mere pastiche—a modern-day battle of the frogs and mice—Tennyson could have employed the simpler form of mock-heroic, invoking truly heroic moments from earlier epic into bathetic contexts. (Byron's "Hail Muse! et cetera" is an example [*Don Juan* 3.1].) Instead, like Alexander Pope in "The Rape of the Lock," Tennyson preferred to maintain a sense of grandeur even among the foolery. To achieve such an effect, Pope had turned to those moments in Milton that are themselves dubiously heroic or mock-heroic. The sylph who, cut in half during a battle, "soon unites again" recalls the wounded Satan, whose "ethereal substance closed" after being sheared by the sword of Michael ("Rape of the Lock" 3.152; *PL* 6.330); like much in book 6, the episode is both awesome and ridiculous. Pope recognizes that Milton himself mocks heroism, or at least false heroism, throughout his epic; by alluding to such already ambiguous passages, "The Rape of the Lock" is able to present an argument not more but less heroic, while nevertheless investing its subject with the remnants of a certain dignity. *The Princess* performs the same operation, though perhaps less successfully: it invokes and celebrates the semiheroic Milton.

The allusions begin with the first lines of the poem: "Sir Walter Vivian all a summer's day / Gave his broad lawns until the set of sun / Up to the people: thither flocked at noon / His tenants." The phrase "all a summer's day" comes from the description of the devil Thammuz in *Paradise Lost,* "Whose annual wound in Lebanon allured / The Syrian damsels to lament his fate / In amorous ditties all a summer's day" (1.447–49). Thammuz comes forward together with a troop of devils who disrupt sexual order: spirits who "can either sex assume" and who beguile Solomon, "that uxorious king" (1.424, 444). The allusion is therefore apt to a poem of gender bending and "amorous ditties" sung in falsetto, and it is reinforced by the onomastically androgynous "Sir Walter Vivian"—the century's most chivalrous literary name (Sir Walter) joined to the name of Tennyson's chief temptress. But the phrase "a summer's day" reappears later in the opening book of *Paradise Lost,* and the second part of Tennyson's allusion is in some ways even more pertinent. Describing Mulciber the heavenly architect, Milton writes, "from morn / To noon he fell, from noon to dewy eve, / A summer's day; and with the setting sun / Dropped from the zenith like a falling star" (1.742–45). Tennyson apparently had this passage in mind when writing his opening lines, as "noon" and "set of sun" indicate (as well as a direct reference to the Vulcan/Mulciber myth later in the poem [*Princess* 3.56]). Mulciber serves as a Miltonic symbol of the vanity of mere knowledge—"nor aught availed him now/To have built in heaven high towers" (*PL* 1.748–49). Tennyson's earlier reminiscence of the same passage picks up on its mingled sublimity and vanity: Mulciber "like a falling star" is echoed in Ulysses's desperate desire to follow knowledge "like a sinking star" ("Ulysses" 31). The fall of Mulciber, one of the most admired passages in Milton's poem, allows Tennyson to equivocate at the very outset of his poem: Princess Ida's dream of a towered feminine domain of science and art is at once admirable and insufficient.[13]

The nameless Prince, who wishes to see himself as a hero of romance, is granted the same ambiguous treatment. When Satan returns among his hellish peers to report on the success of his grand quest, his heroic triumph is recognized for the hollow victory it actually is: he stands

> expecting
> Their universal shout and high applause
> To fill his ear, when contrary he hears
> On all sides, from innumerable tongues
> A dismal universal hiss.
>
> (*PL* 10.504–8)

The same welcome, reversed, greets the Prince on his return to his father's war tents after his adventure; he hears a sound like the

> lisping of the innumerous leaf . . .
> Each hissing in his neighbour's ear; and then
> A strangled titter, out of which there brake
> On all sides, clamouring etiquette to death,
> Unmeasured mirth.
>
> (*Princess* 5.13–17).

As in Pope, a moment of Miltonic bathos is seized upon and expanded. The Prince had earlier resembled Satan the semi-hero when declaiming about his motives: "O not to pry and peer on your reserve" (*Princess* 4.399); Satan at least is more honest in his admission that the chief aim of his great undertaking is "but to pry" (*PL* 1.655). But the Prince's whole undertaking

---

13. James Kincaid offers a more skeptical reading of *The Princess* as wholly parodic, with Ida as a Satan who falls up (to a "mountain height") rather than down (Kincaid 124).

marks him as a lesser Satan. He can only achieve his quest by adopting an ignoble disguise, and his adventure culminates in an earnest but idiotic battle in
which, as in heaven, nobody is allowed to be seriously wounded. (Tennyson
added a line to the third edition—"I trust that there is no one hurt to death"
[6.225]—to make this clear.) *The Princess* shows that Tennyson was attuned
and attentive to all the "charming," liminal moments in Milton—not only
where heaven meets earth, but where high meets low in other ways.

The two most substantial works of Tennyson's maturity, *In Memoriam* and
Idylls of the King, are both generically unclassifiable. The former is certainly
an elegy, but in length and structure unlike any previous elegy; the latter both
is and is not an epic. It has often been suggested that post-Miltonic English
poets avoided those genres, particularly epic, that Milton had made peculiarly his own—either by not writing in them at all, or else by "swerving"
(in Harold Bloom's term, though Bloom is not alone in holding this view)
and creating new hybrid genres that purposely did not challenge Milton on
his own ground. So Keats abandoned *Hyperion* in mid-sentence because it
was, by his own admission, too Miltonic, and transformed it instead into the
epic-dream-poem *The Fall of Hyperion.* Byron in *Don Juan* harked back to
the pre-Miltonic romance epic of Boiardo and Ariosto. Most notably of all,
perhaps, Wordsworth made autobiography epic in *The Prelude*—taking his
cue from the autobiographical invocations in *Paradise Lost* but expanding
them to comprise the whole epic, not just the digressions.[14]

In Memoriam could be seen as representing a similar swerve, a reaction
in part to Milton's arch-elegy, "Lycidas." Edward FitzGerald recalled that
Tennyson was keenly aware and appreciative of "Lycidas," considering that
it "was a touchstone of poetic taste" (*Memoir* 1:36). FitzGerald also noted
that *In Memoriam* differs decisively from Milton's elegy: in 1845 he offered
his opinion that Tennyson had gone to excess in composing "near a volume
of poems—elegiac—in memory of Arthur Hallam," since "Lycidas is the
utmost length an elegiac should reach" (FitzGerald 1:478). But Tennyson's
expansion of his elegy to near-epic proportions could equally well be considered an attempt, not to avoid Miltonic precedent, but to engage with all of

14. Bloom's definition of the poetic "swerve," which he calls "clinamen," comprises chapter 1 of
The Anxiety of Influence. Writing in the same year as Bloom (1973), Stuart Sperry notes, "Ever since
the later seventeenth century the task of writing any long poem in English, not to mention epic, had
been rendered formidable if not insuperable by the overriding example of *Paradise Lost*" (Sperry 164);
Milton's preemptive effect not only on epic but on other genres is a critical commonplace. But the
practice of composing a generic hybrid, and particularly of hybridizing epic, is itself Miltonic; on this
topic, see Barbara Lewalski, *Paradise Lost and the Rhetoric of Literary Forms.*

Milton, not only with "Lycidas." Milton's great concerns, especially in *Paradise Lost*—the relation of spirit to body, and their interaction; the relevance of cosmological knowledge to daily existence—are Tennyson's concerns too, and throughout *In Memoriam* he turns to his predecessor for guidance.

Although the differences between *In Memoriam* and "Lycidas" were obvious to FitzGerald, early reviewers repeatedly drew comparisons between them (Shannon 142).[15] By 1889 Van Dyke was complaining about the speciousness of the parallel:

> The comparison of *In Memoriam* with *Lycidas* would certainly appear…
> easy and obvious; so obvious, indeed, that it has been made a thousand
> times, and is fluently repeated by every critic who has had occasion to
> speak of English elegies. But this is just one of those cases in which an
> external similarity conceals a fundamental unlikeness. (Van Dyke 102)

The truer source, according to Van Dyke, is *Paradise Lost,* in which Tennyson found poetic precedents for the expression of his doubts and for his belief both in universal salvation and in the ultimate meeting of heaven and earth (Van Dyke 105–7). Van Dyke's objection to the too-easy comparison with "Lycidas" is justified: there are many ways in which *In Memoriam* actively eschews the conventions of pastoral elegy of which "Lycidas" is the great exemplar in English. Tennyson does not, for instance, adopt a mask: he mourns not Astrophel or Lycidas or Adonais, but "my Arthur" (*IM* 9.17), a choice that is all the more striking given his usual preference for classical personation, even in such a heartfelt poem of mourning as "Tithonus." It is equally notable that Tennyson never once depicts Hallam as a promising young poet, as prescribed by elegiac tradition, even though Tennyson sincerely admired Hallam's poetry (Kennedy 358). And even when Tennyson does briefly turn to pastoral tropes, in sections 21 to 23 ("pipes," "Pan," "Arcady"), "Lycidas" does not furnish the most direct parallel. Section 21, in which the speaker continues to sing his lament despite upbraidings from three passers-by, derives neither from Milton nor from the pastoral tradition so much as from the book of Job, of which it is a brief model. Section 23, on the other hand, is distinctly Miltonic; but although the language is pastoral, the chief point

---

15. Among the many Victorian comparisons between *In Memoriam* and "Lycidas" is an 1884 article titled "The three poems 'In Memoriam'" (unsigned but probably written by Robert Matthew Heron), which also includes "Adonais." Heron claims at one point that Tennyson "is quite free from the materialism of sentiment which abounds both in Dante and Milton," tending "not to give a material form to ideas, but to spiritualize material things" (Heron 174n.). As I discuss below, I believe precisely the opposite to be true.

of reference is not "Lycidas." The speaker's cry, "How changed" (line 9), harkens back to Satan at *PL* 1.84 (supported by "falling" in line 6), while the memory of how "old philosophy... divinely sang" (lines 21–22) echoes "divine philosophy" in *Comus* 475, a phrase that is echoed again a little later in the poem (53.14).[16]

The significance of these momentary echoes is their indication that Milton, far from being banished by Tennyson's general avoidance of pastoral conventions, appears throughout *In Memoriam* as a "diffusive power." Tennyson is not alone in thus varying his reference; Percy Shelley does the same thing in "Adonais." Alongside many reminiscences of "Lycidas," Shelley sprinkles a liberal dose of *Paradise Lost* in his elegy: invocations to Urania ("Adonais" 12, 29, 204), references to Paradise (88, 208), and a number of direct quotations (337, 417). He even includes some echoes of Milton's sonnets: "A light is past from the revolving year,/And man, and woman" (472–73) recalls Milton's "Of sun or moon or star throughout the year,/Or man or woman" ("To Mr Cyriack Skinner," 5–6). The end of stanza 8 in the first edition of "Adonais"—"the grave which is her maw"—echoes the closing of Milton's sonnet to Cromwell ("whose gospel is their maw"). But the difference between the Romantic and the Victorian poet is once again one of proportion. "Adonais," for all its diversity of reference, clearly participates in the same tradition that gave rise to "Lycidas": it invites a series of mourners to come to the tomb, it celebrates the poetry of the dead youth, it blames the immediate agent of his death. The use of Milton in *In Memoriam* is at once less obvious and more widespread.

"Lycidas," though it may not be Tennyson's chief model, nevertheless remains an essential point of reference. Joseph Sendry, in an important article, detects the same "emotional and metaphysical" impetus behind both *In Memoriam* and "Lycidas," and he carefully describes the major parallels between the two (Sendry 437). He notes, for instance, a structural parallel in the "intrusions" of non-elegiac passages, commenting that "Tennyson's recurrent apologies for venturing to speculate on philosophical and theological issues follow [Milton's] pattern" (Sendry 438). This is certainly true, although here again the closer parallel seems to be found elsewhere: Tennyson's allusions to the scientific theories of Cuvier, Laplace, and Robert

---

16. Section 22, less pastoral in its diction than those on either side, also contains an echo of *Paradise Lost*. The speaker remembers how the "Shadow," death, "spread his mantle dark and cold,/And wrapt thee formless in the fold" (*IM* 22.12–15). This reverses Milton's invocation to light in book 3, which "as with a mantle didst invest/The rising world of waters dark and deep,/Won from the void and formless infinite" (*PL* 3.10–12).

Chambers, his sudden vertiginous shifts of perspective from the microscopic to the cosmic, are more reminiscent of the introduction of Galileo into the landscape of hell in *Paradise Lost* than of the attack on the Anglican clergy in "Lycidas."[17] But Sendry also discusses a number of more direct echoes: the nostalgia for a shared youth in an Arcadian Cambridge; reflections on the possible vanity of poetic fame; and, above all, the extended address to the ship bearing home Hallam's body in sections 9–18. Sendry points out that this last parallel with "Lycidas" is quite self-consciously manufactured: "though the sea had nothing to do with Hallam's death, Tennyson maneuvers events so that for the greatest part of this sequence, his friend's body is at the mercy of the waves. This puts the poet in much the same predicament as Milton is in *Lycidas:* he must wait helplessly for the remains of the dead to arrive at a safe haven on land" (Sendry 438). He notes that section 9, the earliest-written part of *In Memoriam,* echoes Milton's word "waft" (line 4; "Lycidas" 164), and that "Tennyson's lines, 'we have idle dreams;/This look of quiet flatters thus/Our home-bred fancies' (x.9–11), have the same ring as Milton's 'For so to interpose a little ease,/Let our frail thoughts dally with false surmise' (ll. 152–153)" (Sendry 439). Sendry implies that Tennyson began his poem by inserting himself into the elegiac tradition, even though the parallel between himself and Milton was slightly factitious, and that he did so for the same reasons that other elegists have written in traditional forms: for the comfort that such literary companionship provides.

The most important response to Sendry comes in James Kincaid's *Annoying the Victorians*—a book that admits outright that its arguments are intended to provoke (or "annoy") more than to convince. In a chapter titled "Tennyson, Hallam's Corpse, Milton's Murder, and Poetic Exhibitionism," co-authored with Buck McMullen, Kincaid returns to the question of sections 9–18. "So, why all this about water? Why this glaring irrelevance?" he asks (Kincaid 114). His answer is unapologetically Bloomian, in direct contrast to Sendry's more sentimental reading. Tennyson forces a parallel with "Lycidas" not in order to share his grief with the predecessor poet, but to outdo

---

17. Various parallels have been suggested for Tennyson's use of science in his poetry. T. H. Huxley, noting the presence of many leading scientists at Tennyson's funeral in 1892, remarked, "Tennyson has a right to that, as the first poet since Lucretius who has understood the drift of science" (Huxley 2:338). A. C. Bradley claims that "with the partial exception of Shelley, Tennyson is the only one of our great poets... to whose habitual way of seeing, imagining, or thinking, it makes any real difference that Laplace, or for that matter Copernicus, ever lived" (Bradley 30–31). John D. Rosenberg cites yet another predecessor: "Tennyson, like Donne before him, made poetry out of the 'new science'" (Rosenberg 34). To me seems that Milton, among English poets, figures as Tennyson's chief predecessor in incorporating new scientific knowledge—particularly astronomy—into verse.

him: "Tennyson enters this anxious Oedipal wrestling match with an elaborately unconcealed weapon, Hallam's corpse, and he batters Milton to death with it" (Kincaid 117). Such a gleefully gross accusation is clearly reductive, but it draws attention to the serious claim Kincaid is making: Tennyson's address to the ship that safely bears home Hallam's body points to a contrast with Milton's "Lycidas," not a similarity, as Sendry had suggested. That contrast, as Kincaid explains, is between the bodily and the immaterial:

> [Tennyson] focuses on Hallam's body, both as the corpse now being borne over the seas and as its remembered, animated form, insisting on a rich particularity of the physical to contrast to Milton's abstracting and etherealizing of King. Hallam's body is to be buried on land, a point Tennyson reiterates and distinguishes as elegiacally preferable to the comfortless loss of a body at sea. (Kincaid 116)

Kincaid makes the same point in regard to Tennyson's and Milton's "false surmises": whereas Milton imagines that Lycidas is buried on land, only to find that he is fondly dreaming, Tennyson, in the passage noted by Sendry (section 10), imagines that Hallam is lost at sea, only to comfort himself with the fact of the body's safe return to England (Kincaid 116–17). This contrast is drawn even more clearly at the end of *In Memoriam,* where Tennyson rephrases Milton's "false surmise" as "gracious lies": "Love but played with gracious lies,/Because he felt so fixed in truth" (*IM* 125.7–8). Tennyson's wilful self-delusion, unlike Milton's, is founded in fixity.

Kincaid's argument about Hallam's body draws attention to a phenomenon we have already remarked: Tennyson turns to Milton when he wishes to emphasize a sense of physical presence. Sometimes he achieves this by echoing a Miltonic image of concretion, as in his juvenile "The Coach of Death," which imitates the bridge-building episode when "Death with his mace petrific" smites all things "Solid or slimy, as in raging sea/Tossed up and down" and fixes them into a firm mass (*PL* 10.286–95). Sometimes he does it by contrasting his own image to Milton's less substantial one, as in the case of Mariana's mote-filled sunbeam, so much more tangible than its original in "Il Penseroso." And the same process is at work in the series of ship poems of *In Memoriam,* in the contrast between Hallam's safely wafted body and Edward King's. Within this series the overarching allusion to "Lycidas" is varied by other Miltonic allusions, all tending to emphasize the same materialization. In section 11, for instance, two of the five stanzas begin with the same phrase: "Calm and deep peace on this high wold"; "Calm and deep peace in this wide air" (*IM* 11.5, 13). The repetition draws attention to the phrase and to its source in book 7 of *Paradise Lost,* when out of the "immeasurable abyss/Outrageous as a sea, dark, wasteful, wild" God causes the solid, created universe to emerge:

> Silence, ye troubled waves, and thou deep, peace,
> Said then the omnific Word, your discord end.
>
> (*PL* 7.211–17)

Tennyson called line 216 "a magnificent line," exclaiming, "How much finer than 'and, billows, peace,' the proper scansion, this break is, and the alliteration how subtle, 'and thou, dee*p,* peace'!" (*Memoir* 2:522). The allusion to this line in section 11 is doubly appropriate: the passage in Milton concerns both the calming of "a sea" and also, more importantly, the eliciting of something welcomely tangible, a body rising out of the "abyss."

Section 13 produces a similar effect, but through contrast. It begins with a reminiscence of Milton's sonnet, "Methought I saw my late espoused saint":

> Tears of the widower, when he sees
> A late-lost form that sleep reveals,
> And moves his doubtful arms, and feels
> Her place is empty, fall like these.
>
> (*IM* 13.1–4)

The situation of the "widower" Milton and of Tennyson's speaker are very nearly parallel: both have lately lost their beloved, who is seen only in a dream and cannot be physically recaptured. But Milton's sonnet deals mostly with vision, and only at the end turns to the frustration of touch: "But O as to embrace me she inclined/I waked, she fled, and day brought back my night" (Sonnet 19, lines 13–14). Section 13 of *In Memoriam,* on the other hand, begins with the absence of the body. Yet coming as it does in the midst of the series of ship poems, such insistence on bodily absence points to the slight relief of contrast: Tennyson's series culminates in the return of Hallam to "his native land" (18.4), whereas Milton could find no such comfort, no return for his loss. Moreover, Milton's troubles are for Tennyson only illustrations, however poignant: the loss of Hallam makes Tennyson *like* a widower, or in a later allusion to the same sonnet, *like* a blind man: "His inner day can never die,/His night of loss is always there" (66.15–16; the same section contains an echo of the opening of *Samson Agonistes* when it refers to the blind man as one "Whose feet are guided through the land," rhyming with "hand"

[66.9]). The parallel with Milton is close enough to do double duty: there is both the comfort of precedent, and also the smaller comfort of a slight contrast: Tennyson has the advantage that his physical loss is never so total as Milton's.

The deliberate contrast with Milton begins already in the first section of *In Memoriam*. Alan Sinfield persuasively explains the significance of the opening section's multiple echoes of *Comus,* particularly in the third stanza:

> Let Love clasp Grief lest both be drowned,
>   Let darkness keep her raven gloss:
>   Ah, sweeter to be drunk with loss,
> To dance with death, to beat the ground.
>   (*IM* 1.9–12)

The second line adapts Comus's description of the Lady's song: "At every fall smoothing the raven down / Of darkness till it smiled" (*Comus* 250–51). As Sinfield points out, Tennyson deliberately refuses this etherealization, even at the cost of aligning himself with the evil wizard. The speaker in Tennyson's poem "would not have his darkness of grief and death charmed away even for a moment. The allusion boldly links the poet with Comus, and his determination to resist consolation with opposition to Christian virtue" (Sinfield 43). The identification with Comus is reinforced in the final line, which recalls Comus's "Come, knit hands, and beat the ground, / In a light fantastic round" (*Comus* 143–44). Sinfield comments, "These lines end Comus' speech inciting his 'crew' to wantonly abandon themselves to emotion, and the allusion again fits section i exactly," since the speaker prefers rough manifestations of grief to "smoothing" consolations, "beating the ground" to drowning in bodiless grief (Sinfield 44). In this opening section, at least, Tennyson's speaker rejects the metaphysical consolations of "him who sings / To one clear harp in divers tones, / That men may rise on stepping-stones / Of their dead selves to higher things" (*IM* 1.1–4). Tennyson himself glossed this "him" as J. W. von Goethe, but Sinfield points out that these opening lines also recollect *Comus* and those who "by due steps aspire" to rise to higher things (*Comus* 12; Sinfield 43). In place of the spiritualizing tendency of Milton's masque, Tennyson substitutes an insistence on the here and now, on "clasping" whatever earthly remembrance remains of his lost friend.

At the climax of his poem, in section 95, Tennyson again turns to Milton, this time not for contrast but in order to draw on yet another Miltonic image of concretion. The section begins by locating the speaker firmly on dry land:

> By night we lingered on the lawn,
>   For underfoot the herb was dry;
>   And genial warmth; and o'er the sky
> The silvery haze of summer drawn.
>
> (*IM* 95.1–4)

With typical efficiency Tennyson portrays the whole setting, from underfoot up to the sky and even above, and in the middle an absolute element: "And genial warmth." The phrase, wholly Miltonic in timbre,[18] does not appear exactly thus anywhere in *Paradise Lost,* but it derives most closely from the scene of Creation in book 7, describing the first emergence of the solid world:

> over all the face of earth
> Main ocean flowed, not idle, but with warm
> Prolific humour softening all her globe,
> Fermented the great mother to conceive,
> Satiate with genial moisture, when God said
> Be gathered now ye waters under heaven
> Into one place, and let dry land appear.
>
> (*PL* 7.278–84)

Here the "warm" and "genial" waters are made to yield up something less sublime but more tangible—"dry land." We have already seen Tennyson's fascination with Milton's description of this process: in section 11 he recalls its first stage, when the "omnific Word" commanded "thou deep, peace" (*PL* 7.216–17). He returns to the scene of Creation in section 113, when Hallam himself is cast as the omnific word. Hallam is pictured as "A potent voice... /Becoming, when the time has birth,/A lever to uplift the earth/And roll it in another course," which recalls Adam's description to

---

18. So Samuel Taylor Coleridge felt. In "A Letter to———(Sarah Hutchinson)" he used the same phrase in a context strongly reminiscent of Milton's first description of Creation, in book 1: "Even what the conjugal & mother Dove/That borrows genial warmth from those, she warms,/Feels in her thrill'd wings, blessedly outspread—"(328–30; Coleridge 690). The phrase does not appear in the published version of Coleridge's poem ("Dejection: An Ode"), and there is very little likelihood that Tennyson would have known the manuscript version.

Raphael of the sun's altered course: "thy potent voice he hears,/And longer will delay to hear thee tell/His generation, and the rising birth/Of nature from the unapparent deep" (*IM* 113.11–16; *PL* 7.100–103). The echo at the beginning of section 95, though briefer, is significant: the spiritual climax of the poem is prefaced by concretion and grounded in a setting of physical solidity.

A reminiscence of the same Miltonic scene is used by Wordsworth to preface his own climactic vision in *The Prelude,* his epiphany on Mt. Snowdon. In *Paradise Lost,* right after God has commanded the genial waters of the earth to withdraw and give way to land, "Immediately the mountains huge appear/Emergent, and their broad bare backs upheave/Into the clouds" (*PL* 7.285–87). In Wordsworth's version, "A hundred hills their dusky backs upheaved/All over this still ocean, and beyond,/Far, far beyond, the vapours shot themselves/In headlands, tongues, and promontory shapes,/Into the sea."[19] Wordsworth imitates but exactly reverses Milton's scene, which passes from the mind of the Prime Mover to his cloudy, chaotic materials and results in the creation of solid land. Wordsworth's vision begins when the "real" landscape is "Usurped upon as far as sight could reach" by a layer of shifting cloud (*Prelude* 13.49, 51). This very usurpation then leads to creativity: Nature in such moments is so sublime "That even the grossest minds must see and hear,/And cannot chuse but feel" (13.83–84). Wordsworth has thus extrapolated from the landscape back to the creative imagination, "higher minds" which "can send abroad/Like transformation, for themselves create/A like existence" (13.90, 93–95). His vision therefore culminates in the "soul,/Whether discursive or intuitive"—another Miltonic allusion, recalling Raphael's distinction between "Reason...Discursive, or intuitive" (*Prelude* 13.113; *PL* 5.487–88). Raphael's phrase forms part of his description of a disembodying process, the inverse of the solidification he will describe two books later: earthly beings, including humans, may aspire to a more angelic state, until in the end their "bodies may at last turn all to spirit,/Improved by tract of time, and winged ascend/Ethereal" (*PL* 5.497–99). Wordsworth's experience on Snowdon, then, although it begins by recalling Milton's description of the creation of the physical world, ends with a recollection of the Miltonic concept of etherealization.

Not so Tennyson's spiritual climax in section 95. He too has a moment of bodiless transcendence, when "all at once it seemed at last/The living soul

---

19. *Prelude* 13.45–49; all quotations from Wordsworth's *Prelude* refer to the 1805 version, in the edition of Wordsworth, Abrams, and Gill.

was flashed on mine" (*IM* 95.35–36). But Tennyson's incorporeal encounter is not an end point; rather it is characterized by its transience:

> Aeonian music measuring out
>> The steps of Time—the shocks of Chance—
>> The blows of Death. At length my trance
> Was cancelled, stricken through with doubt.
>
>> (*IM* 95.41–44)

Tennyson's speaker, as so often in the poem, returns to his earthly body with an almost audible thump, and here he does so by cancelling Milton's notion of eventual bodily sublimation. As Ricks points out, this stanza recalls the final line of Milton's early lyric "On Time": "Triumphing over Death, and Chance, and thee O Time." Tennyson first reverses Milton's conclusion (Time, Chance, Death), then cancels it, then strikes it through; his vision of heaven does not concur with Milton's picture of an afterlife for the soul which has "all this earthy grossness quit" ("On Time" 20). Instead Tennyson seizes upon an image from earlier in Milton's lyric—"Then long eternity shall greet our bliss/With an individual kiss" (11–12)—and expands that more congenial notion in section 47; in Tennyson's heaven, we shall retain our physical, embraceable individuality: "Eternal form shall still divide/The eternal soul from all beside" (*IM* 47.6–7). Even though *In Memoriam* is famous as a poem of spiritual evolution ("Move upward, working out the beast,/And let the ape and tiger die" [118.27–28]), nevertheless Tennyson is not nearly so ready as Wordsworth to follow Raphael's proposed ascent from the familiarity of the body to some purely ethereal state. His trajectory in section 95 is from a firm, dry footing to a rapt trance, and back to the same landscape (white kine, dark trees), transfigured. In contrast to Wordsworth, he harks back to the material rather than the immaterial aspects of Milton's sublime.

In short, Milton represents a diffusive power in *In Memoriam* in two closely connected senses. In the first place, he is everywhere and nowhere: although there is no single poem of Milton's that provides the model or counterpoint for Tennyson's elegy, references and parallels to Milton's poetry pulse through the whole length of *In Memoriam*. Secondly, Milton's example, while it provides Tennyson with spiritual consolation, grounds that consolation firmly in the material world, culminating in the verses from near the end on Hallam's physical ubiquity:

> What art thou then? I cannot guess;
>> But though I seem in star and flower

> To feel thee some diffusive power,
> I do not therefore love thee less.
>
> (*IM* 130.5–8)

The discovery of Hallam in the features of the landscape represents a gentle literalization of Lycidas's final transformation (or littoralization): "Henceforth thou art the genius of the shore" ("Lycidas" 183). The process had begun in section 83, where Tennyson invokes a catalogue of flowers, reminiscent of those that are to strew Lycidas's imagined grave: "Bring orchis, bring the foxglove spire,/ The little speedwell's darling blue,/ Deep tulips dashed with fiery dew" (*IM* 83.9–11; cf. Milton's "the pansy freaked with jet" ["Lycidas" 144]). Only once he has assembled the flowers together does Tennyson feel himself ready to "flood a fresher throat with song" (*IM* 83.16), as Milton is ready to move on to "fresh woods, and pastures new" ("Lycidas" 193). The ultimate trajectory of *In Memoriam* is toward spiritualization, as in other elegies; but Tennyson keeps touching the earth, as if to refresh his powers, before singing of higher things.

It is therefore appropriate that the Muse of *In Memoriam* is explicitly "an earthly Muse" (37.13). In section 37 Tennyson stages a confrontation between "my Melpomene" and Urania, the heavenly Muse, whom Milton invokes by name at the opening of book 7. The latter upbraids the former for presuming to speak of things divine and orders her back to "Parnassus"; Melpomene with "a touch of shame" acknowledges the presumption of having "loitered in the master's field" (37.6, 10, 23). Tennyson glossed this last phrase as "God's acre." It is tempting to provide a different identification for "the master," to read this section as Tennyson conceding the field to Milton. But it is important to note that this dialogue represents not Milton upbraiding Tennyson for encroaching on his territory, but Urania upbraiding Melpomene,[20] who is herself a Miltonic muse: Urania may be the inspiration of *Paradise Lost,* but the frontispiece of Milton's 1645 volume shows him surrounded by four muses, with Melpomene in pride of place. Since Tennyson turns to all of Milton for his inspiration, not just the epic Milton, and since Milton was one whom "all the Muses decked," there is no abjuring of Miltonic precedent even in this section. To the contrary: the "high Muse" of *Paradise Lost* returns in section 58 and invites Tennyson to continue, to add spiritual considerations to his "earthly" musings.

The Epilogue to *In Memoriam* invokes Milton yet once more, to characteristic effect. In *Samson Agonistes* Milton's hero in despair begins to "yield

---

20. On the significance of this "Pierian rivalry" (p. 203) in *In Memoriam,* see Albright 195–213.

to double darkness nigh at hand:/So much I feel my genial spirits droop"
(*SA* 593–94). Tennyson, though likewise "drooping," turns this darkness to
light, declaring,

> Let all my genial spirits advance
>   To meet and greet a whiter sun;
>   My drooping memory will not shun
> The foaming grape of eastern France.[21]
>
> (*IM* Epilogue, 77–80)

Tennyson has been (justifiably) ridiculed for the final line, a heavy-handed
and pretentious periphrasis for "champagne"; but it should be remarked in
his defense that the quatrain as a whole is neither heavy-handed nor pretentious. Tennyson implicitly contrasts himself to Samson—his "genial spirits"
are at last rising, not drooping; and to make good the contrast, he orders a
glass of champagne. This represents not only an indulgence forbidden to
Samson but also a light-heartedly material interpretation of Milton's "spirits": Tennyson embodies his new mental state in a form of spirits that by its
nature is the opposite of drooping. The stanza displays in small compass the
interconnectedness of spiritual and physical states that is emphasized in the
Epilogue and in the poem as a whole, and which Tennyson repeatedly reinforces through his use of Milton.

The idea of a national epic about King Arthur is a Miltonic one. As David
Masson records, while Milton was in Italy in 1638–39, he "conceived the
notion of an English epic poem on the subject of the legendary history of
Britain, including the Romance of Arthur and his Knights of the Round
Table, and...for some time at least after his return, this idea still fascinated
him" (Masson, *The Poetical Works of John Milton* [1874], 1:42). This project
figures prominently in two of Milton's Latin poems from the period, "Mansus" and "Epitaphium Damonis." In the former he dreams that he will "call
back into poetry the kings of my native land and Arthur, who set wars raging
even under the earth, or tell of the great-hearted heroes of the round table,
which their fellowship made invincible" ("Mansus" 80–83). A few months
later, he goes into further and darker detail: "I shall tell of Igraine, pregnant

---

21. The allusion is mediated by two major Romantic poems. In "Dejection: An Ode," Coleridge
alludes to Samson out of sympathy: "My genial spirits fail,/And what can these avail,/To lift the
smoth'ring weight from off my breast?" (39–41; Coleridge 699). In "Tintern Abbey" Wordsworth,
like Tennyson, contrasts himself to Samson: "Nor...should I the more/Suffer my genial spirits to
decay" (111–13; Wordsworth [1977] 1:360).

with Arthur as a result of fatal deception: I shall tell of the lying features which misled her, and of the borrowing of Gorlois's armour, Merlin's trick" ("Epitaphium Damonis" 166–68). These plans, though never fulfilled by Milton, were well known to the nineteenth century: Wordsworth in the *Prelude,* seeking for an epic subject, briefly decides to "settle on some British theme, some old/Romantic tale by Milton left unsung" (*Prelude* 1.179–80). "Left unsung" here has nearly the force of "left half-told" in "Il Penseroso"; the implication is not that the subject of Arthur is un-Miltonic, but quite the opposite—that it remains within Milton's domain, which may explain why Wordsworth quickly rejects it.[22] Tennyson, on the other hand, pursued the subject, and to his contemporaries it seemed that *Idylls of the King* was the manifest fulfillment of Milton's early plans. Tennyson's friend Francis Turner Palgrave, for instance, discussing Milton's projected Arthurian epic in an 1872 article, writes that "destiny reserved for a later hand the fascinating dream of 'Arthur come again'" (Palgrave 412). Similarly, E. C. Stedman claims of "the Arthurian legends" that "Milton's dream inconsonant with his own time and higher aspirations, has, at last, its due fulfilment. The subject waited long, a sleeping beauty, until the 'fated fairy-prince' came, woke it into life, and the spell is forever at an end" (Stedman 179–80). Van Dyke in 1889 points out that Milton "was the first to call attention to the legend of King Arthur as a fit subject for a great poem.... The design was abandoned: but it was a fortunate fate that brought it at last into the hands of the one man, since Milton died, who was able to carry it to completion" (Van Dyke 93–94).

To undertake an Arthurian epic, according to these critics, was to follow directly in Milton's footsteps. But at times it has been a vexed question whether such a description applies to Tennyson's poem. "One of the central difficulties of *The Idylls of the King,*" writes Robert Pattison, "lies in deciding exactly what they are" (R. Pattison 135); the very title seems to dissociate the work from the epic tradition. Shortly before the publication of the original volume of *Idylls,* Tennyson wrote to his publishers, "I wish that you would disabuse your own minds and those of others, as far as you can, of the fancy that I am about an Epic of King Arthur" (LT 2:212). On the other hand, the earliest-written section of the poem, the "Morte d'Arthur," appeared in 1842 (and in all reprintings) framed by a poem entitled "The Epic," which refers to the twelve-book poem of which the "Morte" forms a part as an "epic" (28). And when the "Morte" was later incorporated into the *Idylls* as "The Passing of Arthur," Tennyson strengthened the generic association by

22. Wordsworth's line also recalls the invocation to *Paradise Regained:* "unrecorded left through many an age,/Worthy t'have not remained so long unsung" (1.16–17).

inserting a traditional epic formula: Bedivere "saw, . . . Or thought he saw, the [ship] that bare the King" ("Passing" 463–65; cf. *PL* 1.783–84, *Aeneid* 6.454). Hallam Tennyson, conscious of his father's initial doubts about whether the *Idylls* truly constituted an epic, was careful to point out the differences from Homer: "if Epic unity is looked for in the 'Idylls,' we find it not in the wrath of an Achilles, nor in the wanderings of an Ulysses, but in the unending war of humanity in all ages" (*Memoir* 2:130). Yet Hallam begins the same chapter of his *Memoir* by calling the work an epic, in a sentence attributed to the poet himself: "On Malory . . . and on his own imagination, my father said that he chiefly founded his epic" (2:121–22). The *Memoir* goes on, moreover, to imply not only that the *Idylls* is epic, but that it should be seen as a parallel to *Paradise Lost*. In what reads like a deliberate echo of Milton's Trinity Manuscript, in which there appear several outlines for a five-act tragedy on the subject of "Paradise Lost" or "Adam Unparadized," Hallam records, "Before 1840 it is evident that my father wavered between casting the Arthurian legends into the form of an epic or into that of a musical masque" (2:124–25), and he reproduces the outline for the five acts from Tennyson's manuscript. *Idylls of the King* is Miltonic not only in its subject, Hallam seems to suggest, but in its gestation, as well as in its eventual twelve-book blank-verse form.[23]

Yet the matter of Tennyson's poem might still seem un-Miltonic given that, his youthful inclinations notwithstanding, Milton in *Paradise Lost* explicitly rejected martial epic, including King Arthur. In book 1 he mentions "Uther's son," but only to compare him and his knights (to their disadvantage) with the troops of devils in hell (*PL* 1.580); and in the invocation to book 9 he dismisses romances of "gorgeous knights / At joust and tournament" (9.36–37). But despite its Arthurian material, *Idylls of the King* does not fall into the category of martial epic that Milton here renounces. Milton's definition of "that which justly gives heroic name / To person or to poem" (9.40–41) tallies closely with Tennyson's; it is a question of fidelity and self-denial rather than one of knightly prowess. As Pattison rightly points out, "in the complex milieu of the *Idylls* Lancelot is no more fit to be a hero than Satan is in Milton's saga" (R. Pattison 148). Tennyson draws our attention to this very parallel. As we have seen, he was acutely aware of

---

23. Pattison concludes, "That [Tennyson] intended to produce a poem in the epic tradition, and that his contemporaries so perceived the *Idylls*, is clear   Tennyson was at great pains to bring the total number of books up to the traditional epic number of twelve, a feat he accomplished in exactly the same way that Milton had when he converted *Paradise Lost* from ten books to twelve in order to match the Vergilian proportion"—i.e., by dividing one of the previously published books (*Enid*) into two (R. Pattison 140).

the mock-heroic or false-heroic moments in *Paradise Lost,* and in "Lancelot and Elaine" he gives us a Lancelot who resembles the Satan of books 1 and 2—majestic, but in precisely the wrong way. Like Satan, whose "face/Deep scars of thunder had intrenched," so Lancelot shows the marks of both high courage and sin: "The great and guilty love he bare the Queen,/In battle with the love he bare his lord,/Had marred his face, and marked it ere his time" (*PL* 1.600–601; "Lancelot and Elaine" 244–46). Satan, encountering the dreadful shape of Death in book 2, remains unshaken—"God and his Son except,/ Created thing nought valued he nor shunned"; Lancelot, confronted with the loving Elaine, also remains unmoved: "woman's love,/Save one, he not regarded" (*PL* 2.678–79; "Lancelot and Elaine" 835–36). In both cases, a single foregoing, underlying sin renders all further courage vain, however "heroic" or great.

Here we find the true affinity between the two poems. If the power of weakness was the Miltonic theme that most influenced Arnold and was also a model for that influence, then the signature of Milton's influence on *Idylls of the King* is *latent* power. There are fewer verbal echoes and allusions to Milton in the *Idylls* than in *In Memoriam,* but Milton is integral to the very conception of the *Idylls,* as we have just seen, and also to its governing motif. *Idylls of the King* describes not only a fall but one whose ultimate source is at once well-known and unlocatable. Van Dyke points out that both Tennyson's epic and Milton's concern "the power of the slightest taint of evil to infect, pollute, destroy all that is fairest and best" (Van Dyke 98). It may not be quite accurate to say that the "taint of evil" in either poem is "slight," but it is in both cases latent or concealed.

Paradise Lost is a poem of latency in two ways, both of which have attracted much critical attention. In the first place, although the poem explores in great detail the causes and circumstances of the Original Sin of Adam and Eve, it is less forthcoming about what is arguably an even more important originary event: Satan's turn to evil. This is described allegorically by Sin when she recounts her birth in book 2, but that episode is difficult to reconcile with Raphael's narrative in book 5 or to place in the poem's chronology. This discrepancy puzzled William Empson, who was forced to conclude that the birth of Sin—true cause of all our woe—occurred at a conference of angels that is never fully described by Milton, and which must have taken place at some time before the exaltation of the Son—before, that is, the earliest narrated event in the poem (Empson, *Milton's God,* 57–59). If we do not accept Empson's conjecture, we must nevertheless acknowledge that the first hint of any sort of evil in the poem (first in terms of chronology) is mentioned in a dependent phrase, almost as an aside. "Deep malice thence conceiving and disdain" (*PL* 5.666): by this one phrase we learn that Satan has already begun the defiance that will soon have "brought/Misery, uncreated till [his] crime" and "instilled/[His] malice into thousands" (6.267–70). This is not a flaw in Milton's poem, nor even always consciously felt as a gap: we are privy to an allegorical version of sin's entry into the universe, as well as to its first voicing and its earliest effects. But in contrast to the next great fall, the actual moment of Satan's fall—the prime mover of our damnation, and of our salvation as well, since God distinguishes between Satan's being "self-tempted" and humankind's being "deceived" (*PL* 3.130)—is overleapt by the narrative.

In *Idylls of the King* the downfall of Camelot and the shaping force of the narrative is the adultery of Lancelot and Guinevere. But this sin is never shown, nor is its consummation precisely locatable in the story, however often it is alluded to. In the first of the "Round Table" idylls, "Gareth and Lynette," it goes unmentioned, and this consequently furnishes the only purely happy episode in the poem, representing the golden age of Camelot. But just a few lines into the next idyll, the slide has begun—"a rumour rose about the Queen,/Touching her guilty love for Lancelot"—and the whole subsequent action is affected ("The Marriage of Geraint" 24–25). The narrator is quick to point out that this is only a "rumour"—"there lived no proof" (26); it is possible that there is yet no adultery, only "love," which predates Guinevere's marriage to Arthur and which therefore may feel "guilty" but is not sinful. The same rumor then causes the deaths of Balin and Balan a few books later. This time the critic John Rosenberg comes to the lovers' defense: "Their adultery is still unproven, very likely as yet unconsummated" (Rosenberg 82). The mingled assurance and tentativeness of "very likely" is revealing: we really have no way of knowing at any point in the poem whether the crucial event has yet occurred. As in *Paradise Lost,* the most basic flaw, which substantially affects the course of every other event in the poem, is strictly unplaceable.[24]

The second form of latency in *Paradise Lost* consists in Adam and Eve's capacity for sin. Knowing as we do the end of the story, we are able to detect in the human protagonists not flaws—they remain innocent until

---

24. A similar narrative ellipsis occurs in Emily Brontë's *Wuthering Heights*. The origin of the preternaturally strong bond between Heathcliff and Catherine, which governs every part of the ensuing narrative, is conspicuously elided. Catherine originally despises Heathcliff, as does the narrator of this part of the history, Nelly Dean, who is sent away from Wuthering Heights as a result of her mistreatment of him. "On coming back a few days afterwards," however, she finds that "Miss Cathy and he were now very thick" (Brontë 30). In this sense Brontë's narrative seems even closer to Milton's than do the Byronic tales that generally mediate between the two.

book 9—but characteristics that will later make their fall psychologically credible. The same sense of potential characterizes Tennyson's protagonists as well; it differs subtly from the inevitable doom that hangs over Achilles or Hector, and of which they are conscious.[25] In a manner more reminiscent of classical tragedy than of epic, the fate of the chief characters can be detected in every action, however trivial, yet is not necessitated by that action. The first sighting of Arthur and Guinevere, for instance, though neither fateful nor even consequential, is fraught with latent meaning. Arthur immediately recognizes her as his other half, and expresses his desire for her in Miltonic phrasing—"What happiness to reign a lonely king?"; so Adam, seeking for a helpmate, asks God, "In solitude/What happiness?" ("The Coming of Arthur" 81; *PL* 8.364–65). For Guinevere, on the other hand, the effect is less immediate: "She saw him not, or marked not, if she saw" ("Coming" 53). Just as Eve, upon first seeing Adam, turns back in disappointment to her own "smooth watery image" (*PL* 4.480), so Guinevere, having been imprinted first with the image of Lancelot, comes only much later to appreciate Arthur.[26] The initial reactions are in both cases blameless, but both carry the shadow of an eventual, fatal dissociation.[27]

---

25. Fateful forebodings of this more common type are also present in *Idylls of the King:* the opening book, for instance, teems with portents both glorious and dire, including one particularly Miltonic vision. On the night of Arthur's birth, Merlin "Descending through the dismal night—a night/In which the bounds of heaven and earth were lost—/Beheld, so high upon the dreary deeps/It seemed in heaven, a ship, the shape thereof/A dragon winged" ("The Coming of Arthur" 370–74). This represents a conflation of two passages of *Paradise Lost,* both ominous: when Satan, a dragon winged, is compared to a fleet at sea that seems to hang in the sky, and when shortly afterward he views Chaos, a "hoary deep...without bound" in which "time and place are lost" (*PL* 2.636–37, 891–94).

26. Unlike Eve, who quickly comes to prefer Adam's image to her own, Guinevere's change of heart comes only at the end of the poem: "now I see thee what thou art,/Thou art the highest and most human too,/Not Lancelot, nor another" ("Guinevere" 643–45). The process begins when Guinevere prostrates herself before Arthur with her "shadowy hair" on the floor (413), imitating the gesture of Eve, who falls "with tresses all disordered, at [Adam's] feet" (*PL* 10.911). Yet immediately before this scene, Guinevere is still reminiscing over her first journey with Lancelot, before her marriage, and how they used to pause "For brief repast or afternoon repose" ("Guinevere" 392). As J. M. Gray points out, this "echoes Eve's promise to return to Adam 'in best order to invite/Noontide repast, or afternoon repose' with Milton's underlining:'Thou never from that hour in Paradise/Found'st either sweet repast or sound repose' [*PL* 9.402–3, 406–7]. So Arthur's paradise, like Adam's before him, becomes corrupt before it has scarce begun" (J. M. Gray 58).

27. William W. Bonney points out that Eve's story of her own first moments, with its ominous hints of narcissism, is alluded to again in later idylls. A voice tells Eve, as she stares into the lake, "What there thou seest fair creature is thyself,/With thee it comes and goes" (*PL* 4.468–69). The last phrase is repeated in descriptions both of the Holy Grail—"The phantom of a cup that comes and goes"—and of Vivien—"Her eyes and neck glittering went and came" ("The Holy Grail" 44; "Merlin and Vivien" 958; see Bonney 363).

In the same way, Milton rarely exerts a shaping force in *Idylls of the King;* rather, the example of Milton lurks constantly and significantly in the background, as it does, for instance, in "Pelleas and Ettarre." The idyll begins, as Rosenberg points out, with a version of Adam's dream: Pelleas falls asleep hoping to find a woman "fair...and pure as Guinevere" ("Pelleas and Ettarre" 42), and then "[l]ike Adam, he awakens to find his dream of Eve come true" (Rosenberg 70). Unfortunately, Pelleas has dreamed truer than he knows; the woman he finds upon awaking, Ettarre, will betray him like another Guinevere. She soon reveals her nature when, in a curiously reversed reminiscence of Milton's Sin, she removes the bridge and closes the gate that lead to her dwelling: "And when she gained her castle, upsprang the bridge,/Down rang the grate of iron through the groove,/And he was left alone in open field" ("Pelleas" 199–201). Pelleas continues to love her nonetheless, until we reach the crisis both of this idyll and perhaps of the epic as a whole, as according to Rosenberg the episode "marks the Fall, and everything that follows it, the Expulsion" (Rosenberg 107).

> Then was he ware of three pavilions reared
> Above the bushes, gilden-peakt: in one,
> Red after revel, droned her lurdane knights
> Slumbering, and their three squires across their feet:
> In one, their malice on the placid lip
> Frozen by sweet sleep, four of her damsels lay:
> And in the third, the circlet of the jousts
> Bound on her brow, were Gawain and Ettarre.
>   Back, as a hand that pushes through the leaf
> To find a nest and feels a snake, he drew:
> Back, as a coward slinks from what he fears....
>   ("Pelleas" 419–29)

Clearly this contains an allusion to the Fall, and more specifically to Milton's version of the Fall, as shown by the echo, in the closing lines, of Milton's "Back to the thicket slunk/The guilty serpent" (*PL* 9.784–85). But behind the betrayal of Pelleas by Gawain and Ettarre lies an earlier sin, the betrayal of Arthur by Lancelot and Guinevere; and behind the guilty serpent lies an earlier act of treachery, Satan's first conception of rebellion against God. It is therefore significant that the setting Tennyson provides for Pelleas's discovery, in both image and diction, deliberately recalls the passage in book 5 of *Paradise Lost* where somehow, unnoticed, Satan's fall from grace occurs. Ettarre's "pavilions reared" for sleep and marked by "malice" reproduce the angelic "Pavilions numberless, and sudden reared,/ Celestial tabernacles, where they slept" (5.653–54)—all save Satan, who alone wakes and watches and, "Deep malice thence conceiving," begins to plot his betrayal. (The equation of Pelleas in this scene with Satan is soon expanded, when Pelleas like Satan flies to "the north" to set up a rival kingdom.) It is only appropriate that whereas the allusion to Milton's serpent is overt, the more important Miltonic precedent—the pavilion scene—constitutes a more shadowy, diffuse reminiscence.

A similar imitation of Milton and of his tendency to finesse the most significant moments of his narrative comes in "Merlin and Vivien." As has often been noted, this is the most transparently Miltonic of the idylls. Vivien herself "combines the roles of Eve and Satan" (Rosenberg 114), in such passages as this:

> And lissome Vivien, holding by [Merlin's] heel,
> Writhed toward him, slided up his knee and sat,
> Behind his ankle twined her hollow feet
> Together, curved an arm about his neck,
> Clung like a snake.
>
>   ("Merlin and Vivien" 236–40)

Like a second Eve, Rosenberg comments, Vivien "lusts for Merlin's forbidden knowledge, and in grasping his heel, like the serpent in Genesis who bruises man's heel, she brings death into the world" (Rosenberg 114). Merlin himself remarks upon her resemblance to Eve: he blames himself for having "stirred this vice in you which ruined man/Through woman the first hour" ("Merlin" 360–61). Yet this wily temptress, however much she may derive from the Eve of patristic tradition, bears little resemblance to Milton's Eve. She does, however, closely resemble Milton's Satan. When she spies on Lancelot and Guinevere in their garden, she is said to be "Peering askance" (98), just as Satan spying on Adam and Eve in their bower "Eyed them askance" (*PL* 4.504). Thomas P. Adler notes a number of other direct echoes: both Vivien and Satan in the serpent are repeatedly described as "wily," and both carry out their temptations in "wild woods"; even more strikingly, Vivien "lay...all her length and kissed [Merlin's] feet," just as Milton's serpent licks the ground whereon Eve treads (Adler 1398, 1400). Rosenberg points out that Vivien's description of her own birth—"My father died in battle against the King,/My mother on his corpse in open field;/She bore me there, for born from death was I" ("Merlin" 42–44)—contains all the elements of Sin's birth narrative in book 2 of *Paradise Lost,* though in confused order (Rosenberg 113). William Bonney develops Rosenberg's point, noting that Tennyson's allusions purposely obfuscate the moral tendency of their Miltonic source. Hence, "in 'Merlin and Vivien' the tempest ceases upon Merlin's capitulation, . . . whereas in *Paradise Lost* the storm only begins upon the completion of the Fall, a fact that suggests Tennyson . . . uses Miltonic echoes in a partial and distortive manner that can only call into question the legitimacy of Christian teleology" (Bonney 353).

These critics all concentrate on the idyll's echoes of *Paradise Lost,* particularly the temptation in book 9; few have remarked upon its debts to *Samson Agonistes.*[28] Yet the allusion is significant. Samson is the other Miltonic character whose crucial act—the disloyal capitulation that sets the whole tragedy in motion—is practically passed over. The omission is less striking than in *Paradise Lost:* Samson's "fall" is at least described, even if it remains defiantly unexplained:

> perceiving
> How openly and with what impudence
> She purposed to betray me, and (which was worse
> Than undissembled hate) with what contempt
> She sought to make me traitor to myself;
> Yet the fourth time, when mustering all her wiles,
> With blandished parleys, feminine assaults,
> Tongue-batteries, she surceased not day nor night
> To storm me over-watched, and wearied out,
> At times when men seek most repose and rest,
> I yielded, and unlocked her all my heart.
>
> (*SA* 397–407)

The phenomenon Samson describes, the open-eyed, deliberate, yet utterly inscrutable step into self-destruction, is one that fascinated Tennyson from the time of "The Lady of Shalott" (1832), who herself is compared (in a presage of the later figure of Merlin) to "some bold seër in a trance,/ Seeing all his own mischance" ("Lady of Shalott" 128–29). In "Merlin and Vivien" the same sudden and baffling failure, for which Milton's Samson provides the great example, furnishes the unseen climax of the poem. Reminiscences of *Samson* begin to appear early in the idyll: Vivien, pouring her blandishments

---

28. Rosenberg notes in passing "another biblical analogue—Samson and Delilah—for the scene in which Vivien, drawing 'the vast and shaggy mantle' of Merlin's beard across her breast, exclaims, 'Lo, I clothe myself with wisdom' (253–255)" (Rosenberg 163, n. 18).

on the long-haired Merlin, ominously refers to love as "eyeless" ("Merlin" 247); later, mocking King Arthur for conniving at his wife's deceptions, she claims that he "blinds himself" (782). Merlin refuses at first to divulge his secret spell, lest Vivien be tempted to use it against him out of "overstrained affection, it may be,/To keep me all to your own self,—or else/A sudden spurt of woman's jealousy" (520–22). These are the same reasons Dalila gives for her betrayal of Samson: "the jealousy of love" and the desire to keep her husband "Whole to myself" (*SA* 791, 809).

But the direct and striking echoes come only at the end. Merlin and Vivien are caught in a thunderstorm, during which, unseen, the catastrophe occurs:

> Till now the storm, its burst of passion spent,
> Moaning and calling out of other lands,
> Had left the ravaged woodland yet once more
> To peace; and what should not have been had been,
> For Merlin, overtalked and overworn,
> Had yielded, told her all the charm, and slept.
>
> ("Merlin" 959–64)

Although Bonney compares this storm to the rain that follows the Fall in *Paradise Lost,* the phrase "passion spent" points to the more immediate Miltonic source for this scene. The words conclude *Samson Agonistes:* "With peace...And calm of mind all passion spent" (*SA* 1757–58). When "Merlin, overtalked and overworn...yielded," he imitates not so much Milton's Adam, "overcome with female charm" (*PL* 9.999), as Samson: because Dalila has continued to "storm" him, "over-watched, and wearied out,/...I yielded" (*SA* 405–7). The Miltonic reference finally crystallizes just when a momentous event occurs without being shown, an event that by the time we are informed of it is already in the past—"what should not have been had been," and Merlin already "Had yielded." The small cluster of verbal echoes at the end of this idyll constitute not just an allusion but a revelation: Milton's tragedy is suddenly shown to have been a model all along, a latent presence recognized only at the close.

So Milton underlies not only the *Idylls* but much of Tennyson's poetry. As Van Dyke notes, Tennyson's early readers and critics did not immediately think to make the comparison. In the poetry of Wordsworth and of other Romantics, the allusions to Milton are often far more thickly layered than in Tennyson, and the parallels more explicit. But the real affinity between the two poets is registered by Victorian critics, not of Tennyson, but of Milton, who tend to employ Tennyson's language to discuss his predecessor. Peter Bayne in 1873, speaking of the death of Cromwell and the Restoration, writes, "It was an evil time for John Milton when he...saw his country self-degraded in the eyes of Europe; and those were evil tongues that reviled 'the great Achilles,' whom he knew" (Bayne 451, quoting "Ulysses" 64). The following year John Addington Symonds, describing assonance in Milton's poetry, remarks, "His blank verse abounds in open-mouthed, deep-chested *a*'s and *o*'s" (Symonds 779, quoting "The Epic" 50–51). At the end of the century, George Serrell paraphrases Milton's sonnet, "How soon hath time," as follows: "He is under the most solemn sense of responsibility, the conviction that God is his 'great Task-Master,' that is, the great appointer of certain work which he is to do in the world: he is certain that there is 'one far-off divine event' to which the whole of his life ought to move, and he steadfastly intends that it shall so move" (Serrell 37, quoting *In Memoriam,* Epilogue 143–44). In each case the quotation is unattributed; the relationship between the two writers, appropriately enough, is not expressly declared, but remains understatedly implicit in the texts.

Chapter 5

Middlemarch and Milton's Troubled Transmissions

George Eliot's *Middlemarch* engages with Milton
as deeply as any work of Victorian literature, and with an aspect of Milton
we have not yet considered. The "Prelude" to the novel begins precisely
where *Paradise Lost* ends, with a pair of figures walking forth "hand-in-hand."[1]
The first chapter then introduces Milton by name: Dorothea Brooke, dreaming of an ideal husband, "felt sure that she would have accepted... John Milton when his blindness had come on" (*M* 10; ch. 1). Already in these opening
pages, Eliot invokes not only Milton's poetry ("hand in hand"), as Arnold and
Tennyson do, but also the story of his life—Milton as a blind man and as a
husband. In the words of Anna K. Nardo, author of the most recent and most
thorough study of their literary relationship, throughout her career Eliot was
just as profoundly influenced by "the stories told about Milton" as by "the
stories Milton told."[2] *Middlemarch* figures centrally in Nardo's thesis, because

---

1. This phrase, which echoes the penultimate line of *Paradise Lost,* describes St. Theresa and her
brother setting out in search of "an epic life" (*M* 3). The two are then compared to a pair of helpless fawns, the same image used by Milton to prefigure Adam and Eve's imminent expulsion from
paradise (*PL* 11.188–89).

2. Nardo, *George Eliot's Dialogue with John Milton,* p. 2. Nardo's informative and insightful
monograph is essential reading for anyone interested in this topic. It fully establishes what earlier critics had asserted in a more piecemeal way—that Eliot was from an early age deeply versed in Milton's
work, and that her major novels and poems constantly and consciously engage with both his life and
his writings. Nardo begins from the axiom that "Milton's language was... for Eliot and her readers,

this novel more than any of Eliot's others displays "the intensity of Eliot's engagement with the Milton legend" as well as "with his poetry" (Nardo 2).

Most of the criticism surrounding the presence of Milton in *Middlemarch* has recognized both these strains of influence, the literary and the biographical. Beginning with Sandra Gilbert and Susan Gubar's *The Madwoman in the Attic,* critics have concentrated on a cluster of themes introduced early in the novel: knowledge (Dorothea like Eve longs after wisdom, which she believes Casaubon, like the angel Raphael, will provide), gender roles (Casaubon plays Milton to Dorothea's daughters of Milton), and marriage.[3] The last forms a particularly fruitful subject of inquiry, because Milton's views on marriage influence the novel at once subtly and pervasively. Although Eliot pointedly mentions Milton's daughters in *Middlemarch,* she never refers specifically to his first wife, Mary Powell. Yet the story of that unhappy union, and the text that emerged from it—Milton's *The Doctrine and Discipline of Divorce,* one of the first extended treatments in English both of the ideal of companionate marriage and of the irreconcilable differences in spirit and intellect that can separate husbands and wives—present a constant parallel to the marital difficulties experienced by both the Lydgates and the Casaubons (Nardo 84–89). George Eliot was fascinated by this episode of Milton's life long before she began to compose her novel. She dedicated a large portion of her first review of Thomas Keightley's *An Account of the Life, Opinions, and Writings of John Milton* (for the *Leader* in August, 1855; she later reviewed the same volume for the *Westminster Review*) to Milton's concept of marriage. Yet Keightley scarcely touches on the subject: the passages from *The Doctrine and Discipline of Divorce*

---

unmistakably authoritative discourse" (25). She proposes that in *Middlemarch,* "Milton's words are, in Bakhtin's terms, both 'dialogized' and upheld as 'authoritative discourse'"—a revision of Gilbert and Gubar's reading (see note 3, below), in which Eliot's response to anxiety-producing patriarchal discourse is not dialogue but "killing off the offending males, like Casaubon, the Miltonic embodiment of all academic culture" (25, 22). My own reading differs from Nardo's in claiming that for Eliot, as for her contemporaries like David Masson, Milton's discourse was "dialogized" a priori, and that Milton embodies the powerlessness as much as the authority of discourse.

   3. All subsequent critics of Milton's role in *Middlemarch* owe a debt to Gilbert and Gubar's analysis of the novel (499–532) and to their governing concept of nineteenth-century women writers as "Milton's daughters" (see especially 214–18). Diana Postlethwaite, for example, writes that "*Middlemarch* and *Paradise Lost* share a fundamental community of themes: knowledge, marriage, and freedom," though she differs from Gilbert and Gubar in her assertion that "Milton is finally an enabler rather than an inhibitor of Eliot's creative voice" (Postlethwaite 200). Lise Kildegaard, who is more concerned than previous critics with "how the gender politics which engage these authors were shaped by the material conditions within which they lived and wrote," considers "labor, gender, and female resistance—those highly charged, interconnected issues with which both [*Paradise Lost* and *Middlemarch*] engage" (Kildegaard 10, 163). Anna Nardo (see note 2, above) considers that Eliot "evaluates Milton's assumptions about gender relations, knowledge, and heroic actions as they might apply in the 'embroiled medium' of life in a middling world" (Nardo 112).

that Eliot cites in her review appear in Keightley's book only in a small-print excursus at the back of the volume ("Note E: Passages in Milton's Writing Relating to his First Wife"), where she must actively have sought them out.[4]

In addition to these topics, however, another major motif, related to the others but less frequently discussed in connection to Milton, pervades the novel. *Middlemarch* is greatly concerned with difficulties of transmission— the transmission of words and wills and intentions; and these difficulties, like the difficulties of marriage, are modeled on the life and works of Milton.[5] In her second review of Keightley's *Account,* which appeared two months after the first, Eliot concentrates not on the divorce tracts but on Milton's "Of Education," and she tries to explain the discrepancy between the magnificent curriculum he sets forth in that pamphlet and the actual reading list he gave to his pupils. Eliot defends the disjunction between word and practice, between high intention and flawed execution, by claiming that Milton (like Tertius Lydgate) possessed an idealistic imagination out of step with the available science of his day.

> Milton's true principle in education, that the reason must be cultivated as well as the imagination and memory, and that it must be cultivated by applying it to the sciences which are of immediate practical value in life, led him into what may seem an erroneous plan simply because the conditions for carrying out that principle were not yet ripe. Modern science had but lately been born, and how limited was the progress it had made even among first-rate minds, may be judged from the fact that Milton himself held fast to the Ptolemaic system. So, in default of the "Principia," he gave his pupils De Sacro Bosco "De Sphæra;" in default of Linnæus and Cuvier, he gave them Pliny; in default of Johnstone's "Physical Atlas," he gave them Dionysius' "Periegesis." (Eliot, "Belles Lettres," 603)

---

4. On this topic see Dayton Haskin, "George Eliot as a 'Miltonist,'" especially pp. 209–15. Haskin argues convincingly that Eliot "[drew] strength" from Milton's divorce tracts when she decided to live with George Henry Lewes, and that this sense of empowerment is evident in *Middlemarch* (220).

5. Various critics have commented on the miscommunications so prevalent in *Middlemarch*. One of the first and best is Robert Kiely, who writes that *Middlemarch* "is a masterpiece of interrupted dialectics, of dialogues broken off . . . out of frustration and a sense of futility" (Kiely 108). Deconstructive readings by J. Hillis Miller ("Optic and Semiotic in *Middlemarch*") and Neil Hertz ("Recognizing Casaubon") expand Kiely's observation to include not just dialogue but the whole range of signs in the novel. As Kiely notes, "Imperfect communication is a literary subject which antedates *Middlemarch* and the novel as a genre. What is striking in *Middlemarch* is the frequency, extent, and finality of the failures of dialogue" (121). Yet no critic has associated these communicative failures with the novel's frequent invocation of Milton. To the contrary, critics of *Middlemarch* have tended to view Milton as a representative of unfallen authoritative discourse (see note 2, above), in contrast to Eliot's Victorian "pessimism about the salvific power of words" (104).

The passage reads like an apt description not only of Lydgate but of Dorothea, whose "true principle" frequently leads her "into what may seem an erroneous plan simply because the conditions for carrying out that principle [are] not yet ripe." (" 'I never could do anything that I liked,'" Dorothea admits at the end of the book. " 'I have never carried out any plan yet'" [*M* 809; ch. 84].) The idea that Milton, too, could be defined as a person whose thoughts and intentions were diffused, or even quite lost, in their translation into action stands at odds with the myth of Milton as the unmoved mover, an absolute source of language and knowledge. But it seemed natural to George Eliot and is typical of Victorian perceptions, particularly once David Masson had begun to present Milton as a product of his time, with all its limitations and encumbrances.

There are three instances or forms of transmission that figure largely in accounts of Milton's life. The first is his vocation: in the numerous autobiographical passages scattered throughout his prose writings, Milton recounts how he recognized early in life his divine calling to be a poet and how he prepared for this great task; and in *Paradise Lost* he describes how the poem is dictated to him as he sleeps by the heavenly Muse, "who brings it nightly to my ear" (*PL* 9.47). But this perfectly successful act of communication, almost of communion, is immediately threatened by the next step: being blind, Milton could not transcribe the Muse's words himself but had to repeat them to a third party. According to a well-known account reprinted by Keightley in the volume Eliot reviewed, Milton was constrained to dictate the poem "in a parcel of ten, twenty, or thirty verses at a time, which [were] written by whatever hand came next" (Keightley 73). This haphazard method of transcription was the more precarious given that, according to a tradition reaffirmed by Keightley, "his amanuenses were probably his wife and daughters" (65). These are the same daughters who, as Dorothea remembers, " 'read Latin and Greek aloud... to their father, without understanding what they read,'" and who, as Casaubon adds, " 'regarded that exercise in unknown tongues as a ground for rebellion against the poet'" (*M* 63; ch. 7). According to the standard biographies known to both Eliot and her characters, therefore, the transcription of *Paradise Lost* depended upon the assistance of those who were "undutiful and unkind" to the poet and unable to understand his mind except superficially (60–61).[6] And even once it had been transcribed,

---

6. A number of biographers disputed whether Milton did indeed dictate *Paradise Lost* to his daughters, including Samuel Johnson, whose life of Milton Eliot reread while composing *Middlemarch* (Eliot, *Letters*, 5:238). Yet the tradition remained so strong through the nineteenth century that Masson found it necessary to dispute it at some length: "It has been the fond fancy of the public, fostered by artists and illustrators of Milton's poetry, that it was chiefly or exclusively Milton's three daughters, Anne, Mary, and Deborah, that served him in this capacity in the composition of his

as Keightley points out, the "great poem...ran a chance of not being allowed to appear in print" because it nearly failed to be licensed by the royal censors (66).

Milton's final act of transmission was his will, which famously left "all his property to his wife" and none to his daughters, save the portion that their mother had bequeathed them (69). Yet here too Milton's intentions encountered problems of execution: "But as his will was merely nuncupative and irregular, [his daughters] disputed it after his death, and [his widow] was obliged to make a compromise with them, giving them £100 apiece" (92–93). Keightley observes, "It seems very strange that, with a brother a lawyer, he should not have made a formal will, but have made such a disposition of his property as was not in accordance with the strict requirements of the law, and, as was the result, liable in consequence to litigation" (69). But Milton's contested legacy is consistent with the other thwartings of his will and his words after his blindness had come on—when his daughters, for instance, "made away with some of his books, and would have sold the rest of his books to the dunghill-women" (61). (Eliot recalls this betrayal in her depiction of Tito's similar treatment of his father-in-law's treasured books in *Romola,* and in Daniel's mother's near-destruction of the papers bequeathed by her father in *Daniel Deronda.*)[7] Milton the poet and testator had as much difficulty "carrying out plans" as did Milton the educator.

Most Romantic accounts of Milton's life emphasize the first form of transmission: Milton is born to be a poet and derives his song directly from the heavenly Muse, "who deigns/Her nightly visitation unimplored,/And dictates to me slumbering, or inspires/Easy my unpremeditated verse" (*PL* 9.21–24). The very ease of the process both inspires and intimidates his successors. Recalling this passage, Percy Shelley exults in the skylark's "unpremeditated art," but he cannot imagine how anyone else "ever should come near" such joyous inspiration ("To a Sky-Lark" 5, 95). William Wordsworth's

---

Paradise Lost. Most of us have seen flummery pictures and engravings representing the blind poet, in a rapt and ecstatic attitude, dictating his sublime epic, in a beautiful trellised arbour, or in an arched Gothic library, to his attentive and revering daughters. Alas! the imagination so suggested little corresponds with the reality" (Masson, *The Poetical Works of John Milton* [1874], 64). Milton's daughters (and wife) did occasionally serve as his amanuenses, according to Masson, but not for his dictation of *Paradise Lost.*

7. In her chapter "Milton and Romola's Fathers" (66–82), Nardo examines Eliot's use of the Milton legend in *Romola,* including the selling of the patriarchal library (72–74). When Daniel goes to collect his grandfather's papers in *Daniel Deronda,* Eliot quotes *Areopagitica:* these are "written memorials which, says Milton, 'contain a potency of life in them to be as active as that soul whose progeny they are'" (Eliot, *Daniel Deronda,* 670; ch. 60). Yet the documents in question are long kept away from the rightful heir, in defiance of the patriarch's will, and are almost destroyed; and they eventually reach Daniel by the merest chance, when he is accidentally recognized by Joseph Kalonymos.

Prelude famously begins, like the Prelude to *Middlemarch,* with a reference to the closing lines of *Paradise Lost:* "The earth is all before me...and should the guide I chuse/Be nothing better than a wandering cloud/I cannot miss my way."[8] But Wordsworth invokes Milton as a foil for himself; whereas Milton never did miss his way (at least according to his own account) but simply pursued his evident vocation from the first, Wordsworth describes over the course of fourteen books a much more erratic career and faltering inspiration. Elsewhere he addresses the example of Milton more directly: "Thou hadst a voice whose sound was like the sea:/Pure as the naked heavens, majestic, free,/So didst thou travel on life's common way,/In cheerful godliness."[9] To Wordsworth, Milton represents one whose voice and whose path were equally clear.

In contrast to these predecessors, Eliot refers to Milton as someone who was repeatedly stymied in his attempts to transmit his ideas as he would have preferred. She not only recalls his miscommunication with his daughters and the ineffectuality of his will, but she reminds us that even his poetic vocation was not so simple as he himself depicts it.[10] As Gilbert and Gubar assert, "Behind the dream-Casaubon, however, lurks the real Casaubon,...just as—the Miltonic parallels continually invite us to make this connection—the 'real' Milton dwelt behind the carefully-constructed dream image of the celestial bard" (Gilbert and Gubar 217). Yet in revealing a Milton frequently hampered in either writing or doing as he wished, Eliot is not oedipally punishing or even necessarily ironizing her precursor. The same failure of intentions, after all, marks not only Casaubon but Dorothea, of whom we are nevertheless told in the "Finale" that "the effect of her being on those around her was incalculably diffusive: for the growing good of the world is

---

8. *Prelude,* 1805 edition, 1.15–19 (Wordsworth, *The Prelude,* 28); cf. *Paradise Lost* 12.646–47: "The world was all before them, where to choose/Their place of rest, and providence their guide."

9. "London, 1802," 10–13 (Wordsworth, *The Poems,* 1:580). Romantic poets did of course recognize that the work even of Milton was subject to time and to misinterpretation. Wordsworth refers to a volume of Milton as a "Poor earthly casket of immortal verse," doomed to eventual obliteration (*Prelude* 5.164). Samuel Taylor Coleridge in "The Nightingale" cites a line from "Il Penseroso"—"Most musical, most melancholy"—and claims that although Milton intended the line dramatically, to reflect the character of his speaker, it has been interpreted by others literally ("many a poet echoes the conceit"). Yet even here Coleridge is zealous for the correct interpretation of Milton's words, because he considers them to constitute the equivalent of a revealed scripture: "The author makes this remark, to rescue himself from the charge of having alluded with levity, to a line in Milton: a charge than which none could be more painful to him, except perhaps that of having ridiculed his Bible" (Coleridge 517).

10. There are, of course, precedents for this skepticism, both in the Romantic notion of Milton's inadvertent Satanism and even in Milton's own expressions of self-doubt concerning the source of his inspiration (*PL* 9.44–47). But Eliot's view of Milton's troubled transmissions is wider than any of these, encompassing his poetry, life, and legacy.

partly dependent on unhistoric acts" (*M* 825). Hence the nature of Milton's influence on *Middlemarch* is dual. On the one hand he is the successful author of an archetypal patriarchal poem, and as critics have often commented, not only the characters of the novel but the author herself struggle with his powerful precedent: Eliot refers to her story as being "no epic" (3; "Prelude") or at best a "home epic" (818; "Finale"). On the other hand, Milton stands not only as the point of contrast for Eliot's thwarted dreamers but as their precursor in frustration. Eliot repeatedly refers both to Milton's own troubled transmissions and also to those moments in *Paradise Lost* when the angels Uriel and Raphael speak in such a way as to defeat their own purposes. Milton's relation to *Middlemarch* is thus more complex than has previously been described. Paradoxically, Milton's failures to write and act as he could wish had perhaps a greater influence on Eliot's novel—an effect more "incalculably diffusive"—than did his successes.

This chapter differs from the preceding ones in obvious ways, apart from its concentration on Milton's biography. It focuses on a novel, rather than on poetry, and on a novel moreover that invokes Milton directly and repeatedly, rather than revealing his influence only obliquely. The first difference is significant: in discussing at some length one of the pivotal novels of the Victorian period, I hope to indicate that the arguments I have been making about Miltonic influence extend beyond poetry to Victorian literature more generally. The second difference, by contrast, is less stark than it appears. *Middlemarch* does refer explicitly to the example of Milton, but he serves above all as an example of influence that is exerted only in a disjointed or accidental manner. Once again, therefore, as in other Victorian works, Milton appears just as important for his weakness as for his strength. Critics of *Middlemarch* have been surprisingly willing to treat Milton as an exception, as an emblem of singularly authoritative discourse within a heteroglossic multi-plot novel. But closer inspection reveals how acutely Eliot discerned the confusions of voice and authority that characterize both Milton's life and his poetry.[11] As a consequence, Eliot treats Milton with neither extreme resistance nor extreme reverence, but rather with the sympathy that typifies *Middlemarch* and is one of its most appealing aspects.

Within a year of the completion of *Middlemarch,* critics were already invoking Eliot's novel to reflect upon Milton. In an 1873 article on Milton,

---

11. On the similar shift in later twentieth-century Milton criticism from readings that posit a unified authoritative voice in *Paradise Lost* (Anne Ferry, Stanley Fish) to readings that emphasize dissonance and multivocality, see Sauer 3–13.

Peter Bayne comments on the practical impossibility of Milton's notion of "the high intellectual and moral ends of marriage": only "A Dorothea Brook [*sic*] and a John Milton might on these terms have realised an ideally perfect marriage union" (Bayne 446–47). Bayne's article appeared soon after the publication of volume 3 of Masson's biography, which covers the period of Milton's first marriage.[12] Masson himself also felt the influence of Eliot's fiction. In the "Introduction" to *Paradise Lost* that opens his three-volume edition of Milton's poetical works, Masson pauses to exclaim upon the depth of learning that the blind poet brought to the composition of his epic. "Nothing is more striking in the poem," he writes in the first edition, "nothing more touching, than the frequency, and, on the whole, wonderful accuracy, of its references to maps. Now, what ever wealth of geographical information Milton may have carried with him into his blindness, there are evidences, I think, that he must have refreshed his recollections of this kind after his sight was gone" (Masson, *The Poetical Works of John Milton* [1874], 1:55). In the second edition Masson slightly expands this passage: "there are evidences, I think, that he must have refreshed his recollections of this kind by the eyes of others, and perhaps by their guidance of his finger, after his sight was gone" (Masson, *The Poetical Works of John Milton* [1893], 2:24). The change is small—a dozen words about the eyes and fingers that assist the helpless Milton—but it is all the more striking for that reason. Masson clearly intends to give his conjecture more vividness, and he does so through a reminiscence of the memorable scene near the very end of *Middlemarch* in which Dorothea suddenly decides to pore over some of Casaubon's maps. In a touchingly belated gesture, she seeks to provide herself with the requisite geographical knowledge to be of use to her late husband and therefore sets "eagerly to work, bending close to her map . . . and marking the names off on her fingers" (*M* 794; ch. 83).

Masson's edition was first published in 1874, hence after the appearance of the final installment of Eliot's novel (December 1872); but his introduction was written and ready for publication much earlier, which would explain why the echo of *Middlemarch* did not appear until the second edition.[13] It is only appropriate that this instance of Eliot's influence on contemporary Milton

---

12. Bayne notes that he received Masson's volume, which begins with Milton's separation from Mary Powell and his composition of the divorce tracts, only after his article was complete (Bayne 446n.).

13. Masson writes in his preface that "Mr. R. C. Browne's excellent edition of the English Poems for the Clarendon Press series had not appeared when the Introductions in the present volumes went to press" (Masson [1874] 1:ii). The book to which Masson refers was already in its second printing by 1872, so Masson's Introduction was probably in press by the beginning of that year at the latest.

scholarship should be one that emphasizes Milton's dependence on others, the extent to which his most inspired work was subject to outside mediation. Eliot had long been aware of the awkward material circumstances that surrounded the creation of *Paradise Lost*. The first of her two 1855 reviews of Keightley opens with a Hazlitt–like single-sentence biography—an account of Milton's life as a well-known classic, such as we have already seen repeatedly:

> The principal phases and incidents of Milton's life are familiar to us all: the sentence of rustication passed on him at the university; the bright, idyllic days at Horton when his early poems were produced; the journey to Italy where he 'found and visited the famous Galileo, grown old, a prisoner'; the prosaic transition to school-keeping in London City and inharmonious marriage with Mary Powell; his Latin secretaryship; his second and third ventures in matrimony, and small satisfaction in his daughters; the long days of blindness in which the *Paradise Lost* was poured forth by thirty lines at a time when a friendly pen happened to be near[.] (Eliot, *Essays,* 155)

In Eliot's unromanticized rendering, *Paradise Lost* sits beside Milton's "prosaic...school-keeping" (which she goes on to describe as falling below his own stated principles), his "secretaryship," and the failures represented by his "inharmonious marriage" and his "small satisfaction in his daughters." Above all, *Paradise Lost* comes into being only as chance permits—when a transcriber "happened to be near."

Eliot's familiarity with David Masson was of long standing, and their influence appears to have been mutual. She was an admirer of his scholarship from as early as 1852, when she urged John Chapman to try to recruit him for the *Westminster Review;* she first met him a year later, and he remained a friend of hers and George Henry Lewes's throughout their lives (Eliot, *Letters,* 2:48, 89; Haight 107). Eliot reviewed Masson's *Essays, Biographical and Critical* (1856), which includes two early pieces on Milton, for the *Westminster,* and in 1874 she was given a copy of Masson's Milton edition and wrote to him with her comments about it.[14] Most significantly, Masson was a visitor just at the time

---

14. The book was a gift from the publisher Alexander Macmillan. In his note on Eliot's letter to Macmillan thanking him for the gift, Gordon Haight misidentifies the book as a volume from Masson's biography (Eliot, *Letters,* 6:88). But Masson's reply to Eliot a few weeks later (her original letter to him has unfortunately been lost) mentions her comments about the "verse discussion" (6:96)—i.e., the section on "Milton's Versification, and his Place in the History of English Verse" that appears in the introduction to Masson's edition of Milton, not his biography. This is the edition that Eliot "read, and carefully annotated in the margins" as she prepared to write *Daniel Deronda* (Nardo 15).

that Eliot began mulling over her novel. Eliot's journal for July 18, 1869, records a visit from "Prof. Masson"; the next day she is "Writing an introduction to *Middlemarch,*" and at the end of the week she again "Meditated characters for Middlemarch" (Eliot, *Journals,* 136).

The journals do not record what they discussed on this or other occasions, but Masson had new information concerning Milton at this time that would have particularly intrigued George Eliot. For nearly two centuries, the accepted chronology of Milton's first marriage had been the one provided in the biography written by Edward Phillips, Milton's nephew; this is the account followed by Keightley. According to Phillips, Milton married Mary Powell in June of 1643. A few months later she asked for permission to visit her family near Oxford, which he granted on the understanding that she would return to him in London before Michaelmas, at the end of September. When she refused to return, despite repeated demands on his part, he set to work writing *The Doctrine and Discipline of Divorce,* which appeared before the end of the year. But Masson made a startling discovery when investigating this part of Milton's life, which appeared to cast serious doubt on the sequence of events as presented by Phillips: "There is proof, however (and I do not think it has been observed before), that Milton's first Divorce Tract was already published and in circulation two months *before* the Michaelmas in question" (Life 3:44). The evidence is a copy of Milton's pamphlet dated August 1—which indicated that Milton's plea for freedom of divorce was not a response to his wife's desertion but was written while she was still living with him in London, and within weeks of his wedding. Masson reluctantly and poignantly considers the implications of his finding.

> That a man should have occupied himself on a Tract on Divorce ere his honeymoon was well over—should have written it perseveringly day after day within sound of his newly-wedded wife's footsteps and the very rustle of her dress on the stairs or in the neighbouring room—is a notion all but dreadful. And yet to some such notion, if Phillips's dating is correct, we seem to be shut up. But, if so, more is involved than Phillips knew. The cause of Milton's thoughts about divorce, in that case, must have been the agony of a deadly discovery of his wife's utter unfitness for him when as yet she had not been two months his wife. It must have been the unutterable pain of the dis-illusioned bridegroom, the gnawing sense of his irretrievable mistake. (Life 3:46–47)[15]

---

15. Volume 3 of Masson's biography, in which this revelation is made, was published in 1873, after *Middlemarch* was complete. But again, publication lagged well behind the actual writing. In

Masson's discovery would have interested Eliot for two reasons. In the first place this picture of a marital disaster based not on desertion but on "utter unfitness," discovered almost immediately and yet too late, closely parallels Eliot's account of the Casaubons' honeymoon. Yet Masson's revised dating of Milton's divorce pamphlet only confirms what Eliot herself had already conjectured: discussing the pamphlet in her review of Keightley, she writes, "We seem to see a trace of [Milton's] own experience when he says, 'Who knows not that the bashful muteness of a virgin may ofttimes hide all the unliveliness and natural sloth which is really unfit for conversation?' " (Eliot, *Essays*, 157). Secondly, Masson's discovery suggests to what extent Milton's words are subject to accidents of transmission. The account of Phillips—that Milton wrote his tract after having been abandoned—was universally accepted for two hundred years and only called into doubt by Masson's having stumbled across a forgotten manuscript. The question of the pamphlet's dating, Masson writes,

> is set at rest by a manuscript note on the title-page, "*Aug. 1st.*" The note was put there by, or by the direction of, the collector, Thomason, to indicate the day on which the copy came into his hands, and is to be relied on implicitly. The Tract, it will be observed, was anonymous; but the words "*Written by J. Milton,*" penned on the title-page by the same hand that penned the date "*Aug. 1st.*," show that the authorship was no secret from the all-prying Thomason. In short, on evidence absolutely conclusive, Milton's first Divorce Tract was in print and on sale in London on the 1st of August, 1643, or two months before Phillips's fatal Michaelmas. (Life 3:44–45)[16]

Yet even here Masson is merely reaffirming something Eliot already knew. She notes in 1855 that Milton's "complete...theological and ethical views" came to be known to posterity only through an accidental discovery in 1823,

---

the preface to volume 2, which was published in 1871, Masson writes, "It was my wish to publish Volumes II. and III. together; and, though Volume II. now appears by itself, Volume III. is ready for the press, and will follow speedily" (Life 2:ix). In volume 3 Masson refers to the marriage "of Milton and Mary Powell two hundred and twenty-eight years ago," which puts the date of composition of that chapter in 1871 (Life 3:51). Masson's discovery of the new chronology cannot be dated precisely, but it was most likely before Eliot began the section on Dorothea in December 1870, and perhaps as early as his visit to Eliot in 1869.

16. Masson's chronology became the standard account for over fifty years. Twentieth-century scholars, however, determined that although Masson's revised dating of the pamphlet (August 1, 1643) was correct, the traditional date of the wedding was off by a year: Milton and Mary Powell were married in June of 1642, and therefore—as far as we now know—Milton did not necessarily write his first divorce tract within weeks of his own wedding.

"when Mr. Lemon, during his researches in the Old State Paper-office, happened to lay his hands on a Latin manuscript which proved to be the Treatise on Christian Doctrine, known to have been written by Milton" (Eliot, *Essays,* 155). It is by chance that Mr. Lemon "happened to lay his hands" on the manuscript, as it is by chance that the collector Thomason recorded the date on which *The Doctrine and Discipline of Divorce* "came into his hands," and did so "in the same hand" that recorded the author's name. Each of Milton's later works—none of which is written in his own hand—becomes known or remains hidden based on the accident of the other hands it necessarily passes through.

Hands form as important a motif in *Middlemarch* as they do in *Paradise Lost,* beginning with Eliot's echo of Milton's "hand in hand." The first thing we learn about Dorothea is that "Her hand and wrist were...finely formed" (*M* 7; ch. 1). (Lydgate similarly has "finely-formed fingers" [570; ch. 58].) Eliot also uses "hand" to refer to writing: Dorothea "piqued herself on writing a hand in which each letter was distinguishable" (44; ch. 5), whereas Fred Vincy has "a hand" that is legible only "when you know beforehand what the writer means" (552; ch. 56). The effect of Eliot's intense focus on these hands, especially Dorothea's, is the same as Milton's: the hands are both a sign of agency and just the opposite—an unpredictable intermediary, a hand that knows not what its owner is doing. When Milton refers to the flowerbeds of paradise metonymically as "the hand of Eve" (*PL* 9.438), "hand" means an identifying signature, an extension of Eve's very self. When the word next appears, however, at the moment of the Fall, Eve's hand seems to act in defiance of her better self: "her rash hand in evil hour/Forth reaching to the fruit, she plucked, she ate" (9.780–81). Similarly, book 4 of *Middlemarch* ends with another echo of the end of *Paradise Lost,* as Dorothea and Casaubon join hands in the last gesture of true spiritual communion between them: "She put her hand into her husband's, and they went along the broad corridor together" (*M* 419; ch. 42). But the next page begins a new book entitled "The Dead Hand," in which "hand," referring to Casaubon's attempt to exert power from the grave by means of the codicil to his will, now indicates dissociation and self-thwarting futility. When Casaubon posthumously reveals his hand, seeking "to keep his cold grasp on Dorothea's life," his words backfire, "defeat his own pride," and eventually alienate Dorothea's affectionate loyalty (484; ch. 50). Even the real Milton, let alone a pale imitation, is subject to the vagaries of the written word when it passes out of his hands.

Hands figure largely in chapter 29, the chapter that includes the Casaubons' argument in the library—their first since the unhappy honeymoon in Rome—and ends with Mr. Casaubon's collapse. The episode is filled with Miltonic allusions that are bound up as much with questions of textual transmission and its uncertainties as with marriage. The chapter begins by outlining the rationale behind Casaubon's choice in marrying Dorothea.

> On such a young lady he would make handsome settlements, and he would neglect no arrangement for her happiness: in return, he should receive family pleasures and leave behind him that copy of himself which seemed so urgently required of a man—to the sonneteers of the sixteenth century. Times had altered since then, and no sonneteer had insisted on Mr Casaubon's leaving a copy of himself; moreover, he had not yet succeeded in issuing copies of his mythological key; but he had always intended to acquit himself by marriage[.] (*M* 272; ch. 29)

All of these well-laid plans go awry: Casaubon does not make a handsome settlement on his wife, does not arrange for her happiness, does not receive pleasure from her, and above all is unable to issue "copies" either of himself or of the work that is meant to represent him. For Casaubon, reproduction is equated with composition, and both are fruitless. Like Milton, moreover, who employed not only his daughters but his wife as amanuenses, Casaubon conflates authorship with marriage as well as with procreation. "The book is Casaubon's child, and the writing of it his marriage, or so Dorothea believes as she realizes how completely textuality has been substituted for sexuality in her married life" (Gilbert and Gubar 505). Casaubon even enlists biblical language (Genesis 2:18: "It is not good that man should be alone; I will make him a help meet for him") to convince himself that God has ordained Dorothea to be his connubial secretary: "she might really be such a helpmate to him as would enable him to dispense with a hired secretary, an aid which Mr Casaubon had never yet employed and had a suspicious dread of.... Providence, in its kindness, had supplied him with the wife he needed" (*M* 272).

But these optimistic reflections are soon interrupted by actual circumstances. Casaubon unintentionally offends Dorothea as they sit working in the library, and from being a Milton who transmits his works through the willing help of a daughter-wife, he becomes instead the object of filial-uxorious rebellion: "Dorothea had thought that she could have been patient with John Milton, but she had never imagined him behaving this way; and for a moment Mr Casaubon seemed to be stupidly undiscerning and odiously unjust" (276). The immediate result of Dorothea's revised view of Casaubon-as-Milton is that his work becomes illegible:

> "We will, if you please, say no more on this subject, Dorothea. I have neither lesiure nor energy for this kind of debate." Here Mr Casaubon

dipped his pen and made as if he would return to his writing, though his hand trembled so much that the words seemed to be written in an unknown character. (276)

Dorothea's writing, by contrast, only grows stronger. The would-be Milton is usurped by his own secretary, even as Dorothea continues to reconsider her earlier Miltonic conception of her husband:

> She began to work at once, and her hand did not tremble; on the contrary, in writing out the quotations which had been given to her the day before, she felt that she was forming her letters beautifully, and it seemed to her that she saw the construction of the Latin she was copying, and which she was beginning to understand, more clearly than usual. In her indignation there was a sense of superiority, but it went out for the present in firmness of stroke, and did not compress itself into an inward articulate voice pronouncing the once "affable archangel" a poor creature. (277)

Yet Dorothea, in revising her idealized version of Milton's biography as well as her idealization of Casaubon as the "affable archangel" Raphael out of Milton's poem (*PL* 7.41), nevertheless does not reject the Miltonic model. As she returns to her secretarial work with a suddenly enhanced comprehension of Latin, she resembles not Milton's rebellious daughters—who famously did not understand Latin—but Milton himself. In the thumbnail history of Milton's life in her review of Keightley, Eliot mentions his "Latin secretaryship"—that is, the years Milton spent under Oliver Cromwell in the laborious work of translating state papers and official correspondence into Latin. We do not usually think of Milton as someone else's secretary (except the Muse's, perhaps), but Eliot was keenly aware of this phase of his life. Mr. Brooke, for instance, compares Will's secretarial powers to those of Milton.

> "Well, you know," interposed Mr Brooke, "he is trying his wings. He is just the sort of young fellow to rise. I should be glad to give him an opportunity. He would make a good secretary, now, like Hobbes, Milton, Swift—that sort of man." (*M* 322; ch. 34)

Mr. Brooke's offhand comment illustrates the wide difference between himself and Mr. Casaubon, as well as the widely divergent available views of Milton. Whereas Mr. Casaubon takes on the role of Milton in viewing Dorothea as both angel in the house and amanuensis, Mr. Brooke describes

Will similarly as both a winged creature and a secretary, yet in doing so makes Will, rather than himself, the Miltonic figure.

As Nardo notes, Will Ladislaw's secretaryship under Mr. Brooke distinctly resembles Milton's under Cromwell—Mr. Brooke is even "the descendent of one of Cromwell's generals" (Nardo 107). But in both cases the secretarial duties they undertake represent a postponement or even imperilment rather than a fulfilment of true vocation. Milton's employment entailed his "Abandoning," as Masson puts it, "all his great schemes of literary preparation and performance" (Masson, "Works," 314); and if Milton's activities as secretary had indeed led to his execution after the Restoration (as almost happened), *Paradise Lost* would never have been written. Similarly, Will's journalism renders him, to most minds, unfit to associate with Dorothea, whom consequently he almost never sees after taking up his post. Moreover, although Mr. Brooke loosely refers to Milton (among others) as "a good secretary," his secretaryship was not only personally dangerous but inefficient. As Eliot would have read in Keightley's account and elsewhere, Milton went blind early in his service to the Commonwealth, and for years he carried out his secretarial functions only with the help of an assistant (Keightley 53–54).

Eliot constantly reminds us that to put one's writings into the hands of an assistant is to risk a serious miscarriage of intention. Will's secretaryship itself results from Dorothea's delegation to her uncle of the task of writing: since "Mr Brooke's pen was a thinking organ, evolving sentences, especially of a benevolent kind, before the rest of his mind could well overtake them," Will is invited to Middlemarch instead of disinvited (*M* 285; ch. 30).[17] And Eliot repeatedly associates such errors of textual transmission with Milton. In Rome, for instance, when Dorothea is discovering the unfitness of her marriage, Will earnestly garbles Milton to her: "'You *are* a poem—and that is to be the best part of a poet—what makes up the poet's consciousness in his best moods,' said Will, showing such originality as we all share with the morning and the spring-time and other endless renewals" (218–19; ch. 22). Eliot's gently ironic comment alludes to the fact that Will is here half-quoting Milton's oft-quoted assertion that "he who would not be frustrate of his hope to write well hereafter in laudable things, ought him selfe to bee a true Poem, that is, a composition, and patterne of the best and honourablest things"

---

17. As a scholar Casaubon is acutely aware of such clerical lapses and even remarks upon them in one of his few attempts at humor. Early in the novel, Celia banteringly wonders whether, in wishing his subjects "a fowl in every pot," Henry IV of France intended specifically "fat fowls." "'Yes, but the word has dropped out of the text, or perhaps was *subauditum;* that is, present in the king's mind, but not uttered,' said Mr Casaubon, smiling and bending his head towards Celia, who immediately dropped backward a little, because she could not bear Mr Casaubon to blink at her" (*M* 76; ch. 9).

(Prose 1:890).[18] Milton's dictum, in his *Apology for Smectymnuus,* concludes a consideration of the necessity of perfect chastity in an artist; Will's paraphrase on the other hand comes when he has deliberately contrived to see his cousin's young wife at home alone. But Will is clearly no more conscious of the context of Milton's quotation than he is of its exact content.

In quoting, or misquoting, Milton to Dorothea, Will is textualizing her much as Casaubon does; yet to do so is not necessarily to contain or limit her.[19] The first person to treat Dorothea as a text is not Casaubon but the narrator, in the opening paragraph of the novel: "her profile as well as her stature and bearing... gave her the impressiveness of a fine quotation from the Bible,—or from one of our elder poets" (*M* 7; ch. 1).[20] Eliot does not say which of "our elder poets" she resembles, although one of them springs to mind when Dorothea immediately afterward begins to fantasize about marrying Milton. But it would be wrong to say that Dorothea is compared to a quotation from Milton; it is not even clear that she is compared to a quotation from an English poet at all. The "or" in Eliot's sentence ("a fine quotation from the Bible,—or from one our elder poets") does not indicate that Dorothea is *both* biblical and poetic, but rather suggests a single quotation of uncertain biblico-poetic origin. Eliot herself comments on the phenomenon of Milton-as-Bible, noting that "perhaps to the majority of English minds at this moment, it would be difficult to say how much of their belief about Satan, about the temptation of our 'first parents,' and the consequences of the Fall, is gathered from the Bible, and how much from Paradise Lost" (Eliot, "Belles Lettres," 604). Milton is at once the most authoritative and the most misremembered of poetic texts. In comparing Dorothea to a text that may be Miltonic, Eliot does not fix her character but rather the opposite. Like all texts, including Milton's—especially Milton's—Dorothea is liable to uncertainties, misinterpretations, and unpredictable alterations as time goes on.

Caleb Garth qualifies as one of those English minds Eliot mentions that possess a strong yet textually untraceable conception of the Bible:

---

18. The sentence is repeatedly cited by Victorian critics; Masson, for instance, quotes it in an article ("Works," 308) that was later reprinted in the 1856 volume reviewed by Eliot.

19. Pace Gilbert and Gubar, who cite Will's line when asserting that "women are denied the status of artist because they are supposed somehow to become works of art themselves" (450).

20. The same collocation reappears in a letter of 1873—"A quotation often makes a fine summit to a climax, especially when it comes from some elder author, or from the Bible" (Eliot, *Letters,* 5:404)—and is picked up by Cross in his biography: "The Bible and our elder poets best suited the organ-like tones of [Eliot's] voice, which required, for their full effect, a certain solemnity and majesty of rhythm. Her reading of Milton was especially fine" (Cross 3:340).

"The soul of man," said Caleb, with the deep tone and grave shake of the head which always came when he used this phrase—"the soul of man, when it gets fairly rotten, will bear you all sort of poisonous toadstools, and no eye can see whence came the seed thereof."

It was one of Caleb's quaintnesses, that in his difficulty of finding speech for his thought, he caught, as it were, snatches of diction which he associated with various points of view or states of mind; and whenever he had a feeling of awe, he was haunted by a sense of Biblical phraseology, though he could hardly have given a strict quotation. (*M* 401; ch. 40)

Harold Bloom speaks of later writers who "misread" their precursors as a willful and necessary act of resistance. But not all misreading derives from conscious or unconscious resistance. It is in the nature of texts to be altered in retelling, and also, as here, to be misremembered in good faith; and the greater—the more "classic"—the text, the more liable it is to popular misconception. Caleb's little speech concludes a chapter; the next chapter opens with the narrator's reflections about the accidents of textual transmission, in language derived not from the Bible but from its near twin, Milton.

Who shall tell what may be the effect of writing? . . . As the stone which has been kicked by generations of clowns may come by curious little links of effect under the eyes of a scholar, through whose labours it may at last fix the date of invasions and unlock religions, so a bit of ink and paper which has long been an innocent wrapping or stop-gap may at last be laid open under the one pair of eyes which have knowledge enough to turn it into the opening of a catastrophe. To Uriel watching the progress of planetary history from the Sun, the one result would be just as much of a coincidence as the other. (402; ch. 41)

Eliot is referring here to the letter signed by Bulstrode that Raffles picks up by accident at Stone Court. This signed slip of paper leads Raffles back to Bulstrode and so eventually precipitates Bulstrode's downfall—a true Aristotelian *hamartia* in the literal sense of "missing the mark." In commenting on the miscarried letter, Eliot refers pointedly to Milton, citing Milton's Uriel, not only because as angel of the sun he has the widest view of planetary history, but because even he could not see or predict the result of his own words. "Uriel, though regent of the sun, and held/The sharpest sighted spirit of all in heaven," is unable to penetrate Satan's disguise when the latter questions him (*PL* 3.690–91). He therefore gives Satan directions to the earth and so by his words helps bring into our world a world of woe.

The "Uriel" or conveyor of knowledge in this case is Peter Featherstone's illegitimate son, Joshua Rigg, who unknowingly supplies Raffles with the fatal letter.[21] Rigg himself, Eliot reminds us, is an accidental document. Reverting once again to her textualized image of procreation, and again quoting Milton ("in prose or numerous verse" [*PL* 5.150]), Eliot writes, "Socially speaking, Joshua Rigg would have been generally pronounced a superfluity. But those who like Peter Featherstone never had a copy of themselves demanded, are the very last to wait for such a request either in prose or verse" (*M* 402; ch. 41). Yet Featherstone is as disappointed in his offspring and as foiled in his will as Milton: Rigg is no true copy, prose or verse, but acts in a manner counter to his father's intentions, selling Stone Court to a man Featherstone hated.

Even when a copy is quite exact, it does not always convey the same impression as its original. The longest quotation from Milton in *Middlemarch* is the epigraph to chapter 3; Eliot does not, like Will, mistake Milton's words, but by quoting selectively she manages to change the grammar and the meaning significantly. Her epigraph reads as follows:

"Say, goddess, what ensued, when Raphaël,
The affable archangel...
                              Eve
The story heard attentive, and was filled
With admiration, and deep muse, to hear
Of things so high and strange."
                                    (23; ch. 3)

In *Paradise Lost* the grammatical subject of the second sentence, and the real subject of the whole invocation, is not Eve but Adam:

Say goddess, what ensued when Raphael,
The affable archangel, had forewarned
Adam by dire example to beware
Apostasy, by what befell in heaven
To those apostates, lest the like befall

---

21. Nardo notes that Rigg stands "turning his back" on Raffles, just as Uriel's "back was turned" on Satan; she goes on to suggest a possible analogue for this chapter of *Middlemarch* in Milton's *Areopagitica* (Nardo 17–20).

In Paradise to Adam or his race....
     He with his consorted Eve
The story heard attentive, and was filled
With admiration, and deep muse to hear
Of things so high and strange[.]

                                    (*PL* 7.40–53)

Eve, central to Eliot's quotation, is much more marginal in Milton's account
of Raphael's address to "Adam [and] his race." When Eliot refers again to
the same passage further down the page, in the second paragraph of the
chapter itself, she seems to reflect upon her own disruption of Milton's text.
Mr. Casaubon "had been as instructive as Milton's 'affable archangel;' and
with something of the archangelic manner he told [Dorothea] how he had
undertaken to show...that all the mythical systems or erratic mythical fragments in the world were corruptions of a tradition originally revealed" (*M* 23;
ch. 3). Eliot's use of Milton confirms Casaubon's point, that even the truest
fragment, erring from its original context, quickly becomes a "corruption."

Eliot's choice of this particular passage to "corrupt" is a pointed one: she
allows us to hear only some of Milton's words, just as Eve herself hears only
some of Raphael's words. Eve is not privy to the whole scene of archangelic
instruction but leaves at the beginning of book 8, intending to learn the rest
through the mediation of Adam (*PL* 8.39–57).[22] This adds yet another layer
to what is already a multi-layered process of transmission (God to Raphael to
Adam to Eve), which some critics have seen as singularly ineffective, even cul-
pably countereffective. William Empson, notably, asserts that "Adam and Eve
would not have fallen unless God had sent Raphael to talk to them, suppos-
edly to strengthen their resistance to temptation. Merely cheating his own
troops [i.e., Uriel] to get Satan into Paradise would not have been enough"
(Empson, *Milton's God,* 147). Empson's claim may be highly debatable, but it
is certain that as soon as Raphael leaves, his words are as liable to being lost,
ignored, misconstrued, or disobeyed as Milton's own words were.[23] At the
beginning of book 4 the poet longs for a "warning voice...that now,/While

---

22. On the significance of Eve's departure in book 8, see Revard 71–72 and Nardo 93–94. Nardo
offers a reading of the epigraph (90–94), though she does not note Eliot's alteration of Milton's syn-
tax. David Leon Higdon attributes the elliptical epigraph to Eliot's desire to heighten the ironic contrast between Casaubon and Raphael: "Three characters and one action figure in the original passage
in Milton. George Eliot used only five of the lines, and, by means of ellipsis marks, she reduced the
actors to two. This purposeful distortion provided a focus necessary for the irony" (Higdon 142).

23. For a recent reformulation of the case against Raphael, and an account of the many critics
since Empson who have similarly found Raphael's instruction misleading, see Kent Lehnhof, "Uncertainty and 'the Sociable Spirit.'"

time was, our first parents had been warned/The coming of their secret foe, and scaped/Haply so scaped his mortal snare" (*PL* 4.1–8). But no such voice is granted—only Raphael's, which proves insufficient to defeat Satan's mortal snare.

Dorothea too longs to hear an authoritative voice immune to contradiction or misunderstanding. When the painter Naumann in Rome compares Mr. Casaubon to Aquinas, we are told, "As for Dorothea, nothing could have pleased her more, unless it had been a miraculous voice pronouncing Mr Casaubon the wisest and worthiest among the sons of men. In that case her tottering faith would have become firm again" (*M* 210; ch. 22). Yet when Dorothea does at last hear what seems to her an incontrovertible voice, Mr. Casaubon himself contradicts it. After lengthy reflection, Dorothea decides that there is an absolute right and wrong to the writing of wills: "Was inheritance a question of liking or of responsibility? All the energy of Dorothea's nature went on the side of responsibility—the fulfilment of claims founded on our own deeds, such as marriage and parentage" (363; ch. 37). Having reached this conclusion, she phrases it to her husband in terms of a divine imperative: "if one has too much in consequence of others being wronged, it seems to me that the divine voice which tells us to set that wrong right must be obeyed" (365). But Casaubon does not recognize the voice as divine; instead, he thinks it belongs to Will ("Mr Ladislaw has probably been speaking to you on this subject?" [366]), and he chooses to disregard it. Both the "divine voice" that speaks to Dorothea and her own "diviner" voice (186; ch. 19) are as ineffective as Raphael's "potent voice" (*PL* 7.100), or as the celestial "voice" that tries to lead Eve to Adam (4.467), or as Milton's voice, fragmented in Eliot's text and relegated to the ambiguous status of an epigraph, a position at once authoritatively capital and impotently marginal.[24]

To say that Dorothea longs for a miraculous voice confirming Mr. Casaubon's work, and hence her own—as opposed to her "inward articulate voice pronouncing the once 'affable archangel' a poor creature" (*M* 277; ch. 29)—is another way of saying that she longs for a true vocation. As has often been observed, not only Dorothea but all the major characters in the novel seek a vocation, a calling to direct their energies.[25] Will and Fred and to a lesser extent Mr. Farebrother all flounder in search of one; Lydgate and

---

24. The other epigraph in *Middlemarch* with a Miltonic association is also misrepresented. The epigraph to chapter 52 derives from the final lines of Wordsworth's sonnet "London, 1802," addressed to Milton ("Milton! thou shouldst be living at this hour"), but Eliot has altered the pronouns.

25. The question of vocation in *Middlemarch* is amply explored by Alan Mintz, who notes, "The most important literary source for the idea of vocation is the great writer of the culture that originated the institution: Milton" (Mintz 69–70).

Mr. Casaubon discover a vocation early on but fail in their pursuit of it. Bulstrode feels a calling to the ministry but hearkens only selectively, just as he listens selectively to Lydgate's medical instructions (and in both cases the partial or fragmentary transmission leads to "corruption"). Only Caleb Garth, that eminent misquoter, both hears a calling and responds to it successfully. All of the others, beginning with Mr. Casaubon, would seem to be contrasted with Milton, and to some extent they are.[26] But perhaps the most surprising effect of Eliot's repeated association of both Milton and his characters with ineffective speech is that it revises the myth of Milton's vocation. Milton's path was not always clear or direct, and his example, so often invoked, serves as a precedent for Eliot's wayward characters as much as a rebuke to them.

This duality comes out most distinctly in Will Ladislaw. Soon after his first appearance Will begins to usurp Mr. Casaubon's role as the novel's stand-in for both Milton and his angels. Yet as we might expect by now, neither association carries consistent authority. In physical appearance, Will resembles Milton's angels, who are able to assume "what shape they choose" (*PL* 1.428): "Surely, his very features changed their form. . . . When he turned his head quickly his hair seemed to shake out light, and some persons thought they saw decided genius in this coruscation. Mr Casaubon, on the contrary, stood rayless" (*M* 203; ch. 21). Mr. Casaubon, deprived of rays and hair and genius, has gone from being Raphael to being the fallen Lucifer, "Shorn of his beams" (*PL* 1.596). But Will's glancing "genius" ensures nothing. The angel he most clearly resembles is the hapless Uriel—"Of beaming sunny rays, a golden tiar/ Circled his head, nor less his locks behind/. . . Lay waving round" (*PL* 3.625–28). For much of the novel, moreover, Will too fears "becoming dimmed and for ever ray-shorn in [Dorothea's] eyes" (*M* 360; ch. 37). In his actions, meanwhile, Will resembles Milton himself. As Nardo details, not only his secretaryship but the whole of Will's haphazard career— his dilettantish travels in Italy, supported by a father figure; his return to England and taking up the cause of reform; his eventual entry into political life in London—clearly follow a "Miltonic pattern" (Nardo 107). Nardo concludes that "Will—no more a modern-day Milton than was Casaubon—stumbles toward a life that takes the shape of Milton's" (107). But in Eliot's view, such

26. According to Francis C. Blessington, "To the reader the similarities between Milton and Casaubon must be ironic" (Blessington 29); Haskin agrees that "the reader finds in [Casaubon's] interior life only a parody of Milton" (Haskin 215). Sister Bridget Marie Engelmeyer rejects even an ironic comparison, since "suggesting parallels between Milton and the pseudo-scholar Casaubon . . . asperses Milton" (Engelmeyer 103).

blind stumbling is as characteristic of Milton as eventual success. Will, who goes "rambling in Italy sketching plans for several dramas, trying prose and finding it too jejune, trying verse and finding it too artificial" (*M* 453; ch. 46); Casaubon, who makes an unhappy choice in marriage; Lydgate, who does the same, and whose true high calling is interrupted by political dissension[27]— these figures *are* modern-day Miltons, or at least one side of Milton that in Eliot's time was more and more being recognized.

The most memorable image of Milton in *Middlemarch* depicts him simultaneously as the greatest man of his age and as one who is subject to inevitable distortion.

> If to Dorothea Mr Casaubon had been the mere occasion which had set alight the fine inflammable material of her youthful illusions, does it follow that he was fairly represented in the minds of those less impassioned personages who have hitherto delivered their judgments concerning him?...I am not sure that the greatest man of his age, if ever that solitary superlative existed, could escape these unfavourable reflections of himself in various small mirrors; and even Milton, looking for his portrait in a spoon, must submit to have the facial angle of a bumpkin. (*M* 82–83; ch. 10)

The point is not that Casaubon is a mere grotesque caricature of Milton; nor is it that Casaubon's critics are all distorting spoons, whereas Dorothea provides a true mirror to Casaubon's Miltonic greatness. The point is that reflection in a spoon is inevitable. Eliot's use of Milton in *Middlemarch* reflects in the first place on Milton: with characteristic sympathy she reminds us that he too was a human figure, who often necessarily "must submit" to seeing himself and even his writings distorted. In turn, this view of Milton reflects compassionately upon the characters of the novel. Milton is not merely an intimidating figure whose precedent implicitly condemns the characters— no more than does the precedent of St. Theresa. To the contrary, even more than St. Theresa, Milton represents a proto-Dorothea, often frustrated and misunderstood, "struggling amidst the conditions of an imperfect social state, in which great feelings will often take the aspect of error, and great faith the aspect of illusion" (824; "Finale")—but leaving a legacy of good nonetheless.

---

27. Bulstrode, with whom Lydgate allies himself politically and whose fall precipitates Lydgate's own, consciously models himself on Cromwell (*M* 604–05; ch. 61).

❧ Chapter 6

The Heirs of Milton

Personal legacies, as George Eliot reminds us in *Middlemarch* (with Milton's example in mind), can be at the same time powerful and fragile—fragile precisely because, by the time they take effect, they have necessarily passed out of our personal control. The same is true of literary legacies, or influences, and in this concluding chapter I consider the ways in which Milton's relation to the Victorians can help us understand the complexities of literary influence more generally. The chapter is divided into two parts. The first places this book in the context of other studies of Milton's influence and of broader debates about literary relations. I argue that the Victorians' response to Milton, as delineated in the preceding chapters, is significant, because it exemplifies with special clarity the paradoxical nature of literary influence—at once potent and fractured, personal and impersonal. The second part then illustrates this argument by exploring an important Miltonic motif that embodies these same paradoxes. The Victorian Milton is of interest, I suggest, not only for itself but for the insight it provides into the workings of literary history.

Throughout this book I have repeatedly offered models for Milton's influence that derive from his own writings, suggesting that the nature of Milton's influence on the Victorians can best be understood by examining representations of similarly oblique, diffuse, or hidden influence in Milton's poetry and prose. This may seem an unusual critical method, but it represents a recurring trope in Milton criticism. The clearest precedent comes from Harold Bloom who, as discussed in chapter 1, takes Milton as providing not only the chief source of the "anxiety of influence" but its best account, since Bloom views later poets as responding to Milton precisely as Milton's Satan does to God. And Bloom is not alone: Sandra Gilbert and Susan Gubar, whose *The Madwoman in the Attic* is also discussed in the opening chapter, similarly draw their models of Miltonic influence from Milton himself. In their account, nineteenth-century women writers relate to Milton either as Eve does to God in *Paradise Lost,* or else (turning to Milton's biography, rather than his poetry) as Milton's daughters did to their father.

Like Gilbert and Gubar, Leslie Brisman, in *Milton's Poetry of Choice and Its Romantic Heirs,* disagrees with Bloom's theory yet adopts his method. Brisman claims that the Romantic fascination with Milton is a matter of choice rather than of anxious obligation: "If we think in terms of a bequest rather than a burden, we open ourselves to discover...the element of volition" in the Romantics' "conscious, controlled turning to a Miltonic way" (Brisman 298). But once again the chief model for this poetic relationship is to be found in Milton himself. As Brisman explains in his opening sentences, the Romantics choose a poetic precedent that is itself characterized above all by choice: "Milton is everywhere concerned with the act of choosing.... This book explores the way the experience of alternatives is expressed in Miltonic usage and the way poetic influence is expressed in the activity of choice" (1). Lucy Newlyn, who cites Brisman's book as "the nearest critical analogue" to her own, takes a similar approach (Newlyn 15). According to Newlyn, Romantic poets' allusions to Milton display an open-ended ambiguity that is itself Miltonic and derives directly from the very poetry to which they are alluding. All of these critics thus seem to agree that the influence of Milton can most fruitfully be understood through models drawn from Milton's own work.[1] And yet there are obvious risks in making these arguments. They might seem at the very least over-ingenious; at worst, such arguments run the risk of seeming to mystify literary history—as if to suggest that Milton had somehow composed a prophetic allegory of his own reception. The question therefore presents itself: Why have critics (myself included) continued so

---

1. Similar examples abound. Joseph Wittreich, for instance, proposes that one of Milton's chief legacies to his successors was a model of how to read his poetry and to continue its visionary tradition. "What the Bible was to Milton, Milton was to the Romantic poets: they took from him what he took from it, the biblical aesthetic to which he had accommodated his poetry" (Wittreich, *Visionary Poetics,* xx).

consistently to derive their models of Miltonic influence from Milton's own life and writings? There seem to me to be three main reasons.

The first possibility is simply that these models are historically true. It requires no great leap of faith to believe that, either by conscious identification or unconscious association, writers may structure their literary relationship to predecessors on models provided by those predecessors. Thus a poet much influenced by Virgil might well be tempted to imitate the example of Aeneas (as Dante obviously seeks to do) by treating Virgil with filial piety even while regretfully leaving him behind. An author who is deeply indebted to *Hamlet* is likely to conceive of that influence in terms of haunting or oedipal anxiety, and a follower of Cervantes in terms of literary obsession. A writer influenced by Milton, moreover, is all the more likely to respond in such a fashion because Milton himself is so self-conscious about his relationship to predecessors, and because his poetry is so rife with possible models: every poem from *Comus* and "Lycidas" onward is filled with scenes of instruction and assertions of authority. If critics tend to see nineteenth-century writers as Satanic rebels against Milton's precedent, or as Adams faced with a crucial choice between conflicting poetic authorities, it is because of similar perceptions, conscious or unconscious, on the part of the writers themselves.

A second reason for describing Milton's influence in Miltonic terms is that it gives critics a means of vividly reinforcing a claim about Milton's own poetry. This is not to say that the parallels are purely factitious. But rather than asserting some causal connection between a trope or aspect of Milton's poetry and its apparent recurrence in the attitude of later writers toward Milton, critics will use the latter as an opportunity to underline an important point—about the role of women in *Paradise Lost,* for instance; or about the complex and open-ended nature of Miltonic allusion; or else about the way in which power in Milton's writings tends to be exerted indirectly. The first reason for adopting this critical method, then, has to do with communicating a truth about the later writers and their self-perception, whereas the second aims to establish a point about the precursor poet. These aims are not of course incompatible, and both are reasons for my own use of this style of argument. My chief motive, however, has been the third advantage of this method, which is that it stakes an implicit claim about the nature of literary influence. To describe a process of influence in terms that are derived from the source of that influence is to posit a literary history that is both (in a good sense) "messy"—that is, it is necessarily multiple, historically contingent, and hence irreducible—and at the same time "neat" or self-contained. This is the point on which I wish to dwell, because it helps explain not only why Milton has been especially liable to this sort of analysis, but also why the study of the Victorian Milton can be of particular use in helping us understand the value of influence study at the present time.

The great change in literary criticism over the past three or four decades could be called a shift from "neat" to "messy": from formalism to historicism. The former approach tends to treat the literary text as something essentially self-sufficient, a closed system of signs relating primarily to each other; the latter sees the meaning of a work of literature as determined by endless filiations to circumstances that exist outside the text and that change over time. In practice, of course, neither approach is as absolute, or as mutually opposed, as such a brief, schematic comparison suggests. Even in the heyday of New Criticism, nobody proposed that a literary text could be considered in total isolation from its context, nor did New Historicism entirely jettison the practice of close reading or the lessons of structuralist and poststructuralist analysis. Nevertheless, it is fair to say that historicism has recently been triumphant in the debate that has long been taking place in anglophone criticism between these two broad critical schools. Milton has always figured prominently in this debate, not only because of his importance in the history of English poetry, but because of the starkly dual nature of his reputation. Is Milton inextricably bound up, even more than other poets, in a literary, historical, and political context from which it would be foolish (and impossible) to try to separate him? Or, to the contrary, is Milton best understood in the way that he repeatedly depicted himself, as standing alone and essentially self-sufficient?[2]

These views of Milton have alternated—as, very generally speaking, have the critical schools that they exemplify—over the centuries. Poets and critics of the eighteenth century, up through Samuel Johnson in his life of Milton (1779), generally did not dissociate Milton's poetry from the seventeenth-century politics in which he was embroiled. At the same time, they also viewed Milton as firmly embedded in a literary context: for the Augustans, Milton was the great imitator and adapter of classical models (Newlyn 40–45).[3] The Romantics, by contrast, tended to admire Milton above all as

2. The same questions have from the beginning surrounded the Romantic poets, with their similarly dual reputation as political activists and solitary dreamers. The latter perception, which Romantic poetry promulgated as part of what Jerome McGann labeled "the Romantic Ideology," resembles Milton's self-depiction in his poetry (though much less in his prose). This uneven self-accounting may explain why Milton and the Romantic poets, particularly Wordsworth, were among the first major English authors to be subjects of historicist analysis when the resurgence began in the late 1970s and early 1980s. Victorian poetry, by contrast, did not experience such a resurgence until at least a decade later (Harrison 6).

3. As Newlyn goes on to explain, critical debate about originality—including Milton's—began in earnest in the 1750s; yet it was not until the early Romantic period, at the end of the century, that critics began to feel a need to apologize for Milton's imitation of the ancients (46–49).

an originator—as someone whose visionary poetry and politics equally existed apart from and beyond the age in which he lived. This view of Milton as sui generis, an exceptional and solitary genius, returned in the twentieth century, notably in the criticism of T. S. Eliot—for whom, however, it constituted Milton's greatest drawback rather than his glory. "As a poet," writes Eliot, "Milton seems to me probably the greatest of all eccentrics. His work illustrates no general principles of good writing; the only principles of writing that it illustrates are such as are valid only for Milton himself to observe" (Eliot, *On Poetry and Poets,* 155).[4]

In between these Romantic and Modernist views of Milton's self-sufficiency came the Victorian Milton. One could see the Victorian response, exemplified most clearly in David Masson's historicizing biography, as representing a return to the contextual appreciation of Milton (such as would occur again in the 1980s, after a period of more hermetic interpretation that reached its zenith in the reader-response criticism of Stanley Fish). It was certainly that; and yet it is crucial to recognize that the Victorian treatment of Milton was much more than a straightforward recontextualization. It has been the contention of this study that Victorian writers managed to emphasize the two sides of Milton's position—his self-relying agency and his historical contingency—equally. All periods of course display some mixture of both attitudes; but the Victorian period was unusual in embodying opposite extremes at once. The more Milton was viewed as part of a wider context, the more singular he seemed to be in his tendency to stand out from that context; the more he appeared to blend into the literary background, the more poetic influence he exerted. Each of the foregoing chapters has sought to demonstrate that Milton's influence on the Victorians was simultaneously diluted and concentrated, and that critics, including Masson, recognized this duality.

The reason the dual nature of the Victorian Milton is significant is that influence studies have become similarly split in recent decades. Robert Douglas-Fairhurst, in his book on the "shaping of influence" in Victorian literature, distinguishes two "theoretical models...[that] offer mirror-reverses of the way 'influence' has come to be understood" (Douglas-Fairhurst 2–3). At one

---

4. Eliot's contention that Milton writes by rules that apply only to himself (and may therefore exert a baleful influence on later poets) dates back to the eighteenth century; the difference is that Eliot applies his criticism much more widely in asserting that Milton illustrates "no general principles" but is exceptional in every respect. Voltaire, by contrast, singles out Milton's autobiographical digressions in *Paradise Lost,* concluding that such poetic egotism "is to be forgiven in *Milton;* nay, I am pleas'd with it.... But this however is a very dangerous Example for a Genius of an inferior Order, and is only to be justified by Success" (Shawcross, *Milton: The Critical Heritage,* 252).

extreme Douglas-Fairhurst locates Harold Bloom, who concentrates on authors and whose model is Freudian, essentialist, and individual (28–43), and
at the other extreme Jerome McGann, who concentrates on texts and whose
model is evolutionary, historically variable, and collaborative (59–78).[5] A few
years earlier, Patrick Hogan described the same divide in more general terms,
noting that "writers on this topic have tended to focus on social aspects of
influence to the exclusion of psychological aspects, or vice versa" (Hogan xi).
In *Wordsworth and the Victorians,* Stephen Gill characterizes the dichotomy in
terms of diffusion and concentration. Gill identifies his book as "an essay in
two kinds of literary and cultural history. The first tries to document as fully
as possible…the ubiquity of Wordsworth," whereas "[t]he second form of
literary history essayed is of a more familiar kind," describing Wordsworth's
particular influence upon individual works of later literature (Gill 4–5).

All of these studies owe a debt to Jay Clayton and Eric Rothstein's important collection *Influence and Intertextuality in Literary History,* the title of
which provides what remain the most useful terms to describe the camps into
which the study of literary history has divided. In Clayton and Rothstein's
pithy summation, "influence has to do with agency, whereas intertextuality
has to do with a much more impersonal field of crossing texts" (Clayton
and Rothstein 4). The split between the two approaches, they explain, has
been largely generational. Influence, which conceives of literary history in
terms of individual authors and tends to provide a relatively "neat," dia-
chronic narrative, was favored by an older generation of critics and theorists
(including Bloom), whereas intertextuality, which expands the number and
nature of the texts under consideration and tends to work synchronically,
has appealed to more recent critics.[6] As a result, the former approach has not
only fallen out of fashion but, in the words of Gill, "has been denigrated
and its necessary death foretold" (Gill 5). The perceived problem with traditional studies of "influence," according to Clayton and Rothstein, was that
they "smacked of elitism, the old boy networks of Major Authors and their

---

5. Douglas-Fairhurst observes that the Victorians themselves recognized the latter model, quite
as much as the former: "the notion that influence was at its strongest where it was exercised indirectly, through a dispersed communion of readers, already formed a sharp focus of Victorian critical
debate" (122).

6. The critical chronology is slightly complicated by the fact that the major theorists of
intertextuality—including Julia Kristeva, who introduced the term, and both Wolfgang Iser and Hans
Robert Jauss, whose reception theory has been so formative in Milton studies—published many of
their important statements already in the 1960s. But their influence in anglophone criticism truly
began about a decade later; see Clayton and Rothstein 17–29. Another good account of the history
of influence studies, published at the same time as Clayton and Rothstein's, appears in chapter 1 of
Robin Jarvis's *Wordsworth, Milton and the Theory of Poetic Relations* (3–28).

sleek entourages." More generally, the study of influence has declined due to "a falling off, among many critics, of interest in its central figure, the author as agent" (Clayton and Rothstein 3, 12).

And yet despite all these distinctions and oppositions, "influence" and "intertextuality" prove to be as difficult to disentangle as formalism and historicism. "Strictly, influence should refer to relations built on dyads of transmission from one unity (author, work, tradition) to another"; but in practice, "influence studies often stray into portraits of intellectual background, context," and the other traditional appurtenances of intertextual studies (3). The slippage occurs just as much in the other direction. As Andrew Elfenbein acutely points out in *Byron and the Victorians,* critics who cast the greatest doubt on the role of individual agency in literary history are very willing to accept it when discussing critical history. For this reason, "Influence, understood as the way that the work of one author shapes that of a later one, now has the peculiar status of being everywhere and nowhere. As an approach to literary analysis, it has become intellectually suspect and professionally unfashionable. Yet a glance at footnotes of books or articles in the field reveals that the discipline of literary study is obsessed with documenting influence" (Elfenbein 3)—so much so that a study that failed to recite its own critical genealogy would itself seem "intellectually suspect." Elfenbein concludes that the attempt to promote one of these two approaches to literary history at the expense of the other is ultimately untenable, taking it "as axiomatic that the pull between treating texts as the products of individual authors and as the products of larger systems of discourses, practices, and institutions is not simply a problem that can be solved by thinking about it hard enough" (8). Rather, the problem is itself historical. As I have already suggested, different periods of literature and criticism have shown themselves more or less willing to conceive of influence as chiefly direct and personal, or chiefly indirect and diffuse.

The study of Milton and the Victorians can be particularly illuminating because it showcases the necessary interrelationship between these two modes of influence. The point is not merely that influence and intertextuality coexist; as I have just mentioned, most studies of literary history display a mixture of both approaches, many of them (like Gill's) self-consciously.[7]

---

7. Clayton and Rothstein note that even Bloom occasionally "sounds very much like a theorist of intertextuality," although they go on to position him, as Douglas-Fairhurst does, at the extreme of influence (Clayton and Rothstein 9). For a fine recent example of a study that alternates between the two models, dividing its chapters between studying what Gill calls "ubiquity" and discussing direct influence on individual authors, see Adrian Poole, *Shakespeare and the Victorians.*

My point, rather, is that the perceived opposition must be deconstructed—
that the notion of influence as emanating from particular sources and that
of influence as circumambient and impersonal are mutually dependent, even
mutually reinforcing. And nowhere is this cooperation more vividly expressed than in the works of Milton. Does Milton propound the power of
individual agents to sway human affairs? On the one hand, the answer is very
obviously yes; that is the subject of both of his great epics, as he summarizes
them himself.

> I who erewhile the happy garden sung,
> By *one man*'s disobedience lost, now sing
> Recovered Paradise to all mankind,
> By *one man*'s firm obedience fully tried.
>
>   (*PR* 1.1–4, emphasis added)

On the other hand, when Michael gives these same glad tidings to Adam,
telling him that Messiah will defeat Satan and redeem humankind from sin,
Adam asks when and where the fight will occur in which (according to
prophecy) the Son will crush the Serpent's head and his heel be bruised in
return—only for Michael to correct his misconception about the personal
and particular nature of the confrontation.

> To whom thus Michael. Dream not of their fight,
> As of a duel, or the local wounds
> Of head or heel.
>
>   (*PL* 12.386–88)

The lines could stand as a rebuke as much to Harold Bloom as to Adam.
Influence is exerted not through battle or the terrible agon of mighty champions, nor even through a single act of apparent weakness at the Crucifixion,
but rather through the ongoing response to that act by innumerable human
beings, by "as many as offered life/Neglect not, and the benefit embrace"
(12.425–26). Satan is ultimately defeated, Michael explains, by the united
force of all those who choose to accept Christ's sacrifice.

And yet Adam could be excused for thinking of the triumph over Satan
in terms of one-to-one confrontation, since he has just recently heard the
story of how Michael himself (though Adam is unaware of his instructor's
identity) entered into single combat with Satan, hoping by his solitary power
to decide the outcome of the war in heaven. On the other hand, the description of that particular duel, as Raphael is careful to point out (6.296–301),

is merely an accommodation to human understanding; and in any case, Michael's personal "victory" proves trivial, since Satan soon recovers and returns to fight, and even temporarily to gain advantage, the next day. And yet—returning once more to the argument in favor of individual agency—when the war does end on the third day, it does so through the actions of the Son alone, conquering the forces of Satan in his triumphal chariot. And on the other hand yet again, this triumph, as we have noted before, although literally central to *Paradise Lost,*[8] is unique in Milton's poetry: elsewhere even God—especially God—exerts his influence not directly but through myriad hidden sources. To the original question about individual agency, then, the answer is both yes and no; power, in Milton, is irreducibly a two-handed engine.

The duality that Milton exhibits is reflected in the Victorian treatment of him, more than in that of any other period. Masson's multi-volume *Life* exalts Milton as an individual to an unprecedented extent, treating his biography not as a supplement to the poems but as a worthy object of study in its own right. Yet at the same time that Masson uses his enormous knowledge of historical context in order to illuminate Milton's life from every possible angle, he also subsumes Milton into that context. In the poetry of Alfred Tennyson, meanwhile, Milton figures as a direct precursor: *Idylls of the King,* for instance, was viewed already by contemporary critics as representing the completion of a poem "by Milton left unsung." Yet this perception is itself equivocal, since it suggests that Milton's chief influence on Tennyson's epic was exerted through a poem he never wrote. The greatest debt of the *Idylls* to *Paradise Lost,* moreover, takes the form of an elision; and in general, Milton appears in Tennyson's poetry in such multifarious aspects—Tennyson draws from so many different (and often unfamiliar) parts of Milton's work, and he so consistently mingles Milton's voice with that of other predecessors—that Milton's influence appears in the end largely incidental. Or again: Milton exerts an obvious influence on George Eliot's *Middlemarch,* which makes pointed and repeated allusion to his life and work. And yet the figure of Milton transforms over the course of the novel from one of omniscience and patriarchal authority to something quite different: one whose influence, though great, is erratic, mediated by others, and contingent on outward circumstances. Thus, although at the beginning of the novel Dorothea perceives only one Milton figure in the world of Middlemarch (Casaubon), by the end Milton serves as a precedent for nearly every character in the novel—including Dorothea herself, who exchanges her dreams of effecting change

---

8. As Fowler notes, the description of the Son's chariot, at least in the first edition, comes at the precise center of the poem (*PL* 6.761–62n.).

in the world through direct personal intervention for a form of influence
that is instead "incalculably diffusive" (*M* 825; "Finale"). The same pattern
emerges whenever Milton is treated by the Victorians as a classic, or as a bible,
or as a mighty weakling: his influence is both personal and impersonal, direct
and "diffusive." If we wish to understand the interdependent nature of influence and intertextuality, the Victorian Milton helps show the way.

For a model to help illustrate the dual nature of both Milton and his influence, we can turn one last time to a notable feature of Milton's own life and
poetry: his hair. An entire monograph could be written about Milton and
hair—both his own fascination with hair, as reflected in his poetry, and also
the fascination later ages have shown with Milton's hair both in fable and in
fact.[9] In Anne Manning's novel *The Maiden and Married Life of Mary Powell*
(1849), for instance—the fictional diary of Milton's first wife, which became
a Victorian favorite and was frequently reprinted—the heroine first meets
her future husband when she nearly runs him over with her horse; yet she
has time nevertheless to be struck by the appearance of his hair. "Just at the
Turne of *Holford's Close,* [I] came shorte upon a Gentleman walking under
the Hedge, clad in a sober, genteel Suit, and of most beautifulle Countenance,
with Hair like a Woman's, of a lovely pale brown, long and silky, falling over
his Shoulders" (Manning 6–7). His hair becomes Milton's defining feature
in Mary's eyes: when her mother objects to the notion of her "wedding this
round-headed Puritan," Mary replies, "Not round-headed... his Haire is as
long and curled as mine" (55). The motif runs throughout the novel and
takes on a life of its own. When Milton and Mary separate shortly after their
wedding, a cousin of hers casts the conflict in terms of their hair, remarking,
"I verilie think she loves everie one of those long Curls of hers more than
she loves Mr. *Milton*" (169).[10]

Anna Nardo has described the revival in the nineteenth century of a number of fancifully romantic stories about Milton's early life, many of which represent Milton as a beautiful youth "with hyacinthine locks" (Nardo 36). But
the fascination is not restricted to the nineteenth century. *The Story of Marie*

---

9. The subject is discussed briefly in Clymer, "Cromwell's Head and Milton's Hair"; Newman, "Entanglement in Paradise"; and Gray, "The Hair of Milton." Interestingly, Claudius Salmasius,
Milton's opponent in the regicide debate, wrote an entire treatise (*Epistola ad Andream Colvium*) about
the appropriate length and adornment of hair for both men and women.

10. The novel as a whole is a classic Miltonic narrative of mighty weakness: Mary conquers her
husband's heart by leaving him. The hair motif runs right through to the end, where Milton equates
hair with books (arguing that both should be free); objecting to "the Press-licenser's Authoritie," he
exclaims, "License! I suppose they will shortlie license the length of *Moll's* Curls" (259). On the novel
and its sequel, *Deborah's Diary* (the fictional journal of Milton's daughter), see Nardo 44–46, 61–65.

Powell, Wife to Mr Milton (1943), Robert Graves's peevish rewriting of Man-ning's novel, similarly focuses on hair. Graves, however, although he frequently mentions Milton's own locks and the pride he takes in them, highlights even more Milton's obsession with women's hair. The first time Milton and Mary are left alone together, these are the first words he addresses to her:

> "Your hair delights my eye, pretty child. Without doubt, Eve had tresses like yours. . . . After I had seen you for the first time, your hair became an obsession of my mind: for it wreathed itself between my eye and what book soever I studied, though it might be the Holy Bible itself, coming with a gadding or serpentine motion until it choked the sense of my reading."
>
> "I am sure that I am heartily sorry if I inconvenienced you," said I, playing the simpleton.
>
> "Yours was neither the first nor the only hair that ensnared my eye," said he, "but certainly, it drew its snare the tightest; however, when I found experimentally that by no act of ratiocination, nor any ascetic exercise, could I circumvent or remove this strange affection of the eye, and also that only the hair of virgins had the same grand compulsion for me, I was no longer dismayed. I concluded it to be God's will that I should render humble submission to Him, and so enter into wedlock, wherefrom for certain choice reasons I had conscientially refrained: for thus I should be able to gloat upon your hair legitimately, and soon (because of its daily and nightly familiarity) I would be no more plagued with it in my visionary sense, than I am now by my own ears."
> (Graves 134)

Here we can begin to perceive the significance of hair in the popular percep-tion of Milton. Over the course of this passage, hair transforms from some-thing extrinsic—a snare, a complication, an interference from the outside world—to something private and internal to Milton himself—an inward prompting given by God, ultimately as personal and native to Milton as his own ears. This duality is essential to the ongoing fascination of hair. Is your hair really a part of you? In one sense, the answer is very much yes: not only does hair grow from your body, but it is often used by others to distinguish you and even to define your personality (as happens in both of these novels). Yet unlike any other part of your body, hair can be easily separated from you, and often is—even more so in the days when locks of hair were regularly exchanged, so that one's hair was often in the keeping of one or more other people. In depicting Milton's fascination with hair, Graves appropriately emphasizes this dual nature, at once intensely personal or peculiar and also interpersonal and alienable.

The same duality is revealed in a nonfictional account of Milton's hair, Philip Neve's pamphlet *A Narrative of the Disinterment of Milton's Coffin* (1790). In August 1790, the church officials of St. Giles, Cripplegate, in London, where Milton is buried, decided to search for the exact location of the poet's coffin. Upon finding it, they exhumed and, eventually, opened it in order to view the remains. Predictably, the viewers immediately began to claim relics; yet not all parts of the body were treated equally. One Mr. Laming, for instance, a parish overseer, first takes Milton's jawbone and later a leg bone; but in both cases he thinks better of so disturbing the corpse and throws the bones back into the coffin. Yet he helps himself liberally to some of the "great quantity of hair" that he and the others discover remaining about the head (Neve 18). The hair possesses a double attraction. In the first place, it is more distinctively Milton's: unlike the bones, which cannot be distinguished from anybody else's bones, the hair is incontestably Milton's own, and it is what allows the gravediggers positively to identify the body. Neve presents the evidence for believing the coffin to be indeed that of Milton, and concludes, "But the strongest of all confirmations is the hair, both in its length and color.... In the reign of *Charles* II. how few, besides *Milton,* wore their hair! *Wood* says, *Milton* had light brown hair; the very description of that which we possess" (28–29).[11] Yet at the same time that the hair is more intimately identifiable with Milton than any other part, the taking of hair from the coffin does not seem as great a despoliation: Neve's reference to the hair "which we *possess*" is telling. There is nothing unusual in having someone else's hair in your possession, as there would be in having someone else's jaw; samples of Milton's hair had been circulating since the poet's lifetime. These new samples too quickly entered into wider circulation: within a week one of the grave diggers had "divided his share [of the hair] into many small parcels," which he distributed among his friends (30). A few teeth and other fragments were also taken from the tomb. But the relic seekers concentrated on Milton's hair, both because it was more legitimately his and because it was more legitimately theirs.

---

11. The passage continues, "and what may seem extraordinary, it is yet so strong, that Mr. *Laming,* to cleanse it from its clotted state, let the cistern-cock run on it, for near a minute, and then rubbed it between his fingers, without injury" (29). The sentence ironically echoes two moments in Milton's poetry: the fate of Lycidas—"With nectar pure his oozy locks he laves" ("Lycidas" 175)—and that of Samson, whose hair is likewise surprisingly resilient, and whose father proposes at the end of the play, "Let us go find the body where it lies/Soaked in his enemies' blood, and from the stream/With lavers pure, and cleansing herbs wash off/The clotted gore" (*SA* 1725–28).

The importance of Milton's hair in all of these texts mirrors the central role of hair in Milton's own poetry, where the same qualities are emphasized. It features most obviously in the Samson story that Milton chose as the subject for his tragedy, but it features most pervasively in *Paradise Lost,* where descriptions and images of hair abound. Many of the characters in the epic are first presented and characterized in terms of their hair, from the "humble shrub,/And bush with frizzled hair implicit" (7.322–23) to Uriel, angel of the sun, whose "locks behind/Illustrious on his shoulders fledge with wings/Lay waving round" (3.626–28).[12] Most notably, Adam and Eve themselves are introduced into the poem by their hair.

> His fair large front and eye sublime declared
> Absolute rule; and hyacinthine locks
> Round from his parted forelock manly hung
> Clustering, but not beneath his shoulders broad:
> She as a veil down to the slender waist
> Her unadornèd golden tresses wore
> Dishevelled, but in wanton ringlets waved
> As the vine curls her tendrils, which implied
> Subjection, but required with gentle sway,
> And by her yielded, by him best received,
> Yielded with coy submission, modest pride,
> And sweet reluctant amorous delay.
>
> (4.300–311)

Milton here highlights both aspects of hair we have already noted. In the first place, hair expresses inherent characteristics. We have already learned of Adam and Eve that he is "For contemplation... and valour formed,/For softness she and sweet attractive grace" (4.297–98), and their hair ("manly" in his case, "gentle" in hers) reflects these attributes. At the same time that hair expresses the essential self, however, it also serves as a common site of contact between that self and the outside world. There is no other part of the body that is so often given up—or in Milton's word, "yielded"—into the hands of others, either voluntarily (it is very difficult to cut one's own

---

12. The changing position of Satan is also conveyed through hair imagery. In book 1 he appears before his fallen host like "the sun... Shorn of his beams" (1.594–96); in book 2, defying Death, he is "like a comet... That fires the length of Ophiucus huge/In the Arctic sky, and from his horrid hair/Shakes pestilence and war" (2.708–11); in book 3, as he poses hypocritically before Uriel, "his flowing hair/In curls on either cheek played" (3.640–41).

hair, and even arranging it is often left to someone else) or involuntarily. This description of hair thus encapsulates the great Miltonic dichotomy of autonomy and contingency. At first glance—though this view will later be complicated—the dichotomy seems to be clearly divided between the two characters: Adam's hair is self-contained, clustering together of its own will; Eve's is subject to outside sway.

When Satan, whose first view of Adam and Eve is the same as ours, begins to tempt Eve, the effect is first registered in her hair. The morning after Satan has crouched whispering into Eve's sleeping ear, Adam wakes at his customary hour and is surprised "to find unwakened Eve/With tresses discomposed, and glowing cheek" (5.9–10). Eve's disordered hair and flushed cheek are disturbing, but not in equal degree. The latter springs only from internal causes—from bad dreams which, though caused by Satan, Eve at least is aware of and can discuss with Adam. The "tresses discomposed," by contrast, indicate both the same internal causes—unquiet dreams that have caused Eve to move restlessly during the night—and also, potentially, an external, physical cause. The latter is merely a possibility: there is no explicit indication that Satan in the form of a toad disturbed Eve's hair by squatting on it; and it may seem trivial whether or not the Author of Evil has mussed up Eve's hairdo. Yet the possibility that Satan may have physically interfered with Eve's tresses is unnerving specifically because it would be so easy. Hair is the only part of our bodies that someone else can touch without our being aware of it. It is therefore the only part that can be harmed in our sleep without our being woken, as happens with Samson: had Samson's strength been lodged in his jawbone, Dalila could not so easily have divested him of it while he slumbered. Hair then—for all Adam's reassurances to Eve that we cannot be tainted without the participation of our own will—serves as a symbol of our vulnerability to outside interference, to the construction (or destruction) of others.

Eve's flowing hair represents both her strength and her weakness. In the words of St. Paul, "if a woman have long hair, it is a glory to her" (1 Cor 11:15), and Eve's is the outward sign of her natural grace and innocence.[13] At the same time it stands as a sign that she is incomplete in herself and dependent upon others. The latter quality is not a fault, much less a sin. Yet right

---

13 Even the most suspect language in the description of Eve's hair—her "wanton ringlets," growing "As the vine" without restraint—merely reminds the reader how innocent such words and images are before the Fall. Compare, for instance, the parallel description of Eden: "nature here/Wantoned as in her prime, and played at will/Her virgin fancies, pouring forth more sweet,/Wild above rule or art" (5.294–97).

away the description of Eve's hair does call to mind the loss of independence that will accompany the Fall. Secrecy and clothing are two of the initial signs of humanity's lapse; both are suggested by the word *veil,* the first word used to describe Eve's hair ("She as a veil down to the slender waist..."). Similarly, after Eve recounts her dream to Adam, she "silently a gentle tear let fall/From either eye, and wiped them with her hair" (5.130–31). This reference, as usual, goes both ways. Handkerchiefs are a postlapsarian invention, and it is a sign of Eve's innocence and self-sufficiency that she does not use one or need one. And yet the effect would be quite different if she had "wiped them with her hand": hair is halfway between hand and handkerchief, between total self-sufficiency and dependence upon extrinsic support.

In contrast to Eve, Adam seems entirely self-contained: he has no veil, nothing requiring the tendance or sway of another. When Raphael arrives in Eden, Adam is able to walk forth to welcome him "without more train/Accompanied than with his own complete/Perfections, in himself was all his state" (5.351–53). Yet Adam is not, in fact, wholly self-sufficient; to the contrary, his definitive human characteristic is his need for companionship. When Adam pleads with God for a helpmeet, he distinguishes thus between deity and humanity:

> Thou in thyself art perfect, and in thee
> Is no deficience found; not so is man,
> But in degree, the cause of his desire
> By conversation with his like to help,
> Or solace his defects. No need that thou
> Shouldst propagate, already infinite;
> And through all numbers absolute, though one;
> But man by number is to manifest
> His single imperfection.
>
> (8.415–23)

The partner that Adam seeks will be his crowning glory and also, necessarily, his point of greatest weakness, the manifestation of his "imperfection." In short, Eve is Adam's hair. She is bone of his bone, flesh of his flesh, an intrinsic part of his being. But unlike any other part of his body or mind, she can be easily separated from him and can even be appropriated by another. After the Fall, Adam laments that Eve was his downfall—that had she never been created, he would have "persisted happy" (10.874). Yet the claim is meaningless, because without Eve, Adam would not be Adam in the first place, would not be complete (in the words of Paul again, "neither is the man without the woman, neither the woman without the man, in the Lord" [1 Cor 11:11]). Interpersonal relations, what Adam calls "conversation," define humanity.

The point holds just as true in the other direction: Adam is Eve's hair too. After Eve has wiped away two tears with her hair, Adam takes the office upon himself, kissing away the next two "ere they fell" (5.133). The argument could easily be made that Adam is the source of Eve's weakness, as much as the other way around—that had she existed without him (if that can be conceived), she would never have fallen either. But in both cases, their "weakness" is also their glory. The very thing that makes Adam and Eve vulnerable—their relationship to and dependence upon someone outside themselves—is also what makes them Adam and Eve; it individuates them, setting them apart from God and above the rest of creation.[14] Just as their obedience derives its true value from their fallibility, so their identity and self-determination are all the stronger for their mutual contingency.

This is the same point I wish to emphasize about Milton. Perhaps more than any other English poet, Milton is a singular force: unmistakable, self-sufficient, autonomous. Yet he is also, perhaps more than any other poet, enmeshed in history, subject to influence, interpretation, and intertextual diffusion. And the fact that a single symbol, hair, aptly represents both these aspects of Milton shows them to be not separate but the same. When modern critics describe Milton's influence in terms that he himself provides, they are acting in a manner similar to Eve's when she wipes her tears with her hair—that is, describing a process that is simultaneously external and internal to Milton. And when the Victorians find Milton "dark with excessive bright," they are recognizing the same phenomenon—that Milton is at his most Miltonic, not only when he remains aloof and isolated, but also when he is most dispersed amongst other texts and contexts.

The relationship between Milton and the Victorians is perhaps best encapsulated in (ironically) a reliquary, now at the Keats-Shelley House in Rome. The reliquary contains a lock of Milton's hair—not one of those pillaged from his coffin in 1790, but part of a lock with a much finer pedigree. It belonged to no less a Miltonist than Joseph Addison, and later passed into the possession of Samuel Johnson and then, eventually, to Leigh Hunt.[15] In

---

14. The case is similar with Samson. Just as Samson's native strength is lodged in the weakest and most alienable part of his body ("God, when he gave me strength, to show withal/How slight the gift was, hung it in my hair"), so his greatest weakness—his desire to marry into alien society—arises from "intimate impulse" and ends up being the key to his most defining achievement (SA 58–59, 223).

15. For a fuller account of the reliquary and its contents, see Origo 458 and Gray, "The Hair of Milton."

1818 Hunt showed the hair to Keats, who responded with "Lines on Seeing
a Lock of Milton's Hair," which concludes as follows.

> For many years my offerings must be hush'd.
>   When I do speak, I'll think upon this hour,
> Because I feel my forehead hot and flush'd—
>   Even at the simplest vassal of thy power;
>   A lock of thy bright hair—
>   Sudden it came,
> And I was startled, when I caught thy name
>   Coupled so unaware;
> Yet at the moment, temperate was my blood—
> Methought I had beheld it from the Flood.
>
>   (32–41; Keats 165)

Keats's reaction to this, his most direct encounter with Milton, is rather confused. In the final couplet, Keats treats Milton as a classic: the lock of hair
seems perfectly familiar, as if he had known it all his life—indeed, had known
it almost since the beginning of time. Yet the preceding lines display a more
typically Romantic reaction: Milton comes upon Keats as a surprise, something "Sudden" and "startl[ing]." This manifestation of Milton seems to exert
a direct, concentrated, and in some sense overpowering force (since it leaves
him "hush'd" and unable to speak) upon the young poet.

Part of the lock of hair that Keats saw remained in Leigh Hunt's possession; it is now housed, along with the rest of Hunt's collection of hair, at the
University of Texas (Keats 436). One half of the original lock of Milton's
hair, then, has been preserved in its original state—separate from all the
others in the collection, as "bright" (Keats's word) and identifiable as ever.
The other half, however, was given by Hunt to Robert and Elizabeth Barrett
Browning; that strand is now in the reliquary, where it can be seen enclosed
together with a much thicker and fuller lock of Barrett Browning's own hair.
It is not known who placed the two strands of hair together; Robert Browning himself kept his wife's hair separate, in a "faded folder," until his death
(Origo 458). But that is part of the nature of hair, just as it is part of the
nature of texts: they pass out of your control, becoming subject to invisible
forces and shifting contexts. Appropriately, the lock of Barrett Browning's
hair with which Milton's is paired is not just any lock, but one with strong
literary and intertextual connections: the very lock that she gave to Robert
Browning at his urging during their courtship, as described both in her letters
and in *Sonnets from the Portuguese.*

I never gave a lock of hair away
To a man, Dearest, except this to thee,
Which now upon my fingers thoughtfully,
I ring out to the full brown length and say,
"Take it."

(18.1–5)

The sense of vulnerability and reluctance in these lines, as the speaker submits to the necessity of foregoing her self-imposed isolation and passing into social circulation, soon turns to a note of powerful confidence; in the next sonnet she boldly demands a return, a lock of her beloved's own hair in exchange for hers.

Later in the sonnet sequence Barrett Browning reflects upon the fact that the more we love someone and the closer we feel, the less visible that person becomes. They seem to disappear, not because their influence or their individual presence has weakened, but because it is all-encompassing. This is what has happened, Barret Browning's speaker says in Sonnet 29, in her relationship to her beloved—although in her image it is she herself who does the encompassing.

I think of thee!—my thoughts do twine and bud
About thee, as wild vines, about a tree,
Put out broad leaves, and soon there's nought to see
Except the straggling green which hides the wood.
Yet, O my palm-tree, be it understood
I will not have my thoughts instead of thee
Who art dearer, better! Rather, instantly
Renew thy presence; as a strong tree should,
Rustle thy boughs and set thy trunk all bare,
And let these bands of greenery which insphere thee
Drop heavily down,—burst, shattered, everywhere!
Because, in this deep joy to see and hear thee
And breathe within thy shadow a new air,
I do not think of thee—I am too near thee.

The image of "shattered" greenery (line 11) comes directly from the opening lines of "Lycidas," where the speaker tells the laurel, myrtle, and ivy that he will "Shatter your leaves" (5). There is nothing unusual about Milton's use of the verb, which simply means "scatter." But by the time Barrett Browning was writing, this meaning had long since become obsolete, and in any case the adjoining word "burst" suggests that she intended this to be a jarring image, and a deliberate allusion.[16] It is appropriate that this reference to Milton should come in a poem that pictures the object of love and veneration standing apart in individual splendor, and yet also pictures that individual "presence" (8) as emerging from a thicket of intertwining relationships. What Barrett Browning says of love is equally true of literary influence, and particularly Milton's: it takes place simultaneously through direct, individual bequests and through diffuse, hidden, and unpredictable channels. It is in recognizing and responding to this dual aspect of their predecessor's legacy that the Victorians are most truly the heirs of Milton.

---

16. The force and poignancy of the allusion comes from Barrett Browning's having kept her lover aloof throughout the first part of *Sonnets from the Portuguese* because of her grief over the death by drowning of her brother, which she says has incapacitated her for love. The unexpected reference to Milton's elegy for a young man who drowned, coming especially in the context of a sonnet about the renewal of love, demonstrates just how much the speaker has changed over the course of the sonnet sequence.

❦ WORKS CITED

Note: In the case of unsigned articles in Victorian periodicals, I have followed the attribution in the *Wellesley Index to Victorian Periodicals;* where the attribution in the index is tentative, I have put the name in brackets.

Abbott, Claude Colleer, ed. *The Letters of Gerard Manley Hopkins to Robert Bridges.* London: Oxford University Press, 1935.

Abrams, M. H. *The Mirror and the Lamp: Romantic Theory and the Critical Tradition.* 1953; New York: Norton, 1958.

Adler, Thomas P. "The Uses of Knowledge in Tennyson's *Merlin and Vivien." Texas Studies in Literature and Language* 11 (1970), 1397–1403.

Albright, Daniel. *Tennyson: The Muses' Tug-of-War.* Charlottesville: University Press of Virginia, 1986.

[Allon, Henry.] "Masson's *Milton and His Times." British Quarterly Review* 59 (1874), 81–100.

Anonymous. "Masson's *Life of Milton." British Quarterly Review* 29 (1859), 185–214.

Anonymous. "Masson's *Milton." Dublin University Magazine* 53 (1859), 609–23.

Anonymous. "Milton and the Commonwealth." *British Quarterly Review* 10 (1849), 224–54.

Anonymous. "Milton's Prose Writings." *New Monthly Magazine* 40 (1834), 39–50.

Armstrong, Isobel. *Victorian Poetry: Poetry, Poetics and Politics.* London: Routledge, 1993.

Arnold, Matthew. *Culture and Anarchy and Other Writings.* Ed. Stefan Collini. Cambridge: Cambridge University Press, 1993.

———. *The Letters of Matthew Arnold.* Ed. Cecil Y. Lang. Charlottesville: University Press of Virginia, 1996–2001.

———. *The Poems of Matthew Arnold.* Ed. Kenneth Allott; 2nd ed., ed. Miriam Allott. London: Longman, 1979.

Arseneau, Mary. "Pilgrimage and Postponement: Christina Rossetti's *The Prince's Progress." Victorian Poetry* 32 (1994), 279–98.

Bagehot, Walter. "John Milton." 1859; repr. *Collected Works of Walter Bagehot,* ed. Norman St John-Stevas. Cambridge: Harvard University Press, 1965–86, 2:109–48.

Bate, Walter Jackson. *The Burden of the Past and the English Poet.* Cambridge: Belknap Press, 1970.

Bayne, Peter. "Milton." *Contemporary Review* 22 (1873), 427–60.

Bentley, D. M. R. "The Meretricious and the Meritorious in *Goblin Market:* A Conjecture and an Analysis." In *The Achievement of Christina Rossetti.* Ed. David A Kent. Ithaca: Cornell University Press, 1987, 57–81.

Bidney, Martin. "Of the Devils's Party: Undetected Words of Milton's Satan in Arnold's 'Dover Beach.'" *Victorian Poetry* 20 (1982), 85–89.

Blessington, Francis C. "The Portrait in the Spoon: George Eliot's Casaubon and John Milton." *Milton Quarterly* 20 (1986), 29–31.

Bloom, Harold. *The Anxiety of Influence: A Theory of Poetry.* New York: Oxford University Press, 1973.

———. *A Map of Misreading.* New York: Oxford University Press, 1975.

———. *Poetry and Repression: Revisionism from Blake to Stevens.* New Haven: Yale University Press, 1976.

———. *The Ringers in the Tower: Studies in Romantic Tradition.* Chicago: University of Chicago Press, 1971.

Bonney, William W. "Torpor and Tropology in Tennyson's 'Merlin and Vivien.' " *Victorian Poetry* 23 (1985), 351–67.

Boyle, Robert, S. J. " 'Man Jack the Man Is': *The Wreck* from the Perspective of *The Shepherd's Brow.*" In *Readings of* The Wreck: *Essays in Commemoration of the Centenary of G. M. Hopkins'* The Wreck of the Deutschland. Ed. Peter Milward, S. J., and Raymond Schoder, S. J. Chicago: Loyola University Press, 1976, 100–14.

Bradley, A. C. *A Miscellany.* London: Macmillan, 1929.

Brisman, Leslie. *Milton's Poetry of Choice and Its Romantic Heirs.* Ithaca: Cornell University Press, 1973.

Broadbent, J. B. "Milton and Arnold." *Essays in Criticism* 6 (1956), 404–17.

Brontë, Emily. *Wuthering Heights.* Ed. Richard J. Dunn. New York: Norton, 2003.

Browning, Elizabeth Barrett. *The Complete Works of Elizabeth Barrett Browning.* Ed. Charlotte Porter and Helen A. Clarke. New York: Thomas Y. Crowell, 1900; repr. 1973.

Browning, Robert. *The Poems.* Ed. John Pettigrew and Thomas J. Collins. New Haven: Yale University Press, 1981.

Burke, Edmund. *A Philosophical Enquiry into the Origin of our Ideas of the Sublime and Beautiful.* Ed. David Womersley. Harmondsworth, UK: Penguin, 1998.

Burnet, Gilbert. *History of My Own Time.* Ed. Osmund Airy. Oxford: Clarendon Press, 1897–1900.

Burnett, Archie. "Tennyson's 'Mariana': Two Parallels." *Notes and Queries* 27 (1980), 207–08.

Chandler, James K. "Romantic Allusiveness." *Critical Inquiry* 8 (1982), 461–87.

Clayton, Jay, and Eric Rothstein. "Figures in the Corpus: Theories of Influence and Intertextuality." In *Influence and Intertextuality in Literary History.* Ed. Jay Clayton and Eric Rothstein. Madison: University of Wisconsin Press, 1991, 3–36.

Clymer, Lorna. "Cromwell's Head and Milton's Hair: Corpse Theory in Spectacular Bodies of the Interregnum." *The Eighteenth Century: Theory and Interpretation* 40 (1999), 91–112.

Coleridge, Samuel Taylor. *Poetical Works.* Ed. J. C. C. Mays. Princeton: Princeton University Press, 2001.

Cross, J. W. *George Eliot's Life: As Related in her Letters and Journals.* Boston: Dana Estes; repr. Grosse Pointe, MI: Scholarly Press, 1968.

Culler, A. Dwight. *The Poetry of Tennyson.* New Haven: Yale University Press, 1977.

D'Amico, Diane. *Christina Rossetti: Faith, Gender, and Time.* Baton Rouge: Louisiana State University Press, 1999.

Dawson, Carl, ed. *Matthew Arnold, the Poetry: The Critical Heritage*. London: Routledge and Kegan Paul, 1973.

Dennis, John. "Milton and Wordsworth." *Temple Bar* 60 (1880), 106–15.

De Quincey, Thomas. *The Works of Thomas De Quincey*. Ed. Grevel Lindop et al. 21 vols. London: Pickering and Chatto, 2000–2003.

Donne, W. B. "The Youth of Milton." *Edinburgh Review* 111 (1860), 312–47.

Douglas-Fairhurst, Robert. *Victorian Afterlives: The Shaping of Influence in Nineteenth-Century Literature*. Oxford: Oxford University Press, 2002.

Dowden, Edward. "The Idealism of Milton." *Contemporary Review* 19 (1872), 198–209.

Durling, Robert M., tr. and ed. *Petrarch's Lyric Poems: The* Rime Sparse *and Other Lyrics*. Cambridge: Harvard University Press, 1976.

Elfenbein, Andrew. *Byron and the Victorians*. Cambridge: Cambridge University Press, 1995.

Eliot, George. "Belles Lettres." *Westminster Review* 64 (1855), 596–615.

———. *Daniel Deronda*. Ed. Graham Handley. Oxford: Clarendon Press, 1984.

———. *Essays of George Eliot*. Ed. Thomas Pinney. London: Routledge and Kegan Paul, 1963.

———. *The George Eliot Letters*. Ed. Gordon S. Haight. New Haven: Yale University Press, 1954–78.

———. *Impressions of Theophrastus Such*. Ed. Nancy Henry. London: William Pickering, 1994.

———. *The Journals of George Eliot*. Ed. Margaret Harris and Judith Johnston. Cambridge: Cambridge University Press, 1998.

Eliot, T. S. *On Poetry and Poets*. New York: Farrar, Straus, and Cudahy, 1957.

———. *Selected Essays*. London: Faber and Faber, 1951.

Emerson, Ralph Waldo. *The Collected Works of Ralph Waldo Emerson*. Ed. Alfred R. Ferguson et al. Cambridge: Harvard University Press, 1971–.

Empson, William. *Essays on Shakespeare*. Ed. David B. Pirie. Cambridge: Cambridge University Press, 1986.

———. *Milton's God*. London: Chatto and Windus, 1961.

Engelmeyer, Sister Bridget Marie. "In Defense of Milton, Aspersed." *Milton Quarterly* 21 (1987), 103–04.

Evans, B. Ifor. "The Sources of Christina Rossetti's 'Goblin Market.'" *Modern Language Review* 28 (1933), 156–65.

Everett, Barbara. "The End of the Big Names: Milton's Epic Catalogues." In *English Renaissance Studies: Presented to Dame Helen Gardner*. Ed. John Carey. Oxford: Clarendon Press, 1980, 254–70.

Ferry, Anne. *Milton's Epic Voice: The Narrator in Paradise Lost*. Cambridge: Harvard University Press, 1963.

Fish, Stanley. *How Milton Works*. Cambridge: Harvard University Press, 2001.

———. *Surprised by Sin: The Reader in Paradise Lost*. 2nd ed. Cambridge: Harvard University Press, 1998.

FitzGerald, Edward. *The Letters of Edward FitzGerald*. Ed. Alfred McKinley Terhune and Annabelle Burdick Terhune. Princeton: Princeton University Press, 1980.

Fitzgerald, F. Scott. *This Side of Paradise*. Ed. James L. W. West III. Cambridge: Cambridge University Press, 1995.

Fletcher, Harris Francis. *Contributions to a Milton Bibliography 1800–1930*. University of Illinois Studies in Language and Literature, vol. 16. Urbana: University of Illinois Press, 1931.

Gelpi, Barbara Charlesworth. " 'Verses with a Good Deal about Sucking': Percy Bysshe Shelley and Christina Rossetti." In *Influence and Resistance in Nineteenth-Century English Poetry*. Ed. G. Kim Blank and Margot K. Louis. London: Macmillan, 1993, 150–65.

Gilbert, Sandra M., and Susan Gubar. *The Madwoman in the Attic: The Woman Writer and the Nineteenth-Century Literary Imagination*. New Haven: Yale University Press, 1979.

Gill, Stephen. *Wordsworth and the Victorians*. Oxford: Clarendon Press, 1998.

Glavin, John J. " 'The Wreck of the Deutschland' and 'Lycidas': ubique naufragium est." *Texas Studies in Literature and Language* 22 (1980), 522–46.

Grass, Sean C. "Nature's Perilous Variety in Rossetti's 'Goblin Market.' " *Nineteenth-Century Literature* 51 (1996), 356–76.

Graves, Robert. *The Story of Marie Powell, Wife to Mr Milton* and *The Islands of Unwisdom*. Ed. Simon Brittan. Manchester, UK: Carcanet, 2003.

Gray, Erik. "Faithful Likenesses: Lists of Similes in Milton, Shelley, and Rossetti." *Texas Studies in Literature and Language* 48 (2006), 291–311.

———. "The Hair of Milton: Historicism and Literary History." In *Romanticism, History, Historicism: Essays on an Orthodoxy*. Ed. Damian Walford Davies. New York: Routledge, 2009, 32–42.

———. "Nostalgia, the Classics, and the Intimations Ode: Wordsworth's Forgotten Education." *Philological Quarterly* 80 (2001), 187–203.

Gray, J. M. *Thro' the Vision of the Night: A Study of Source, Evolution and Structure in Tennyson's* Idylls of the King. Edinburgh: Edinburgh University Press, 1980.

Griffin, Dustin. *Regaining Paradise: Milton and the Eighteenth Century*. Cambridge: Cambridge University Press, 1986.

Guillory, John. *Poetic Authority: Spenser, Milton, and Literary History*. New York: Columbia University Press, 1983.

Haight, Gordon S. *George Eliot: A Biography*. New York: Oxford University Press, 1968.

Hallam, Arthur Henry. "Sorelli's Italian Translation of Milton." *Foreign Quarterly Review* 10 (1832), 508–13.

Harrison, Antony H. *Victorian Poems and Romantic Poets: Intertextuality and Ideology*. Charlottesville: University Press of Virginia, 1990.

Haskin, Dayton. "George Eliot as a 'Miltonist': Marriage and Milton in *Middlemarch*." In *Milton and Gender*. Ed. Catherine Gimelli Martin. Cambridge: Cambridge University Press, 2004, 207–22.

Havens, Raymond Dexter. *The Influence of Milton on English Poetry*. 1922; repr. New York: Russell and Russell, 1961.

Hazlitt, William. *Complete Works*. Ed. P. P. Howe. London: J. M. Dent, 1930.

Herman, Peter C. *Destabilizing Milton: "Paradise Lost" and the Poetics of Incertitude*. New York: Palgrave Macmillan, 2005.

Heron, Robert Matthew. "The Three Poems 'In Memoriam.' " *Quarterly Review* 158 (1884), 162–83.

Hertz, Neil. "Recognizing Casaubon." *Glyph* 6 (1979), 24–41.

Higdon, David Leon. "George Eliot and the Art of the Epigraph." *Nineteenth-Century Fiction* 25 (1970), 127–51.

Hogan, Patrick Colm. *Joyce, Milton, and the Theory of Influence.* Gainesville: University Press of Florida, 1995.

Hollander, John. *The Figure of Echo: A Mode of Allusion in Milton and After.* Berkeley: University of California Press, 1981.

Hopkins, Gerard Manley. *The Poetical Works of Gerard Manley Hopkins.* Ed. Norman H. MacKenzie. Oxford: Clarendon Press, 1990.

Hunt, Leigh. "My Books, No. II: Originality of Milton's Harmonious Use of Proper Names." *New Monthly Magazine* 14 (1825), 387–92.

Huxley, Thomas Henry. *The Life and Letters of Thomas Henry Huxley.* Ed. Leonard Huxley. London: Macmillan, 1900.

Jarvis, Robin. *Wordsworth, Milton and the Theory of Poetic Relations.* London: Macmillan, 1991.

Jiménez, Nilda. *The Bible and the Poetry of Christina Rossetti: A Concordance.* Westport: Greenwood Press, 1979.

Johnson, Samuel. *Lives of the English Poets.* Ed. George Birkbeck Hill. Oxford: Clarendon Press, 1905.

Keats, John. *Complete Poems.* Ed. Jack Stillinger. Cambridge: Harvard University Press, 1982.

——. *The Letters of John Keats.* Ed. Hyder E. Rollins. Cambridge: Harvard University Press, 1958.

Keightley, Thomas. *An Account of the Life, Opinions, and Writings of John Milton.* London: Chapman and Hall, 1855.

Kennedy, Ian H. C. "*In Memoriam* and the Tradition of Pastoral Elegy." *Victorian Poetry* 15 (1977), 351–66.

Kent, David A. "'By Thought, Word, and Deed': George Herbert and Christina Rossetti." In *The Achievement of Christina Rossetti.* Ed. David A. Kent. Ithaca: Cornell University Press, 1987, 250–73.

Kermode, Frank. *The Classic: Literary Images of Permanence and Change.* Cambridge: Harvard University Press, 1983.

Kiely, Robert. "The Limits of Dialogue in *Middlemarch.*" In *The Worlds of Victorian Fiction.* Ed. Jerome H. Buckley. Cambridge: Harvard University Press, 1975, 103–23.

Kildegaard, Lise. *Home Epics, Home Economics: George Eliot Reads Milton.* PhD Diss. University of Chicago, 1995.

Kincaid, James R. *Annoying the Victorians.* New York: Routledge, 1995.

Kintner, Elvan, ed. *The Letters of Robert Browning and Elizabeth Barrett Browning, 1845–1846.* Cambridge: Harvard University Press, 1969.

Knoepflmacher, U. C. *Laughter and Despair: Readings in Ten Novels of the Victorian Era.* Berkeley: University of California Press, 1971.

Kolbrener, William. *Milton's Warring Angels: A Study of Critical Engagements.* Cambridge: Cambridge University Press, 1997.

Lehnhof, Kent R. "Uncertainty and 'The Sociable Spirit': Raphael's Role in *Paradise Lost.*" In *Milton's Legacy.* Ed. Kristin A. Pruitt and Charles W. Durham. Selinsgrove: Susquehanna University Press, 2005, 33–49.

Lewalski, Barbara Kiefer. Paradise Lost *and the Rhetoric of Literary Forms.* Princeton: Princeton University Press, 1985.

Macaulay, Thomas Babington. "Milton." *Edinburgh Review* 42 (1825), 304–46.

Machacek, Gregory. "Allusion." *PMLA* 122 (2007), 522–36.

Maginn, William, and John Wilson. "Mr. Prendeville's *Milton.*" *Blackwood's Magazine* 47 (1840), 691–716.

Manning, Anne. *The Maiden & Married Life of Mary Powell, Afterwards Mistress Milton.* London: Hall, Virtue, 1849.

Mariani, Paul L. *A Commentary on the Complete Poems of Gerard Manley Hopkins.* Ithaca: Cornell University Press, 1970.

Marsh, Jan. *Christina Rossetti: A Literary Biography.* London: Jonathan Cape, 1994.

Martin, Robert Bernard. *Tennyson: The Unquiet Heart.* Oxford: Clarendon Press, 1980.

Masson, David. *Essays Biographical and Critical: Chiefly on English Poets.* London: Macmillan, 1856.

——, ed. *The Poetical Works of John Milton.* Boston: Little, Brown and Co., 1866.

——, ed. *The Poetical Works of John Milton.* London: Macmillan, 1874.

——, ed. *The Poetical Works of John Milton.* New ed. London: Macmillan, 1893.

——. "The Three Devils: Luther's, Milton's, Goethe's." *Fraser's Magazine* 30 (1844), 648–66.

——. "The Works of John Milton." *North British Review* 16 (1852), 295–335.

Maxwell, Catherine. *The Female Sublime from Milton to Swinburne: Bearing Blindness.* Manchester and New York: Manchester University Press, 2001.

——. "Tasting the 'Fruit Forbidden': Gender, Intertextuality, and Christina Rossetti's *Goblin Market.*" In *The Culture of Christina Rossetti: Female Poetics and Victorian Contexts.* Ed. Mary Arseneau, Antony H. Harrison, and Lorraine Janzen Kooistra. Athens: Ohio University Press, 1999, 75–102.

Mayberry, Katherine J. *Christina Rossetti and the Poetry of Discovery.* Baton Rouge: Louisiana State University Press, 1989.

McGann, Jerome J. *The Beauty of Inflections: Literary Investigations in Historical Method and Theory.* Oxford: Clarendon Press, 1985.

McInerney, Peter. "Satanic Conceits in *Frankenstein* and *Wuthering Heights.*" *Milton and the Romantics* 4 (1980), 1–15.

Milbank, Alison. *Dante and the Victorians.* Manchester, UK: Manchester University Press, 1998.

Miller, J. Hillis. "Optic and Semiotic in *Middlemarch.*" In *The Worlds of Victorian Fiction.* Ed. Jerome H. Buckley. Cambridge: Harvard University Press, 1975, 125–45.

Mintz, Alan. *George Eliot and the Novel of Vocation.* Cambridge: Harvard University Press, 1978.

Najarian, James. *Victorian Keats: Manliness, Sexuality, and Desire.* New York: Palgrave Macmillan, 2002.

Nardo, Anna K. *George Eliot's Dialogue with John Milton.* Columbia: University of Missouri Press, 2003.

Nelson, James G. *The Sublime Puritan: Milton and the Victorians.* Madison: University of Wisconsin Press, 1963.

Neve, Philip. *A Narrative of the Disinterment of Milton's Coffin, in the Parish-Church of St. Giles, Cripplegate, on Wednesday, 4th of August, 1790.* London: n.p., 1790.

New, Herbert. "John Milton." *Modern Review* 2 (1881), 103–28.

Newlyn, Lucy. *Paradise Lost and the Romantic Reader.* Oxford: Clarendon Press, 1993.

Newman, Robert D. "Entanglement in Paradise: Eve's Hair and the Reader's Anxiety in *Paradise Lost.*" *Interpretations* 16 (1985), 112–15.

Ong, Walter J., S. J. *Hopkins, the Self, and God.* Toronto: University of Toronto Press, 1986.

Origo, Iris. "Additions to the Keats Collection." *Times Literary Supplement,* April 23, 1970, 457–58.

O'Sullivan, Maurice J., Jr. "Matthew Arnold: *Un Milton jeune et voyageant.*" *Milton Quarterly* 7 (1974), 82–84.

Palgrave, Francis Turner. "Masson's *Life of Milton.*" *Quarterly Review* 132 (1872), 393–423.

Parker, Lois W. "The Milton Window, the Americans, and Matthew Arnold." *Milton Quarterly* 13 (1979), 50–53.

Patterson, Annabel. "No Meer Amatorious Novel?" In *Politics, Poetics, and Hermeneutics in Milton's Prose.* Ed. David Loewenstein and James Grantham Turner. Cambridge: Cambridge University Press, 1990, 85–101.

———. "Milton's Negativity." In *Milton in the Age of Fish: Essays on Authorship, Text, and Terrorism.* Ed. Michael Lieb and Albert C. Labriola. Pittsburgh: Duquesne University Press, 2006, 81–102.

Pattison, Mark. "Milton." *Macmillan's Magazine* 31 (1875), 380–87.

Pattison, Robert. *Tennyson and Tradition.* Cambridge: Harvard University Press, 1979.

Perry, Seamus. *Alfred Tennyson.* Tavistock, UK: Northcote House, 2005.

Pollock, Frederick. "John Milton." *Fortnightly Review* 54 (1890), 510–19.

Poole, Adrian. *Shakespeare and the Victorians.* London: Arden, 2004.

Postlethwaite, Diana. "When George Eliot Reads Milton: The Muse in a Different Voice." *English Literary History* 57 (1990), 197–221.

Potts, Abbie Findlay. "The Spenserian and Miltonic Influence in Wordsworth's *Ode* and *Rainbow.*" *Studies in Philology* 29 (1932), 607–16.

Pyre, J. F. A. *The Formation of Tennyson's Style.* Madison: University of Wisconsin Press, 1921.

Revard, Stella P. "Eve and the Doctrine of Responsibility in *Paradise Lost.*" *PMLA* 88 (1973), 69–78.

Reynolds, Matthew. *The Realms of Verse 1830–1870: English Poetry in a Time of Nation-Building.* Oxford: Oxford University Press, 2001.

Richards, I. A. *The Philosophy of Rhetoric.* 1936; repr. Oxford: Oxford University Press, 1965.

Ricks, Christopher. *Milton's Grand Style.* Oxford: Clarendon Press, 1963.

Riede, David G. *Matthew Arnold and the Betrayal of Language.* Charlottesville: University Press of Virginia, 1988.

Rieger, James. "Wordsworth Unalarm'd." In *Milton and the Line of Vision.* Ed. Joseph Anthony Wittreich. Madison: University of Wisconsin Press, 1975, 185–208.

Rosenberg, John D. *The Fall of Camelot: A Study of Tennyson's "Idylls of the King."* Cambridge: Harvard University Press, 1973.

Rossetti, Christina. *The Complete Poems.* Ed. R. W. Crump and Betty S. Flowers. Harmondsworth, UK: Penguin, 2001.

———. *Poetical Works.* Ed. William Michael Rossetti. London: Macmillan, 1904.

Rumrich, John P. "The Provenance of *De doctrina Christiana:* A View of the Present State of the Controversy." In *Milton and the Grounds of Contention.* Ed.

Mark R. Kelley, Michael Lieb, and John T. Shawcross. Pittsburgh: Duquesne University Press, 2003, 214–33.

Ruoff, Gene W. *Wordsworth and Coleridge: The Making of the Major Lyrics 1802–1804.* New Brunswick: Rutgers University Press, 1989.

Salmasius, Claudius. *Epistola ad Andream Colvium: Super Cap. XI Primae ad Corinth. Epistolae, de Caesarie Virorum et Mulierum Coma.* Leiden: Elzevir, 1644.

Sauer, Elizabeth. *Barbarous Dissonance and Images of Voice in Milton's Epics.* Montreal: McGill-Queen's University Press, 1996.

Seeley, J. R. "Milton's Poetry." *Macmillan's Magazine* 19 (1869), 407–21.

———. "Milton's Political Opinions." *Macmillan's Magazine* 17 (1868), 299–311.

Sendry, Joseph. "*In Memoriam* and *Lycidas.*" *PMLA* 82 (1967), 437–43.

Serrell, George. "Milton as Seen in His Sonnets." *Temple Bar* 121 (1900), 27–42.

Shairp, J. C. "Keble's Estimate of Milton." *Macmillan's Magazine* 31 (1875), 554–60.

Shannon, Edgar Finley, Jr. *Tennyson and the Reviewers.* Cambridge: Harvard University Press, 1952.

Sharp, Ronald A. "A Note on Allusion in 'Dover Beach.'" *English Language Notes* 21 (1983), 52–55.

Shaw, W. David. *Tennyson's Style.* Ithaca: Cornell University Press, 1976.

Shawcross, John T., ed. *Milton: The Critical Heritage.* London: Routledge and Kegan Paul, 1970.

———. *John Milton and Influence: Presence in Literature, History and Culture.* Pittsburgh: Duquesne University Press, 1991.

Shelley, Percy Bysshe. *Shelley's Poetry and Prose.* 2nd ed. Ed. Donald H. Reiman and Neil Fraistat. New York: Norton, 2002.

Shurbutt, Sylvia Bailey. "Revisionist Mythmaking in Christina Rossetti's 'Goblin Market': Eve's Apple and Other Questions Revised and Reconsidered." *Victorian Newsletter* 82 (1992), 40–44.

Sinfield, Alan. *The Language of Tennyson's In Memoriam.* Oxford: Blackwell, 1971.

Smith, George Barnett. "Masson's *Life of Milton.*" *Macmillan's Magazine* 28 (1873), 536–47.

Sobolev, Dennis. "Contra Milton." *English Studies* 84 (2003), 530–44.

Sperry, Stuart M. *Keats the Poet.* Princeton: Princeton University Press, 1973.

Stedman, Edmund Clarence. *Victorian Poets.* Boston: James R. Osgood, 1876.

Stevens, David Harrison. *Reference Guide to Milton: From 1800 to the Present Day.* Chicago: University of Chicago Press, 1930.

Symonds, John Addington. "The Blank Verse of Milton." *Fortnightly Review* 22 [16 ns] (1874), 767–81.

Tennyson, Alfred. *The Poems of Tennyson.* 2nd ed. Ed. Christopher Ricks. Berkeley: University of California Press, 1987.

Terry, R. C., ed. *The Oxford Reader's Companion to Trollope.* Oxford: Oxford University Press, 1999.

Trilling, Lionel. *Matthew Arnold.* Rev. ed. New York: Columbia University Press, 1949.

Trollope, Anthony. *Barchester Towers.* Ed. Robin Gilmour. Harmondsworth, UK: Penguin, 1987.

———. *The Warden.* Ed. David Skilton. Oxford: Oxford University Press, 1980.

Tucker, Herbert F. "Strange Comfort: A Reading of Tennyson's Unpublished Juve-
nilia." *Victorian Poetry* 21 (1983), 1–25.

——. "Swinburne's *Tristram of Lyonesse* as Assimilationist Epic." In *Influence and Resistance in Nineteenth-Century English Poetry.* Ed. G. Kim Blank and Margot K.
Louis. London: Macmillan, 1993, 76–90.

——. *Tennyson and the Doom of Romanticism.* Cambridge: Harvard University Press,
1988.

[Tulloch, John.] "Masson's *Milton and his Times.*" *North British Review* 30 (1859),
281–308.

Twain, Mark. *Following the Equator and Anti-Imperialist Essays.* New York: Oxford
University Press, 1996.

Van Dyke, Henry. *The Poetry of Tennyson.* New York: Scribner's, 1889.

Vejvoda, Kathleen. "The Fruit of Charity: *Comus* and Christina Rossetti's *Goblin
Market.*" *Victorian Poetry* 38 (2000), 555–78.

White, James. "Guizot and Milton." *Blackwood's Magazine* 43 (1838), 303–12.

Wilson, William. "Algernon Agonistes: 'Thalassius,' Visionary Strength, and Swinburne's Critique of Arnold's 'Sweetness and Light.' " *Victorian Poetry* 19 (1981),
381–95.

Winters, Sarah Fiona. "Questioning Milton, Questioning God: Christina Rossetti's
Challenge to Authority in 'Goblin Market' and 'The Prince's Progress.' " *Journal of Pre-Raphaelite Studies* 10 (2001), 14–26.

Wittreich, Joseph Anthony, ed. " 'A Poet Amongst Poets': Milton and the Tradition
of Prophecy." In *Milton and the Line of Vision.* Ed. Joseph Anthony Wittreich.
Madison: University of Wisconsin Press, 1975, 97–142.

——. *The Romantics on Milton: Formal Essays and Critical Asides.* Cleveland: Press of
Case Western Reserve University, 1970.

——. *Visionary Poetics: Milton's Tradition and His Legacy.* San Marino, CA: Huntington
Library, 1979.

——. *Why Milton Matters: A New Preface to His Writings.* New York: Palgrave Macmillan, 2006.

Woof, Robert, ed. *William Wordsworth: The Critical Heritage. Volume I: 1793–1820.*
London: Routledge, 2001.

Wordsworth, William. *The Poems.* Ed. John O. Hayden. Harmondsworth, UK: Penguin, 1977.

——. *The Prelude.* Ed. Jonathan Wordsworth, M. H. Abrams, and Stephen Gill. New
York: Norton, 1979.

❧ INDEX